Cheyenne Ti

Between the Rivers

By

Tom McMullen

Preface

The Cheyenne followed their own way of life on the Great Plains of the United States of America until the end of the 19th Century. The coming together of three great natural phenomena – the horse, unlimited grasslands and the buffalo – must have seemed heaven sent; the Cheyenne embraced it wholeheartedly. Their life of hunting and war, underpinned by spirituality, was not of course without risk or danger. Surviving nature's occasional scarcities and warfare with other tribes for horses or captives was natural to the Cheyenne. A less natural struggle was the resistance to the gradual encroachment of Europeans who were determined to turn America into their own form of continental Paradise. The Cheyenne, in common with all other native peoples, eventually succumbed. Despite that, the Cheyenne are still with us today – on the Northern Cheyenne Reservation in Lame Deer, Montana.

This book has fictional characters set against a real culture with a real history. Some of the tribal structures and ceremonies are fictional though they are set in the same pattern of those that actually existed. Most of the historical events are true and well documented; I just wanted to add the Cheyenne perspective.

This book is neither a hagiography of the Cheyenne nor a condemnation of US expansion. It is about human beings dealing with hunger and plenty, war and peace, friendship and enmity, birth and death.

Tom McMullen
Cumbria
England
2015

Book One

Chapter One

---- o o o ----

Otter turned his head and forced himself to look, though the sight in his remaining eye was grainy. His left eye lay on a flat stone on the ground beside him in his family's lodge. The arrow shaft had been removed from it and the badly damaged globe quivered and flattened slightly as it started to dry out.

He turned again and lay back on the buffalo robe bed, the heel of his palm covering his good eye, shutting out all painful light. When he had been carried there, his mother had put a cottonwood twig between his teeth before she had taken her sharp skinning knife and sliced at the remaining pink tendrils which joined the damaged eye to the socket. His eye was dead and she knew it, it had no place in his head. There had been a lot of blood and Otter had almost chewed the twig in half. His mother had tapped a moist, poultice inside the eye socket to soak up the excess. Otter had then vomited over his mother; she just tutted soothingly.

Now, red lights danced in his head as he squeezed the fleshy part of his palm into his good eye. He eased the pressure and the lights flickered out, darkness returned. But there was something else in the background – a murmuring of low voices in his father's *tipi*. He peeked through his fingers and turned his head both ways; he had an audience.

His mother knelt to the left of his head, leaning over the fire preparing something. It was summer and odd to have a fire inside the lodge, but Otter couldn't dwell on why this was so, he just wanted the pain to stop. His father watched anxiously at his feet while Yellow Bear, the medicine man, muttered incantations and used an eagle wing fan to waft sage grass smoke from a burning twist across Otter's bed.

Sitting across the far side of the lodge, representatives of the tribal elders sat impassively watching the process. Otter wondered what they were doing there; perhaps it was out of respect for his father. It was hard to make out who was there through the smoke though he did recognise Broken Knife, the war leader of the Thunder Bear soldiers' society. Otter sighed bitterly; Broken Knife would have little interest in his condition or if he would recover but probably just wanted to see how he withstood the pain.

Yellow Bear's chants now got louder. Otter watched through spread fingers, though it was like looking up from the bed of a slightly muddy lake; he could only see the bottom of the man's angular chin and skinny neck, the rest was lost in swirling smoke and the poor light.

Otter liked Yellow Bear – he was a man who had followed his own mind and his own trail in life; a new spirit diviner for the Otter's band of the *Suhtai* Cheyenne.

Otter's father once told him that Yellow Bear had been one of his warriors. Smoke on the Moon had watched him in battle with the Pawnee and Crow on several occasions and thought that Yellow Bear's heart lay elsewhere. Not that Yellow Bear was cowardly, Smoke had stressed, he was just not as committed to fighting as the others. Riding back from a raid once, Yellow Bear had admitted that battle and policing the tribe on the hunt or when the village moved were not for him. He had never disgraced himself and no-one took it amiss when he withdrew from the warrior society and went to fast and dream alone in the wild country.

Visions and prophecies had been his reward. The skinny dreamer could often sense where the buffalo would be and after a dream during one bad winter, when starvation stalked the camp, had led hunters to a band of elk stranded in freezing mud. This had earned him great acclaim and the People now sought his opinion on many matters. Though as far as Otter could recollect, he was Yellow

Bear's first peacetime patient. His good eye watered as he watched him invoke the spirits.

Yellow Bear raised his burning twist of sage grass high and circled it around his head. Picking up a turtle shell rattle to attract the attention of the good spirits, he called on them to restore Otter to health and fitness and heal the wound. The seated elders nodded in assent and shuffled into more comfortable positions. Rituals took a while.

Otter turned his head again and looked at his mother; she could be a very impatient woman if the notion took her. Sure enough he saw Badlands Walking Woman grit her teeth and drum her stubby fingers on her thigh. She was a skilled healer in her own right; she would want to clear the tipi of the crowd so she could apply her own remedies.

The medicine man then stopped his chants and focused his attention on the eyeball lying on the stone. Surprisingly, he spoke to the assembled adults:

"I once cut out the eyeball of a dying buffalo and took it to the far side of a small hill, out of sight of the animal. I held up the eye in front of my face and wondered if the buffalo could still see me. Of course I was young then and not yet your spirit diviner. Buffalo only spoke to great chiefs or those with spiritual powers, so I couldn't know if the animal saw me through its removed eye or not."

The small crowd in the lodge leaned forward with interest as they detected a departure from the usual rituals over the wounded. Otter wondered what was coming next.

"Now that I have some powers for the use of the People, I would like to use the eye of the son of Smoke on the Moon to see if any sight is left in it when it has been taken from his head. The boy will be able to tell me yes or no."

There was a ripple of consternation – it was a departure from normal healing ceremonies, but Yellow Bear was not to be stopped. The medicine man knelt down on his skinny legs and put his own hand over Otter's remaining eye. Otter peeked through a gap in Yellow Bear's fingers and saw him wave his eagle wing fan in front of the detached eyeball by the side of his bed.

"What do you see?" he asked. Otter was tempted to say that he saw the fan but the pain had deadened his usual humour and flippancy would not sit well with his parents when company was present. Yellow Bear closed his fingers and darkness returned.

"What do you see?" asked Yellow Bear again. Otter could feel the wafts of air from the fan moving more wildly in front of his dead eye. Otter stopped thinking about the pain for a moment and spat out the twig.

"Nothing" he croaked. His mother noted the dry rasp of his voice and gave him a drink of water from a skin pouch.

Otter could not see what was happening but guessed that Yellow Bear would think of something else. He felt the passing of a burning taper next to his cheek. The medicine man was probably waving a flame in front of the dead eyeball.

"And now?" The pain was returning and Otter had lost the twig. He concentrated on getting his pain to retreat:

"I can only see the dark."

There was a slight raised tone amongst those gathered – was it a murmur of approval? Yellow Bear removed his hand from Otter's face and he forced his good eyelid to open. A sprinkling of green pinpoints of light cleared from his eye, though it felt as though someone had thrown a handful of large sand grains directly into it. Lubricating tears came and he brushed them away in case they were misinterpreted.

Yellow Bear, more concerned that he had at least proved that detached eyes were of no use, re-ignited his twist of sage grass and began to wave it about. The tipi flap opened and closed; Broken Knife had slipped out of the lodge without a word.

Otter looked at his mother. She seemed to have remembered something and turned back to her preparations over the fire. Good, despite the pain, he still felt hungry.

Suddenly she turned and slipped something into his mouth. It stuck out either side of his lips and he tried to chew it. Then he realised that it was a rawhide strip and not for eating. His father's hand clamped his jaw shut and strangers lay on top of him. Badlands Walking Woman pulled the bloody poultice from his eye socket and threw it aside.

It was done quickly. Otter's body arched in pain and surprise as the hot stone from the boiling cookpot was pushed into his raw wound. The hide strip in his mouth seemed to expand and fill his jaws, preventing any outcry. Lights flashed in his skull; it seemed like he had been hit with another bigger, jagged arrow. He knew no curses but he tried to shout his indignation out loud. His saliva, however, had turned edges of the rawhide strip into foamy glue and this kept his mouth fixed shut. A stabbing sensation, like a lance into his brain, kept exploding over and over again. Mercifully, under the determined press of bodies, he fainted and lay still.

Chapter Two

---- o o o ----

The leader of the raiding band grunted in satisfaction at the screaming; there was great spiritual power to be had from the pain inflicted on an enemy. As the life force drained from the victim, it strengthened the pain-giver. It was a waste to let enemies die quickly or silently.

He glanced outside at the burning buildings across the dirt clearing that served as a town square. As he looked, the mission roof collapsed inwards, the single bell clanging for the last time. Dust and smoke rose from the wreckage, grey ashes settling on the body of the spreadeagled Black Robe by the village well. The raider looked up - vultures already floated on the warm air, waiting.

His men would need to be back in the saddle soon if they were to lay false trails and confuse any pursuers. He examined his prize from the blacksmith's shop – a slim, two-edged skinning knife and a small whetstone to keep it sharp. The dark skin of his fingers contrasted against the bright metal edges of the blade. The screaming started again and he looked round.

Flames rose from the forge and lapped around the torso of its owner. The man screamed again, louder this time as his blackened flesh sizzled in the hot coals, sweat turning to rancid steam. The four dark skinned men holding him down turned to their leader and laughed. Cruz said:

"See Viajero? These Mexicans are very poor at withstanding pain."

It seemed odd to him that his men had started calling him by his Spanish name but he let it pass. Viajero did not reply but grinned with fierce pleasure, the light from the flames reflecting yellow and red in his silver coin necklet.

A dying Mexican mule trader had once whispered to him before they had stolen his stock. He had called Cruz over to translate. The young man had swept his long hair to one side, put his ear close to the Mexican's lips and listened to the death speech. He looked up:

'The Mexicans call you *El Viajero de la Muerte* – the Traveller of Death. They do not know when or where you will strike. They frighten their children with stories of you. You are famous.' Viajero had smiled at the coincidence of it – his own Apache name meant the Wanderer, so 'Traveller' was close. It seemed to be a good omen.

Outside, another raider draped other plunder across the backs of all six horses. Viajero walked outside to view the spoils. Not much from this rats' nest of a town – some powder, lead bullets, cloth and food. Two stolen mules, alarmed by the screams and smoke, jerked on their headropes tied to the saddles.

"Anyone left in the town?" he asked.

"No," replied the other warrior. "All the houses are empty; the people have fled to the hills." He paused and tied a side of sallow pork onto his pommel. "It's a pity - we could do with some more women."

Viajero snorted in disgust. "The last thing we need is more mouths to feed. Mexican women make poor captives, their town lives make them too soft for our hardships. They soon get sick and have to be abandoned or killed. Survival takes effort in our country; I regard them as well below mules."

"True," said the other, "But my wife is ugly with wrinkled skin, young Mexican women are smooth. A change would be welcome."

Viajero looked at the canvas lean-to. The screaming at the forge had subsided into gasps of pain and he walked back inside. His four companions had dropped the smouldering blacksmith onto the dirt floor and were busy ransacking the shelves for iron tools. They crisscrossed the shack, walking over the prostrate body, using the hard soles of their moccasins to slide lumps of black skin from bubbling red flesh. The man shrieked at each indignity and Viajero recognised the turning point; these shouts were not power-giving, they just showed fear and helplessness. They were the cries of women and children. The power of the Mexican's pain had gone.

Viajero clicked his fingers and pointed to the blacksmith. Cruz was closest and drew his long knife. He was young and headstrong and looked insolently at Viajero:

"Don't click your fingers at me, I am not a slave. Tell me what you want me to do, like any normal human being."

Viajero walked over to the younger man and stood within knife reach. It was a challenge and Cruz knew it. Cruz had been taken as a child from a Mexican settlement by Viajero's people and was sometimes wayward. He had often tried to escape in the early days but he had always been tracked down and returned to the wickiups. Usually, his hamstring would have been cut to prevent any further annoyance but he had proved to be a skilful fighter and shedder of blood. Cruz now killed his own kind as though he had been born a true Apache. Viajero spoke slowly and deliberately, never letting his eyes move from the face of the other man:

"Talking is the curse of the whites and Mexicans, it draws enemies to you. Silence is our discipline; it is part of our life as men of the *N'de*." He clicked his fingers again and pointed to the blacksmith.

Cruz let his head hang for a moment, his own signal to Viajero that he accepted the reproach. Then he knelt, his knee pinning the man's skull to the floor and stabbed the blacksmith through the ear, driving the hilt through the thin bone with the heel of his hand. He rocked the blade up and down until death came. Bracing his foot against the dead man's head, he pulled out the knife and yelled his triumph. Disdaining the scalp, he cut off the Mexican's top lip with its luxuriant moustache and clamped it under his own nose, strutting and laughing at his trophy. Viajero allowed himself a bleak smile to ease the tension. The dead blacksmith grinned in death, his upper jaw a row of small yellow tombstones streaked with blood.

But it was time to go. With more finger-clicking, the raiders were back in the saddle, cumbersome loot banging against their long moccasins as they headed north for the Gila, through the arid emptiness of Sonora.

Silent in the saddle with ponies now at a natural trot, Viajero rode behind the others. It was always this way. He was waiting for the black clouds; they were not in the sky but in his head. The same despondency always descended after a raid – lethargy in his spirit and a lead weight around his heart. Sure enough, as if coming across a familiar landmark, the clouds inside him rose like a thunderhead and made him slump in the saddle. His pony knew him well and always seemed to sense it too, slowing to a dejected walk. It was time to stop.

He reined in his horse and dropped the bridle across the rough mane. Cruz looked around for him and saw that Viajero had stopped; he called to the others. Tightening the red calico bandana around his hair as the raiders drew close, Viajero turned in his saddle and spoke:

"I'll circle to make sure we are not followed. Cruz, you are the leader now. Split up before nightfall, lay false trails south and east, then go home."

The other man nodded curtly but, true to his wayward nature, offered his unwanted opinion:

"Your wife always asks me why you do not return to her. No-one will follow; those Mexicans are like frightened chickens. Come with us – we should all go back together."

Viajero looked hard at him; he did not like to be challenged. Cruz' insolence would get him killed one day. Protecting the back trail was just an excuse; he suspected the others already knew.

"Just ride."

The other man nodded again, a curt dismissive gesture rather than acceptance of orders. He wheeled his pony and joined the waiting group. As if at a signal, the younger ones rode off yelling and screeching with joy at their success and, Viajero knew, at the welcome absence of their dour leader. The mules trotted stiffly behind, spooked by the shouting. The ragged red hills, pockmarked with dusty green scrub, soon swallowed them up.

Viajero dismounted. He made a show of climbing to a rocky outcrop to watch for any pursuit but instead of looking south, settled his stocky frame into a crevice and stared into the setting sun.

Taking a handful of dirt, he sprinkled it onto a flat rock, taking care that *Usen*, the One God of the White Mountain Apaches, could see the distinctive shape of the horned lizard emerging from the particles. Viajero always liked to identify himself before he tried to communicate. The horned lizard was a creature that Viajero admired for its hardiness and simplicity; it suited his description of himself.

His talks with God were a complicated matter – Viajero knew that Usen sent the bleak, roiling inner clouds to him each time after a raid. Viajero wanted to know *why* the One God sent such thoughts; thoughts that kept him in the solitude of the wild places, away from his family. Unfortunately, Viajero already knew the reason and always felt guilty.

"Usen, I know I am restless at the family camp fire…"

He paused. The truth that lay just behind his tongue would be uncomfortable for him to hear, let alone the Life Giver.

"My wife is good but she does not interest me now; the love has passed. I bring her good things from raids – necklaces of blue stones, silver, calico, stock - but she knows that I never fully return to her. We share the same bed in the *wickiup* but she knows that my heart is still in the wilderness. We drift apart like twigs floating in a stream."

Viajero's eyes narrowed and, to his surprise, briefly filled with tears; he knew that hard confessions affected the hardest of men. Physical pain was needed to balance his wickedness. He took out his knife and ripped open his shirt, the sharp point slicing the dark skin above his heart. Blood trickled around his nipple and down his ribcage. He breathed out a long sigh, air hissing through his teeth. It was not with pain but only the realisation that there was worse to come. He grasped the knife firmly by the hilt, point towards his heart – if Usen willed it, he would end his own life, here in a red stone cleft, many days ride from home.

"I was proud of my son when he was born but, out here, I am pleased to be free of his crying and child's ways. I am a worthless father. I look for any small piece of love for my family that remains in me and find none. When I look at my reflection in the stream, I see a face that I do not know. I am empty."

Viajero pushed the knife further into his flesh and now the pain came; more blood joined the first, thin red trail though the wound was not liable to cause death.

"The smell of a settled camp – of children, women and old men – sickens me. We have grown fat and easy to find. We've stopped our life of hardship that builds great warriors and a strong people. Perhaps my days are over."

So it was in the open now, not just confined to his selfish heart. Shame washed over him but he had, at least, admitted his innermost thoughts out loud. For him, it was easier being alone in the wilderness than it was coping with family life. Usen may have created the craving for solitude but Viajero was glad of it.

"Usen, my life is yours. Drive my knife home; I am not fit to live as a man of the N'de."

As so often when Viajero talked to God, there was no reply, no firm instruction. Men must make their own minds up. Viajero eventually took the knife from his flesh; the blade had dried into the wound and had to be pulled out, causing fresh bleeding. The Apache let the blood run, though his own practised eye could tell that he would not die from the flow. He settled down and slept in the rock crevice as darkness crept across the dappled pink and purple sky.

Chapter Three

---- o o o ----

It was a week before Otter could stand unaided. His friends, Little Head and Thorn had visited every day, each taking an arm and leading him outside the tipi so he could at least watch village life going on as normal. Both of the others were a year older than him but they'd all raced around the village in the same wild pack of growing boys; racing ponies, playing games, hunting and trying to impress girls. Now, at sixteen, Otter felt that the year's age gap between them was widening.

The shock of the hot stone in his eye socket still made him shiver when he thought about it. His mother had since applied soothing poultices of dampened tree moss and spiders' webs, moulding them into soft globes to plug the raw wound. It still made Otter flinch but at least his punctured eyelid was healing and he could close this over the strange new eyeball.

The arrow that took his eye had been accidental; a boyish prank that went wrong. The boy had meant it to hit a tree near Otter's head but misjudged the shot. In the seconds before it hit him, Otter had heard the arrow leaving the boy's bow – 'like a panicking bird' as his father described such poor shots; the shaft scrabbling over the bow stave, struggling to get into the air like a startled bird clattered talons on branches to escape. Though only for a heartbeat, he remembered time slowing down and he'd seen the arrow approaching. His limbs seemed to have turned to stone as the shaft bucked through the air towards him. He'd tried to duck but only managed to turn his head to the right; his left eyeball's last image was of a rusted iron arrowhead.

Sitting in the open entrance to the lodge and looking out into the circle of tipis of his village, he practised moving his head moving from side to side as he dealt with the unaccustomed limit to his vision. A calico bandage covered his eye socket now to keep out the dust. Thanks to his father, his courage had been widely reported and many sought him out to give him words of reassurance. Even the taciturn Broken Knife had taken to riding past on his pony and nodding a silent acknowledgement to him.

Smoke on the Moon, back from discussions about moving to the next camp site with Twisted Wolf and Yellow Bear, sat down beside his son:

"You seem to get stronger every day, how is the new eyeball?"

"I'm getting used to it" said Otter, though a dull ache had spread to the back of his skull.

"You handled the pain well, your mother and I are proud of you."

Otter smiled and nodded his head in gratitude; his father only gave praise sparingly. There had been a lot less praise when Otter's own poor work with the bow had been the subject of their talks; many of those 'panicking birds' arrows during tuition had been his. At first it was overlooked; Smoke had patted him on the shoulder and told him not to worry, improvements would come with practice. But they never did.

His father was still speaking, he jerked back to the conversation…

"…your uncle sends a message of sorrow about your eye. He is just back from a hunt but he'll come and see you soon."

Otter nodded and hoped he hadn't missed anything important; Smoke could be easily irritated. He sensed that his father's satisfaction with him in his time of pain might be short-lived so he ventured along a different track while circumstances were favourable:

"Father, I know I've brought disgrace to our family…"

Smoke bristled but Otter continued:

"… with my poor work with the bow. I'm sixteen and still can't be relied on to fill the family cookpot or be taken seriously to go with a war party."

Smoke knew this was true; boys many years younger than his son could hit a running jackrabbit. Some youngsters could steer a pony at a dead run alongside a fleeing buffalo calf and could be relied on to bring it down with an arrow through its heart. Otter could ride well but he lacked the other skills to provide for his family or be trusted on the war trail. The loss of his eye only made things worse. Smoke stroked his chin thoughtfully as he chose his words:

"You do not bring disgrace to us, so no more of that. Your mother and I just worry what trail in life you will take without the skills of a warrior or hunter. Life with the People is hard enough - we always live on the edge of hunger or death. The *Tsis-tsis-tas* are not as numerous as the Lakota but our spirit is the same; all our young men need to find their reputations in life through battle and the hunt…"

"Nonsense!"

Otter whipped his head round; his mother, carrying skin pouches of water, had come up on his blind side. She was a loyal wife but she was an outsider from another tribe so she often ignored Cheyenne custom if it did not benefit her family. Letting her husband frighten her son was not her way. She put the water into the lodge out of the sun and came back. Smoke gritted his teeth as his strong-willed wife gave her unwanted opinions.

"Not all things in life depend on the blood of men or animals on your arrows. Not all of our men fight or hunt; there are those who make the best arrows and shields – people pay them with presents for that. Some can predict the rain coming or know where the buffalo are – others provide for *them* too."

Otter nodded dumbly, aware that his father was being overridden but saw the flaw in his mother's argument:

"Yes, Yes. I know this," he said testily. His mother's pudgy hand swiped him across his shoulder to remind him to respect his parents. Otter continued more cautiously:

"I know that some stay behind but I don't want people to provide for *me*. I want to be a full member of the People – to fight for them, protect them and feed them. I don't want to be…" he searched for the word, "one of the *Hee-man-heh*."

There were no *Hee-man-heh* in Otter's tribal group but he had seen them in other bands of the Cheyenne. They were appreciated for their skilled crafts; decorating with porcupine quills, making jewellery or for their graceful dancing. They were men who lived as women. Otter shuddered at the uncomfortable image in his mind. Surprisingly, it was Smoke who came to their rescue:

"Those who join the *Hee-man-heh* are at least brave. They know their life's trail and follow it. If they have beliefs or faults that keep them from the war trail or hunting parties, they accept it." He looked steadily at Otter, making sure that his son saw him.

"You will need to think about that." He stood up and stalked off, irritated by his wife's interruption in his talks with his son and Otter's petulance. God was trying him today.

When Smoke on the Moon had gone, Badlands Walking Woman sat on her haunches in front of Otter so he could see her without moving his head to and fro. She looked at him steadily, her black eyes boring into his face. His mother was formidable; Otter sighed in resignation.

Smoke had told him that his mother had got her name once the People had been told how she had followed her mother around the hot, arid wastes of her homeland on the southern Plains, collecting herbs and plants. When she had first arrived in their village as a fifteen year-old captive from a raid on the Kiowa Apache, she had screeched her defiance for weeks in her own tongue and had just been known as The Outsider. She had the dark skin of her southern kinfolk and had been thought erratic, unmarriageable and unstable.

"Your father speaks wisely," she said, ignoring the fact that she had just interrupted the flow of her husband's wisdom.

"Your hunting and war skills are coming more slowly for you than the others. Your blindness in one eye won't help. It may be a sign that you may need to consider a different path in your life, to live life differently and make the best of what you have."

Otter shook his head determinedly. No war, no glory; no glory, no wife; no hunting, no family. It was a simple thing. The stepping stones on the way to manhood were many – testing in battle, seeking visions on a quest or even just getting rid of his child's name; Otter wanted them all or he would not be a true Cheyenne. Badlands Walking Woman sensed his turmoil and handed him a piece of buffalo jerky so she could have time to think of the best thing she could do for her beloved son.

"You did manage to bring us some game for the cooking fire the other day" she said," I was very proud of you."

Otter looked at her and, to his own surprise, smiled:

"Mother, it was a *skunk*; one of life's slowest creatures, I nearly tripped over it. Even I couldn't miss that…"

"I *did* wonder – I thought it might have surrendered."

Otter laughed but he knew that even the chubby and cocksure Little Head or Thorn, the crazy one, could always be relied on to fill the bellies of their families. Skunks rarely featured in *their* meals. The act of smiling now hurt his head, as the muscles under his eyes remembered the uncomfortable mossy globe in his eye socket. Badlands saw his discomfort and led him back inside the lodge to his bed.

That night, Twisted Wolf, the camp chief, sent criers round to the family fires; the camp would move the next day.

At dawn, Otter, under instruction from his father, helped Badlands strip the hide covers from the tipi poles, pack the lodge contents and load the travois. He seethed under the imposition of girls' work. Badlands saw his poor temper and lectured him on petulance, then with a dismissive jerk of her head, released him to his other duties.

Otter walked carefully to the horse herd. Normally, he would have found Little Head and Thorn and raced them to the grazing grounds but trying to run these days was a bit more difficult. He'd already slipped down the riverbank when he failed to judge the width of a track. His friends were nowhere to be seen so he found and mounted his bay and helped a five or six younger boys to move the pony herd out to follow the moving village. Out on a ridge he could see his father's Striking Snakes soldiers forming a screen to protect their families during this vulnerable time. Ahead a small dust cloud showed where Broken Knife's Thunder Bears moved in arrow point formation, guarding the main body of the tribal group. Dogs yapped, children scampered between ponies, women laughed and chatted as they walked and his mother, in her own high yip, sang her camp moving song. Otter was strangely comforted.

Chapter Four

---- o o o ----

Viajero lay on the sun-baked red mesa and waited, watching for an opportunity to close in for the kill.

When he was young, his father had once tested him in the ways of Apache life. He'd said:

"When I turn my head, walk up that trail and become a stone. Do not move until I come to fetch you."

Viajero had selected a group of rocks, scattered dust over himself and lay down motionless. He had lain without food or water for two days and nights. On the morning of the third day, another rock nearby got up and tapped him on the shoulder – it was his father. Viajero had passed the test of endurance but had failed the test of being observant. The old man forbade him any food back in the wickiups as a reminder that concealment was of no use unless it was used to advantage.

Up on the mesa, the Apache reflected on his recent talks with Usen after the Sonora raid. His selfishness had come at a high cost. His shallow prayers to Usen now haunted him; he had brought disaster on himself and his family. Now his selfish cravings for solitude had been granted, in full measure and permanently.

He had had been returning from a hunt when he had seen the smoke column. It was too big for a family fire and too obvious for his secretive people. He had charged back, rifle at the ready, to the campsite and found his family circle in ruins; smouldering wickiups with collapsed frames, broken pottery, torn skins and clothing. He couldn't bear to touch the flesh of his dead family, not even to remove the thorns where they had been dragged through the cholla cactus. He had wrapped his wife and her mother in a stolen trade blanket and dragged them to a hastily dug shallow grave. While he was filling in the scraped earth, a horned lizard had scuttled out from under a rock and looked at him reproachfully; Viajero knew Usen had sent it to remind him where the fault lay for his selfish prayers. He had collected rocks and thorns to keep the coyotes from digging up the newly dead but an owl hooting nearby spooked him and he left without a backward glance. There was no sign of his son.

The attackers had been easy to follow. Ten horses with iron shoes, his stock of sheep and mules and the body of his sister-in-law, dragged along by her feet made a broad trail. He found her the next day - she had been raped many times, killed and casually tossed aside into a shallow ravine. The raiders were not far ahead, making a leisurely pace. They were Mexicans, all well-armed and alert, masters of the moment and enjoying their victory.

Viajero had felt impotent; the Mexicans took strict precautions at their night camps with armed and vigilant sentries. All slept with their bridled mounts picketed to hand. They could not be attacked without grave risk.

He had noticed a small burlap sack near the saddle of one of the Mexicans. He needed food and so, as a show of defiance and despite the armed sentries, he had crept among the sleeping men and stolen the sack. Once opened, he wished he had not taken it – the sack contained the severed head of his son; proof of the raiders' successful foray into the *apacheria*.

He had stared dumbly at his son's face. There was still a look of terror in the boy's eyes; the once chubby flesh was starting to rot in the heat. He examined the brown staring eyes again, muddy now in death, still using the blood-caked burlap to avoid touching the dead skin. There was another hint in the boy's eyes too; it was the same knowing look of reproach that he had seen in the horned lizard at the graveside. Usen was letting him know just who was responsible for this devastation of his life.

Viajero had felt the familiar flames of vengeance rise within him. But behind them was a roiling smoke cloud of guilt. There was the usual blood price to pay but the Apache knew it would need to be balanced by a purging of his soul. These men would have to be left alone for now but other Mexicans would do just as well. How the One-God would cleanse the guilty Apache, Viajero would have to leave that to fate. He had left the sack in an old rattlesnake pit and rode off.

Now, Viajero slipped into a rock crevice out of the harsh sunlight. The shade brought relief but he hadn't gone there for comfort. His target was moving slowly southwards and he wanted to keep track of it. The familiar excitement of the stalk and the chase became more pronounced. Long practice made him breathe slowly and keep his movements to a minimum.

He changed position again on the mesa; it was just after midday and the heat shimmered on the shale plain. Below him, two Mexican *vaqueros* dismounted from their horses and walked them into the shade of a rocky overhang on the far side of a narrow defile. Between them they were driving about twenty head of scrawny scrub cattle that bawled as they too stopped walking, glad of the rest in the scorching heat. The *vaqueros* knew what they were doing – a trickle of water fell lazily into a shallow pool by the rocks and the cattle gathered round, lapping at the dusty surface. The riders took their water bottles down from their saddles and moved under an outcrop where there was shade.

The Apache counted their weapons. Both men carried revolvers in leather holsters on their belts but had no rifles in their hands or in saddle buckets. They were poorly armed. The two horses of the *vaqueros* did not excite much interest; they looked like hard worked mustangs from a ranch *remuda*. They were bony and worn out. One saddle, well kept and soaped, looked to be inlaid with silver platework. It would be a good prize.

One of the *vaqueros* was young, some twenty summers; the other looked about ten years older than Viajero, around forty years of age. Both wore the wide brimmed sombreros common to this part of Mexico. They were both tired. They drank their water sparingly and ate something from a greasy calico wrapping. Drowsy words of Spanish floated up to the Apache as he prepared his plan of attack.

These *vaqueros* had no involvement with the massacre of his family and he knew it; he was just determined to make all Mexicans pay for his loss. Their deaths would give him great satisfaction but their pain before they died, as he exulted in their screams and agony, would give him something even better – spiritual and personal power. It would feed his hatred and give renewal for future killings. His heart beat faster in anticipation.

Viajero had thought much about his life in the days since his family had been killed. He was hard on himself and, as he often reminded Usen in his prayers, rightly so. Any Apache would be doing the same as him, exacting vengeance for the death of his family. But those others would be doing so for an honourable reason; out of unbearable grief and lost love. Viajero delighted in the revenge trail; the stalk, the kills. But he knew that making Mexicans pay a blood price for his family was just a convenient excuse. Raiding was his life and his reputation was built on it; he had never considered stopping. He killed Mexicans because they were there; it was what the Apache were supposed to do. However many he slaughtered, raped or plundered, he knew that there would never be the feeling of an ordinary man – that the blood price had been paid, that vengeance had been fully served or that the hatred would fade. He trusted Usen to tell him when to stop.

Viajero climbed back down to his pony, safely grazing in a small box canyon away from the scent of the Mexican horses. He took out a deerskin pouch tucked into a rawhide saddlebag, poured out a small pile of yellow powder into his hand, spat on the contents and mixed powder and spittle into a bright paste. After dipping his forefinger in the mixture, he traced a bold line from his left ear, under his eye, across the bridge of his nose to his right ear. He made two yellow slash marks on each cheek. The paint was in bright contrast to his dark, sun-flayed skin. He repeated the process using a red dye from another pouch, all the while looking at the markings in a fragment of mirror which he always carried.

Viajero completed his preparations by stripping down to his breechclout, a deerskin vest, his long moccasins and a red linen bandana over his hair to keep it from falling into his eyes during the coming fight. His black eyes glittered fiercely back at him from the mirror as he checked himself for the final time. He sang his death song softly as he spurred his pony in a wide arc, keeping well ahead of the *vaqueros*. He was going to war and needed time to make his plan work.

A short ride brought Viajero to the salt lick. He dismounted and led his pony to a nearby dry streambed, hobbling the animal behind a screen of thorn bushes. Returning to the side of the trail, he took out his knife and dug a shallow scrape, covering himself with a gray blanket that matched the colour of the soil. He pulled mesquite and greasewood fronds through slits in the blanket and, as he settled back, sprinkled dust over the gaps where the blanket was still visible.

The Apache watched the salt lick through a slit in his blanket. He had become as the earth as his father had taught him. The cattle came first, a series of low complaining bawls and snorts coming out of the narrow defile. The younger vaquero rode point, the elder trailed at the rear, bandana over his nose to filter out the dust. The group cast long purple shadows in the setting sun.

Under the blanket Viajero smiled – his plan was working. The crystals of the salt lick twinkled in the fading light; the cattle were glad of the minerals, pushing and jostling to get to the small hollow. They were exhausted and would not wander far overnight. There was no visible water but several of the steers had already smelled the hidden spring and pawed their way through the hard-caked mud to soothe their muzzles in the dampened earth. They wandered off from the salt lick to patches of grazing.

The elder *vaquero* dismounted and threw saddle and blanket onto the hard earth. Taking out a rawhide noose, he moved his animal to a patch of grazing close to the campsite and hobbled both its front legs. As he was in hostile country, he also took out an iron spike and picketed the horse to a rope to keep him close in case of emergencies. The younger man followed his example, the silver brightwork on his saddle giving off a dull red glow as the sun sank lower in the western sky. Both horses munched and tore at the poor grass and ground plants.

The younger man went off to collect mesquite wood for the fire and presently came back with an armful of thin brush for kindling and stouter boughs for a cooking fire. Flames soon illuminated the small campsite; coffee was put on to boil and fatback bacon sliced into an iron skillet. Both men lay around the fire, curling their bodies towards the heat, talking and turning the bacon in the pan with the point of a knife. The older man unholstered his pistol and placed it within hand's reach on his bedding blanket. The younger man did not follow suit but chose to keep his gunbelt around his waist. He pulled his blanket over him as he waited for the bacon to cook. Darkness fell quickly and the night turned chill as the movements of both men slowed and conversation slurred; sleep beckoned. Viajero prepared himself with a last prayer to *Usen*. The men lounged back on their saddles, idly throwing fragments of salt crystals into a circular patch of yellow grass. Then it was time.

The war shriek paralysed both Mexicans with fear, their picketed horses crow-hopped around their tethers, squealing in alarm. Spooked cattle stampeded off into the chaparral. Those short heartbeats of frozen inactivity gave the Apache the advantage he needed.

Viajero threw the blanket from him, scattering the slivers of plants and bushes that he had pulled through slits to aid concealment. The covering of carefully applied dust exploded into a cloud, obscuring the vision of his enemies.

The older *vaquero* died first. Viajero leapt across the small cooking fire and thrust his hunting knife deep into the man's neck. Blood spurted over the hilt and the Apache's wrist. The blood was warm and made a violent black stain on the shoulder of the Mexican's working shirt. The warrior released the knife handle, leaving the weapon inside the jugular. Hanging from the Apache's wrist was a stone war club that he used for close quarter fighting. Turning and flicking the club into the palm of his hand, he turned his attention to the younger man.

This one was white with fear, kicking his spurred heels to get rid of his blanket but only succeeding in tangling himself further. Under the blanket he reached frantically for his pistol but he couldn't unhook the restraining strap over the revolver's hammer. His weapon remained firmly in place. His breath came in urgent grunts of frustration. Now he caught sight of the terrible face of the Apache turned towards him, vermilion and yellow stripes gleaming in the firelight. There was a sharp, acrid smell as the boy's bowels erupted in fear and he soiled himself. Viajero clubbed him hard on the side of the head and his struggles ceased.

He trussed up the younger *vaquero.* He removed the man's boots, tying wrists and ankles together behind the youth's back, then with a rawhide rope looped around a rock, he bound the man around the throat pulling him tight against the red sandstone grunting and squeaking – a pale pig, ready for disembowelling. To keep him quiet, Viajero stuffed the man's mouth with dried grass and horse dung. Ignoring the retching and gagging, he tore off a piece of the *vaquero's* shirt to keep the mixture in place overnight.

The Apache had wanted both men alive but the older *vaquero* was more experienced; his pistol had been unholstered and close to hand. It was too much of a risk, he had to be killed. Still, there was always power to be had from the direct killing of an enemy with your own hands.

Satisfied, he ate the remainder of the fatback bacon then left the glow of the fire to sleep some distance off. Tomorrow, the young *vaquero* would announce his pain to the empty, pitiless hills and Viajero of the White Mountain Apache, would try to fill some of the emptiness of his soul.

Chapter Five

---- o o o ----

Otter was healing and gaining strength. The village had moved a couple of times in quick succession as the swelling horse herd, the rewards from successful raids on the Crow and Pawnee, stripped the pasture quicker than it could grow back. Twisted Wolf was always the first to spot when the resources of the People had dwindled to a dangerous level. But these summer moves were relaxed events and no-one seemed to mind the upheaval of lodges, baggage and families in these times of plenty. Their last campground had been shared with a few lodges of the Arapaho, long-time allies of the Cheyenne, before the horse herds forced another move to the banks of the Tallow river. Otter got the impression that the Arapaho were glad to see the Cheyenne go and take their greedy mounts with them.

Otter's band had not been long in their new camping place when there was a commotion. A rising chatter from women at the river and those out foraging was the first signal of something different; children ran from their games to the centre of the village. A lone horseman was entering the circle of lodges and a small crowd was gathering. Otter was too far away to see who it was but carefully made his way through the tipis and meat drying racks to find out.

Getting closer, he could see that the rider was Little Head. He picked his way round a pegged-out elk skin and asked a woman where Little Head had been. The woman, the pretty wife of one of his father's warriors smiled and said:

"He's back from the mountains. I think he went on his vision quest, his parents will be pleased he has found us again safely."

Otter was slightly petulant that he hadn't known about his friend's trip. Tribal life had continued while he had lain in bed. Little Head's proud father led the young man's pony into the centre of the village smiling and nodding at the greetings of the people as they rejoiced at his son's safe return. Smaller children came up and touched the boy's bare legs in respect. Women, led by Little Head's mother, started an impromptu celebration dance, then bustled away to prepare a homecoming feast. Otter stayed shyly apart from the throng. His friend nodded to him but did not speak. Little Head looked tired and thin; his puppy fat seemed to have disappeared.

Otter walked back to his family lodge. He knew that Little Head must first speak to Yellow Bear in order to report the dreams and visions he had seen. Yellow Bear would then interpret the dreams and try to give the youth a flavour of his destiny. It was a crucial time and, for a moment, made Otter flare with envy. He would have felt better if Little Head had told him that he was off on his quest; perhaps they could have gone together.

He waited by their favourite tree for the feasting to finish. Usually the two boys would swing out on rawhide ropes and splash noisily into the river together, often as a pretty girl went past. But Little Head did not come that day or most of the next. Otter sensed that things were changing.

Eventually they met beside the river; Little Head seemed changed, more adult somehow, as he told Otter how his quest had gone.

He had reached the mountains after a long ride. A pack of wolves had followed him for a while but an arrow fired into one gave him a chance to break away as the others turned and ripped their injured pack mate to shreds. Once in the mountains, he had eaten little but had stared into the sun for three continuous days, standing on a flat rock and moving round to keep the rays in his eyes.

"It must have been hard for you not to eat," said Otter interrupting. Little Head just glared at him; it was the look of a man rebuking a boy.

"Do you want to hear the story of my dream or not?" Otter hung his head.

"Well, I was mounted on an Appaloosa pony…"

"You aren't rich enough to have an Appaloosa; the Snake People make us pay high prices for them…" Otter was continuing his conversation as he would with his friend, chafing, challenging and joking. But now he sensed he was talking to a stranger.

Little Head leant across and cuffed his ear. Otter recoiled; they had often hit each other during their games but this was new. Little Head gritted his teeth and went on:

"For the last time – I was mounted on an Appaloosa on a high rocky cliff in moonlight. The light reflected off the pony's rump…"

Otter opened his mouth but changed his mind about speaking.

"… Wolves and bears came towards me, I thought they would attack but they just slunk off. Enemies fired arrows at me but all missed. Then, as danger got closer, the pony leapt from the cliff with me still on it and we floated safely back to earth."

Otter had an unreasonable thought that Little Head was making it all up but dismissed it guiltily from his mind. This was far too sacred a thing to lie about. He tried to make amends:

"That sounds like a real warrior's dream. I hope I have one like it on my own vision quest."

Appeased, Little Head nodded sagely. Otter sighed; his friend's new air of maturity was annoying.

"What did Yellow Bear tell you about the dream?"

"Well, he told me that the meaning of the dream was only for me to know…"

"Yes, but I'm your friend. I won't tell anyone else."

Little Head paused, unsure of what spiritual sin he'd be committing if he failed to obey Yellow Bear's instructions. He sighed, the interpretation of his dream had been powerful and he would hate to miss the chance of bragging to Otter. He plunged ahead.

"Yellow Bear told me that the Appaloosa pony meant that I would be wealthy, the bears and wolves turning back showed my courage and the enemy arrows missing me meant that I wouldn't die from them…"

Otter looked at his friend with envious respect. Despite growing up together, playing ball games, wrestling and chasing each other across the broad prairie grasslands, Little Head was now leaving him behind. The parting was subtle but still definite as the gulf between his immature boyhood and Little Head's beckoning manhood widened. His friend had found his life trail and was setting out on it while Otter was still grubbing around in the dust trying to find his own.

Little Head continued:

"…and the moonlight on the pony's rump pointed to my man's name." He finished his story with a swift nod of the head.

"What is your man name going to be?"

Little Head got up shaking his head; he had probably already overstepped the medicine man's instructions and couldn't tell Otter that final fact.

"It's too sacred to say before I'm properly named; there'll be a naming feast in a couple of days."

Otter nodded glumly and walked dejectedly home, flinging himself onto the skin robe at the flap.

Smoke on the Moon watched his son from the shade as he picked burrs from his pony's hide. His wife helped him and they conversed in low tones across the animal's spine. A light rain fell and Otter moved back inside the lodge. Smoke had recovered his temper but was disconsolate:

"Your healing was strong. The boy is on his feet and can move around."

"My mother taught me well."

"That's true. Your potions have great power."

Smoke paused and sneezed as the dried mud from his pony's coat rose into his nostrils.

"I have been thinking about our son and his trail in life. He has always been different from the others and now, this difference is greater. His chances for glory and great deeds are few…"

Badlands Walking Woman, quick to defend her own, butted in:

"No! He is not sick or weak – he is not a child. When he recovers there will still be time for him to flourish."

But Smoke was adamant:

"There can be no future for a one-eyed youth as a fully-fledged warrior; his remaining eye will always be a weakness. Even rising pollen or trail dust would render him as good as blind. His poor showing with the bow doesn't matter now; he will never get the chance to test himself in battle."

Badlands opened her mouth to speak again but Smoke cut her off:

"I have spoken with Yellow Bear many times about our son. He has talked to the spirits but has no words of comfort. The boy will be flawed for the rest of his life."

Badlands hissed her disagreement and slapped the pony's rump. It skittered from side to side, until Smoke took its head rope and calmed it. He had had an idea brought on by Little Head's return – though it was just a plan for the short term:

"It is doubtful if the boy will ever go on the war trail or even on his vision quest – I'm not even sure if dreams can come to one-eyed men. If we wait for a great achievement in his life, he may wait forever for his adult name. So I have decided…"

His wife looked quizzical, cocking her head to one side.

"…to give him his man's name. We must do it quickly in the next few days while the People remember his courage during his time of pain. This time…"

He looked meaningfully at Badlands.

"…I will discuss his adult name with others. You are not to interfere. This may be the last useful service that I can perform for him."

Badlands was pleased:

"Just when I think you are a traditional Cheyenne, you surprise me. So - I have a feast to prepare. I'll tell Otter."

Otter saw his parents talking and untether the pony to return it to the herd, walking off together as the drizzle lifted.

Healing gave Otter time to think. He alternated between gloom and hope. Sometimes cast down by recurring pain, sometimes buoyed up by helpful words from his father or other members of the tribe. The words they spoke were kindly and comforting but their hidden, and final, meaning had not yet dawned on him. A spasm of pain returned and he shook his head to be free of it. Things were settling down after his accident, soon the welcome glow of notoriety that it gave him would be gone.

In one of the earlier campsites, Yellow Bear had herded a sheepish group of children into see him. Yellow Bear had pointed to one chubby child of about nine years old and gestured to him to step forward. The boy, who was called Little Snake, began a piping, childish oration:

"My brother, you see that I am only small and not yet ready for the war trail. I was the one who fired the arrow that killed your eye. My father has already punished me for it. I was with my friends…"

He looked around to the others for support but saw only heads hung in embarrassment and shame.

"…and we were playing at stalking the Pawnee. You were the Pawnee. I saw you go into the trees after that deer and we followed you. You did not hear our steps…"

He looked around proudly but saw only Yellow Bear's fierce stare.

"….I meant to fire my arrow into the tree beside you as a surprise but you moved. I cannot bring your eye back to life but I offer you this present in friendship."

The boy handed over a small hunting knife; its steel blade cased in a deerskin sheath with porcupine quillwork on the outer edge. It was probably the boy's prized possession; steel knives were not normally given to children. The boy's father must have thought highly of him. He wished Smoke was of a similar frame of mind. Otter took the knife and tried to smile. The uncomfortable lump in his eye socket turned the smile into a twitching grimace. Little Snake stepped back in alarm. Otter was thinking of something to say when Yellow Bear cut in:

"They have all been punished" he said, gesturing to the children, "Your eye cannot return, they just hope that it does not stop you becoming a warrior". With that, he shepherded the small group away. Relieved of the tension in the lodge, they scattered yelling and screeching their child war cries.

Otter felt sick. He had never considered that the loss of his eye would actually prevent him becoming a warrior, a full Cheyenne. True, it might delay things but hopefully it wouldn't be a permanent obstacle? This was a crushing blow when added to his poor skills with the bow. Then he remembered how he now had to turn his head from side to side just to see everything. That would be bad for a fighting man, Yellow Bear and the others had been warning him to expect the worst. Some of the despair returned and he struggled to his feet. He needed reassurance.

His father would know what to do but Otter hesitated; he did not want to approach his father again. Smoke would give advice that he would be almost duty bound to follow. No, it would be better to seek guidance from his uncle. His uncle always gave him balanced advice, he was the brother of Smoke on the Moon after all, but he had a different way of looking at life. What he had to say may be more palatable than advice from his stern father. Shielding his good eye, he walked to his uncle's lodge.

Otter found his uncle at the edge of the pony herd; Bad Elk had just returned from hunting and had turned his horse out to graze. It joined the hundreds of other mounts in the small valley next to the village, their coats sleek and glossy with the good grass. Nearby on a hillside, women were cutting new lodgepoles from a stand of pine, their high voices carried clearly over to Otter.

Bad Elk saw him, walked over to a rocky outcrop and motioned him over. The warrior was covered in fine dust and was stretching the knots out of his leg muscles. His skill with a rifle was well known and the weapon lay in its buckskin case on the rock next to him. His wife, a plump and ugly woman called Burnt Hair, dragged the hunting trophies – two small Pronghorn antelope – off to the lodge.

Bad Elk had often sung the praises of the Pronghorn when he had taken Otter hunting. The antelope were swift and graceful; they were difficult to shoot under normal circumstances as their eyesight and sense of smell was excellent. However, they had a weakness, they were intensely curious. After wasting much powder and ball on fleeing white rumps, Bad Elk had taken to luring the inquisitive animals by waggling a small piece of cloth on a branch while he lay hidden. He shot them when they came close enough.

Bad Elk asked about his wound. Otter countered with the expected response that it did not hurt much now. Otter sat down and fingered the beaded decoration on the rifle case waiting for the right moment. Bad Elk sat and watched him but still said nothing. He knew Otter had come for a special reason; he would no doubt get round to mentioning it in good time.

"Uncle", Otter suddenly blurted out, "Can I ever be a warrior with only one eye? Will I ever draw a true arrow on our enemies?"

Bad Elk mused on the question and stroked his chin then swatted away horseflies that buzzed and circled around the corner of his eyes. He had been one of Otter's teachers when the boy had progressed from the child's bow, firing blunted wooden arrows, to a man-sized killing weapon. Patient as Bad Elk had been, he knew that Otter's skills were sporadic; luck played a big part in the boy's ability to bring down game with an arrow. It was a risk that most war party leaders were unprepared to take if battle was expected. Even a mundane war task, like guarding their ponies in enemy country, required a youth that was able to put three or four deadly accurate arrows into a target in a short time. Bad Elk knew that Otter's skills could not match that. He needed to be truthful but not to hurt the boy's feelings.

"I once knew a warrior with one eye who still went into battle", Bad Elk recalled. "He lost his eye during a fight with the Crow in the mountains to the west. So these things are not unknown. That man though, was already a warrior when it happened. He did not fight again for a long while until his wound healed but he did return to the war trail. Sickness took him some years back."

His uncle always spoke loudly; it was a strange trait, perhaps he was deaf from the rifle. Otter looked unblinkingly at Bad Elk, he wasn't yet sure whether he was being encouraged or not. Bad Elk had taken his rifle out of its case and was wiping the dust from it with a soft deerskin patch. He continued:

"As you know, your own work with the bow was never good even when you had two eyes…"

Otter knew he would get the truth from Bad Elk but just wished that the blow had landed more softly. He seemed to be staring into a long dark cave where there was no light, no glimpse of a bright future as a Cheyenne fighting man.

"…you tried hard but sometimes these things are not meant to be…"

Otter was crushed; he prayed that Bad Elk would not echo his mother's suggestion of staying in camp while the others went out to fight. He would die of shame. Bad Elk paused when he saw his words had hit hard. He squinted along the rifle barrel, enjoying the blue steel shining in the sunlight. He idly lined up the iron sights on the flank of a horse in the distance. Then, the idea came to him.

"Firing an arrow is not just a question of good eyesight, though that is part of it. No, arrows are fired true and on target by feel. When you were a child, with all the others, you fired many small arrows at targets we had laid out. You got used to the weight of the bow's pull, how your arrows would fly and how the bow was held. Little by little, as you saw where your arrows landed, you learnt the secret.
"

Bad Elk paused; he knew that Otter never did get to understand the fine combination of intuition and skill that marked out the accurate bow shot. But he continued:

"In war often there is no time to aim, either on foot or on the back of a pony. Your training will tell you that if you pull and hold your bow in a certain way, the arrow will find its mark. Firing your bow will have become natural to you but it is a skill that all have to find out for themselves. Your father, when he fights, keeps both eyes open as he is releasing the arrows – he likes to be sure that they have hit properly. Your grandfather though always closed one eye – it was the best way for him…"

Otter's spirits were starting to revive; if his grandfather, Great Horse, could do it then so could he. But Bad Elk hadn't finished.

"A bow, of course, is not the only weapon for a warrior. There is the axe or the lance. The shorter the lance, the closer you will need to be to your enemy to kill him. It brings great honour, though it is not much use for hunting. Your way as a warrior will need to be different to the rest. Remember it was never good enough just to stalk one of those antelope…"

He gestured towards his lodge where Otter's aunt was struggling up a slope with the Pronghorns.

"…they are too quick and we would always be hungry. I had to think and act differently to bring one down. You must think differently too."

Bad Elk leaned forward and picked up the rifle

"There is always the gun. The trapper who used to come to our village showed me how to shoot this. You need to have one eye closed to look along the barrel if you are to be accurate with it. Perhaps the loss of your eye was meant to be – now your right eye is permanently set to aim a rifle. Perhaps you will take a rifle out on the war trail."

Otter beamed and gasped his thanks. His uncle smiled indulgently, secretly pleased that he had found an answer that had some wisdom in it even though there were a few untruths sprinkled around; he would ask God's forgiveness later.

Bad Elk passed over the rifle so that Otter could examine it. Otter hefted it in the palm of his hand, trying to find the point of balance. It was the first time he had seen the gun up close and free of its carrying case. It seemed familiar. The weapon was heavy, the weight of the one-piece barrel made it swing downwards. It was not as long as the old trade muskets which some warriors had. The half stock and butt were of a deep red wood. A curved brass butt plate lined the part that went into the shoulder and a hammer, like the head of a striking rattlesnake, fitted over the nipple that fed the spark from the percussion cap down to the powder charge in the barrel. A ramrod fitted snugly in sockets under the barrel from the stock to the muzzle.

Otter held the rifle in the firing position and, after only a little coaching from Bad Elk, found to his joy that he could easily align the front and rear sights on a target. Of course, Bad Elk would not let him waste precious powder and ball on practice but Otter now knew this was for him. This was a good day; he could scarcely wait to tell his father.

Then he remembered he couldn't afford a gun. He had no furs to trade with the whites at the forts for one and was not allowed to go with the war parties to seize one. It seemed an intractable problem but he would not bother his uncle with it now, Bad Elk was stiffening up from his hunting trip and needed food and a rest. Otter thanked him for his advice, Bad Elk nodded in acknowledgement.

Walking away, Otter paused, turned and asked his uncle where he had got his rifle. Bad Elk shook the buckskin case and inserted the weapon into it, muzzle first. He looked up:

"I took it off a Pawnee breed. He was a scout for a wagon train through our country when you were much younger. You and my brother even spoke to him. I have his scalp in my lodge if you want to see it."

Otter knew now where he had seen the rifle before and a germ of an idea formed in his mind.

Chapter Six

---- o o o ----

Viajero rose early and walked over to the trussed *vaquero*. The rawhide cinch around the boy's neck, binding him to the rock, had tightened with the young man's nervous sweat but he was still alive.

"Did you get any sleep?" he asked mockingly in broken Spanish. The boy just looked at him, wide-eyed with terror and wishing he had been killed like his friend. He had heard of Apache tortures, they were cruel and ingenious. His father's housekeeper, a Mescalero woman, had proudly told of her people's skill at inflicting long lasting pain in order to transfer their enemies' power to themselves.

The Apache slashed at the binding around the throat and the boy slumped into the red dust. Next he took off the gag across the *vaquero's* mouth and stood back as the young man vomited out the grass and dung. The boy pleaded for water but Viajero ignored him. Then, on impulse, he took his goatskin waterbag and poured some down the boy's throat. The young man gulped and spluttered as pieces of grass and horse shit were washed down his gullet. This was no act of mercy on Viajero's part; it was a practical necessity if he wanted to keep the boy alive and hear his screams in the work that lay ahead.

He had planned the day's events in detail. The *vaquero* was young, but still old enough to provide Viajero with great power through the pain he would have to endure. He would keep him alive for as long as he could, draining him of all his youthful strength which would give the Apache renewed fighting zeal and appetite for more reprisals against other Mexicans. He looked across at the young man, who lay face down in the dust whimpering softly. Then it was time.

With his hunting knife, Viajero slit the seams of the vaquero's clothes and ripped them from the boy's spare, brown frame, throwing them into the chaparral. The boy cringed, trying to hide his nakedness, instinctively clamping his knees together to protect his genitals. Normally for Viajero, castration was a good part of these proceedings. But it was usually done in the heat of a raid when retaliation could be close at hand and they had to be back in the saddle quickly. Today though, time was not of the essence and the Apache had other plans.

The boy had squirmed in fear as he saw the big knife slashing down out of the sun but had been surprised when only his clothes and not his entrails had been removed. Then he quailed as he realised the reason for being left alive, there was more to come. The Apache now stood over him with a different knife – this one was smaller, thinner and seemed to have two razor-sharp edges.

The Apache bent over swiftly, tucked the boy's bound ankles underneath his arm and dragged him through the red dust over to a flat rock. At the rock, the Apache took the *vaquero's* own lariat and bound his prisoner's legs to the smooth, even surface, wrapping the rope around many times until he appeared satisfied.

Viajero fingered his skinning knife. He liked the thin, deadly blade. It had been a good war prize; the screams of the roasting blacksmith on the forge coals had amused them all.

The Apache moved behind the flat stone and looked the young man in the face. Then, transferring the two-edged knife to his right hand, he sliced off the soles of the *vaquero's* feet. The young man yelled in agony. Viajero laid the two bloody and calloused pieces of flesh on the *vaquero's* chest so that he could get a better view of his handiwork. The boy subsided into a retching, choking rattle.

Diego de Velasco was the only heir of an important cattle ranching family in Mexico. His father's house was only two day's ride away from where the young man now lay writhing and screaming in agony. His father had insisted that he work himself up through the ranks of the cattle business so that he would understand every element of it. The young man, a dutiful son, had been willing to accept the rigours of a *vaquero's* life, living in the bunkhouse, roping and branding his father's herd and now this unbearable pain was to be his only reward. Noble De Velasco blood spurted onto the flat, red rock as the Apache stood back and observed his pain without pity.

Viajero cut the rawhide thongs that bound the boy's ankles. It would not do to let the pain and screaming subside. He dragged the boy to his feet, put a halter around his neck and made the young *vaquero* walk across the sharp crystals of the salt lick. A bloody trail crossed the shining hollow; the boy could only shuffle across the rocks, tearing more at his flesh and exposed nerves. Loose salt crystals, some big, some small, embedded themselves in his raw feet. Diego had read books that sometimes described pain as 'exquisite'. There was nothing exquisite about this. The agony of the combination of slicing crystals and injections of raw mineral salt was Hell on Earth.

The Apache sang a strange song and beat his chest, shuffling along in a rhythmic dance to music inside his own head. The shrieks of pain from the *vaquero* seemed to renew him like water flooding into a dry creek. Diego fell occasionally and the Apache savagely jabbed a sharpened mesquite twig into his flesh until he stood up and continued his walk. The salt lick hollow was not big but to Diego it seemed like and endless crater of fire. Eventually he could scream no more and collapsed. Before he blacked out, he prayed for death.

The boy was unconscious and would not wake, no matter how hard the Viajero prodded him with his knife. He had tried to get a reaction from the collapsed youth by cutting a strip of skin off the boy's chest that removed both nipples. He pulled this off with small, sharp jerks but still the *vaquero* did not stir.

Then, in the very midst of feeling most alive, the black clouds rose again in his head.

Without warning, he became victim to a great tiredness. It was as if a thick blanket had been pulled across his senses, deadening his normal pleasure in such work. The Apache was puzzled by his disinterest in pursuing the torture further. The clouds only came when he was discontent with life and up to now, living in the arid wastes, raiding and killing had fulfilled him more than at any other time. What was happening?

He felt no ecstatic surge of power, no balm to soothe his vengeance or his solitary bleakness; his limbs became like lead. He sat on a rock next to the youth's body and faced into the sun. Loosening the red bandana from around his forehead, he wiped away the sweat from his exertions. The painted stripes on his face blurred and ran together. He needed to think.

He was a feared warrior; a black avenging shadow that had brought death to many Mexicans. He had not even considered a future when his lust for killing would not eat away at him like a vulture tearing at carrion. His reprisals were always carried out alone; even his tribal brothers were left behind on these raids. He did not want to share the fruits of his vengeance with anyone else. *They* didn't want to go with him as they thought he was going crazy.

Most of the raids had been good and many Mexicans had paid the price of Viajero's revenge with their blood and pain. He had slaughtered rich and poor – men, women and children alike and all without regret. He had dismembered and burned whites and Mexicans, raped their women and dragged their children through cholla cactus. His indifference to the suffering of others had made him a pitiless foe. He was a hated man, both in Mexico and Texas where the authorities of both places tried, without success, to hunt him down. Even the famed Texas Rangers had spared time from quelling the Comanches to try and pick up his trail after he had raided into west Texas. He had revelled in the action and bloodletting where he was bold and often reckless.

All this had now suddenly palled and he didn't know why. He was not affected by the suffering of the young *vaquero*. He knew the boy's father owned the big cattle ranch not far distant. He had often stolen his stock. The warrior had toyed with the idea of mutilating the boy and hoisting him up on the crosspiece of the ranch gate for his father to find him. Now he sighed and felt uneasy, as though he recognised that something in his life had come to a halt. If there was to be no benefit to his powers from killing or torturing why should he continue with it? The deadness inside him was puzzling. He was sure that his hatred of Mexicans was still there; they were, after all, the One-Above's lowest forms of creation and he hoped that he would never tire of killing them. But he *was* tired of seeking constant revenge.

Vengeance was like a fire; it had to be constantly refuelled to retain the heat. To satisfy it took all his energy and required much personal risk. Others of the N'de had also followed the trail of vengeance but no-one had done it for so long. Something was steering him away from this trail. In his stillness, he recognised what it was. It was a voice.

It was difficult to pin down; he felt that a small creature, living inside his head, had whispered a message to him. Usen, the One God, had, of course, sent it. The Apache sat still, deep in thought with his eyes closed. Outside things were blacked out as he concentrated on searching inside his head to see what the form the creature took. He knew that this was important – if he could see a raven or a fox then the message could be false. Both those animals often used their cunning to make humans do crazy things. Raven and Fox were known to watch and then laugh as humans acted on their wicked advice. No, if his life was to change, Viajero needed to be sure that it was not a joke. He concentrated harder. Then, he saw it, poised in mid-step in the darkness inside his skull. He sighed with relief. The creature was reliable; it was a horned lizard. Viajero would listen to it; Usen had sent a dependable messenger.

His thoughts crystallised slowly and he now came to a decision. He had no home or family and did not wish to join his tribal group back in their wickiups near the Gila. No, something in his life was not yet fulfilled – he didn't know what it was or where it lay but he would set out and see if he could find it. Usen would tell him when the time came.

The *vaquero* at his feet stirred back into life and, as his pain returned, began a long, keening wail of agony. Viajero got up from the rock and fetched his pony from the thick chaparral some distance away. He glanced at the body of the older *vaquero,* lying where he had bled to death by the ash circle of the fire. Walking over, he picked up the pistol that lay just out of reach of the dead man's hand. The pistol was old and rusty, the revolving chambers did not move well when Viajero cocked the hammer. It was a weapon that was untrustworthy. Still, a gun was a gun. It may have value later.

He buckled on the gunbelt of the younger man and checked the pistol, walking over to him, past the severed work trousers and shirt that flapped from a bush. This pistol was better kept. Its revolving chambers clicked smoothly round when the hammer was cocked, all were fully loaded with powder and ball and a bright copper percussion cap was on the nipple of each chamber. It was an old weapon but at least Viajero knew how to load and fire it. It was a good addition to his arsenal.

Diego de Velasco stopped his screaming long enough to register that the Apache was again standing over him, pointing the barrel of his Colt revolver at him. Diego looked at the exposed chambers of the gun on each side of the barrel. He could plainly see the dull grey lead balls, each with a full charge of powder behind it. His father had given him the gun when he had needed to ride out in wild country to bring back cattle – the old man had said it would be good protection against snakes or bandits. He hadn't mentioned Apaches.

Viajero had resolved to start his quest immediately. He felt no kindness or humanity towards the boy. The young man remained only as an unfinished vestige of his recently abandoned past – he was a burden now.

Without pity or regret, Viajero cocked the hammer on the pistol and shot the boy through the forehead. A gout of grey smoke and bright flame spurted from the muzzle, red sparks from excess burning powder blossomed out of the barrel landing on the boy's open eyeballs as they registered the realisation that death had arrived. The heavy ball smashed out through the back of his skull and a puff of red dust spurted out beneath his head. Blood seeped slowly from the exit wound and reddened the Mexican soil. A curl of blue powder smoke rose from the neat entry wound.

The Apache strolled back to the dead campfire. He hoisted up the boy's ornate Mexican saddle and cinched it on to his own pony. The saddle bucket was empty so Viajero transferred his rifle to it. Unhobbling the better of the two mustangs to take along as a spare mount, he tied the head rope to his saddle.

He considered what to do about the stray cattle that still bawled and swished around in the nearby bushes – it was against Viajero's nature to leave them, he had always plundered stock. He forced himself to think of the new trail in his life that he was about to take – the coyotes and wolves could have the beef. Then, tying both sets of saddlebags across the second horse he realised he was ready for his quest. He had weapons, powder and ball, food and even a shirt from the baggage of the older *vaquero*.

A horned lizard darted out from under his feet. Viajero smiled, it was the only thing he had been lacking – a sign of which direction to take. Usen seemed to be busy with lizards today; this one, at least, did not look at him with any reproach. The morning sun cast a shadow to the left of the reptile's body as it scurried away, Viajero too would follow the direction indicated by the lizard's path. He mounted his newly saddled pony, tugged on the head rope of the packed horse and swung off north at an easy walk.

Chapter Seven

---- o o o ----

Otter watched them all arrive. Guests had made the effort to dress well for his naming feast. His mother was wearing her best deerskin shift; white, after much washing in alkaline water. It was heavily fringed and intricately decorated with quill work and bright metal discs. A red blanket tied around her waist kept most of the grease off her favourite garment. She fussed around the many cookpots.

He looked at his mother fondly. If Badlands Walking Woman had been a true blood Cheyenne, her sisters and her mother would have helped with the preparations for such a large gathering. But Cheyenne arrows had killed all her family many years before, so now other women helped her keep the pots boiling and meat grilling. She did not often reflect on her past life or her lost relatives but she had told Otter that she knew that her Kiowa Apache mother would have been content with her marriage and proud of the grandson she would never meet.

Smoke spent all afternoon braiding his hair and had helped Otter choose a suitable style, appropriate for a youth about to receive his man's name. Thick applications of bear grease helped keep Otter's locks well-shaped for the occasion.

The boy had been delighted by Smoke's decision to award him a man's name. He knew that his father was making an exception for him but had decided not to question it; especially now that Little Head had got his. It was good to try and catch him up.

"Where shall I hang your war shirt? " he asked his father as he helped decorate the lodge for the feast.

"Up there," said Smoke, pointing to the lodgepole above his willow backrest. It would be above his head when he sat down at the centre of the celebrations.

"The People will need to remember whose lodge they are in".

He smiled slightly. Unlike others, Smoke was not given much to boasting about his exploits but the painted designs and scalps on his war shirt would tell them all they needed to know. He dug around behind his bed and brought out the buckskin case containing his red stone pipe; the pipe would be passed round during the feast. Smoke squatted on his heels and filled the pipe bowl with his sumac mixture.

Badlands was outside, presiding over several cooking fires and cookpots.

"How many are coming to the naming?" Otter asked.

"Ask your mother," said Smoke, still preparing refills for the pipe. "I invited the important ones but knowing her, the whole village will turn up..."

Otter felt a question rise to his lips; it was not the right time to ask it. But he prepared the way, just in case.

"Thank you for giving me my adult name now; I know it is not traditional."

He sensed his father shifting uncomfortably as he straightened his hanging war shield. Otter thought that he might test Smoke on when he could start on warrior duties despite his shortcomings.

"I am your father. I thought that this was the best time, especially as your friends are getting theirs…"

"Friends?" Otter knew about Little Head of course but which other friend?

"Thorn came back late last night from his quest. He'd been away for longer than Little Head but didn't see any visions – he seems unconcerned about it. He's just told his father that he prefers to keep his child name. His father is upset and will take him to see Yellow Bear tomorrow."

"I like Little Head's new name," said Otter.

"Yes," said Smoke "Shining Horse is a suitable name for a young warrior."

Otter hadn't been invited to the Little Head's naming feast but Smoke, as an influential member of their tribal band, had. Shining Horse was a perfect name and he would have to get used to using it with his friend. But Thorn worried him. It now made sense to Otter why he hadn't seen Thorn much during his time of sickness. That boy was really crazy, keeping his child name. His family would be in despair, it went against all the traditions.

Smoke interrupted his thoughts and told him to receive the guests. There was no time to press his father on his warrior duties; his future there would have to wait. In the warm twilight, the People came to celebrate. One or two of his father's soldiers had come; he was particularly pleased to see Spotted Buffalo, though this was mainly because he had brought his pretty wife White Rain Woman to help his mother. White Rain glanced at him occasionally and Otter glowed; she was probably impressed by his new hairstyle.

The crowded tipi represented a cross-section of the rich and poor of the tribal group, though Badlands had kept the old, infirm and scruffy to the darker part of the lodge. Latecomers sat outside around the cooking fires. Smoke had ensured that all would be well fed and praise the feast later. It was always important to be seen as generous and open-handed. Boiled buffalo hump and roasted tongue, ribs dripping with seared fat and venison flavoured with wild onions filled many willing bellies. An unsuspecting white dog had been unceremoniously clubbed to death to provide the tastiest treat. Stories were told and brave deeds recalled, though all eyes were now on Otter as his white teeth tore into the scorched meat.

Otter's limited vision made him turn his head from side to side so he could see who had turned up for the feast. Yellow Bear, of course,

Smoke had already discussed the new name and its importance with him; Broken Knife, who would preside as the name giver; Twisted Wolf, the camp's chief and some members of Broken Knife's soldier society. Smoke seemed pleased with the audience.

When the tobacco pipe had been passed to him, Smoke on the Moon indicated that he wished to speak. He reminded them that they were here to give his son a new name. He recalled the occasion that had led to his son's child name – how Badlands Walking Woman had been playing with the boy by the swimming hole and she had taken him out of his cradleboard. The boy could not yet walk or even crawl but, unafraid, seemed to try and move towards the deep water. She had been amused by this and had dipped him in the warm pool. The child had not cried out but had seemed to want to go deeper. Intrigued, she had waded out several steps then laid him on the surface, still holding him with one hand underneath his belly. She let him sink a little and watched as his chubby brown arms instinctively started to swim. Badlands had laughed and told her husband. His name would be Otter.

The women in the feasting group nodded knowingly to each other. The strength of Smoke's wife's will was legendary. In this small band of the Suhtai, women usually played no part in naming their children. Smoke glossed over the acute embarrassment he had felt by allowing his wife to give their son his first name. He had later reprimanded her but she was adamant that their son should not be named by a stranger; Smoke had stayed outside the lodge for two days pretending to make a new bow. Only the foolhardy argued with Badlands Walking Woman.

Otter's father concluded his reminiscences and passed the pipe to Broken Knife of the Thunder Bear Soldiers. Smoke watched his war companion closely. Broken Knife was not known as a great orator but he was highly valued as a fighting man. He was tall with an austere, almost aloof presence. He had never taken a wife, though rumours that he had once taken someone else's dogged him as an adult. Being from a union of an Oglala Lakota woman and a Cheyenne father, he understood both languages and used these skills often. For him, battle was everything and his life was dedicated to being better at it than anyone else. His war deeds were well known; he had counted many coups and killed many enemies.

Broken Knife sat impassively and collected his thoughts, his best blue blanket across his knees. His words would have power and strength. The Thunder Bear soldier chief would have to be careful though; to give a boy his man's name before any of the recognised rituals of manhood had been passed was rare. Still, Smoke on the Moon was wealthier than many in the tribe and he could throw a feast whenever he wished for whatever reason pleased him. He had been given a fine pony by Smoke to preside as the name-giver and he was happy to do this, especially as he had witnessed Otter's courage after the loss of his eye.

Otter was brought to the front and put in the centre of the circle. His mother roughly elbowed two elderly men out of the way so she could get a better view.

"This young man" said Broken Knife, pointing a greasy finger at Otter," has reached a point on life's trail where he should have his man's name. He has not yet been tested in war or had the opportunity to travel on his vision quest but he has already shown great courage against pain."

This was met by murmurs of agreement by the assembled feasters. Smoke had made sure that news of his son's dogged determination not to succumb to the pain of his ravaged eye had been spread widely about the village.

Quick hands used the break in speaking to reach into pots for extra morsels of food. Smoke looked on benevolently and Otter smiled shyly, a soft deerskin bandage across his empty socket giving him a more mature look. Broken Knife continued:

"We, the People, live free. Every man has a choice of how to live his life; it is a matter for him. Courage is highly valued and it comes in many forms – it can be in battle, on the buffalo hunt or…."

Broken Knife's voice trailed away slightly – he was getting into sensitive territory, using images that perfectly explained what the Cheyenne *were* but what Otter could never be. He regained his composure, noting that Smoke had bristled slightly at the direction of his words.

"..against the many tests of life here in our country. The son of Smoke on the Moon has shown this and his bravery should be saluted and marked."

High pitched yells of encouragement and agreement greeted this statement; Otter's mother started a low song of praise in her own tongue. More food was brought; hands plunged into bowls to resume the feast.

"The son of Smoke on the Moon and Badlands Walking Woman," continued Broken Knife "has already spoken his new name during his trial of pain. It was a sign. I, as the name-giver, announce that he shall henceforth be known as See the Dark as a remembrance of that time."

The crowd in the lodge hooted with joy, Otter squirmed with pleasure whilst his parents looked proudly on. His words during his time of pain had taken on an added meaning and depth that was unplanned. From beneath his shirt, he took out a small symbolic otter made out of sage grass and threw this on the fire. The flames crackled briefly and then it was gone. His childhood was past.

Smoke picked out an overlooked portion of dog meat and chewed it carefully. Some thought must now be given to finding a tribal role for his son.

In front of him, Otter still sat cross-legged, contentedly receiving the plaudits of the crowd. Behind him, Badlands Walking Woman deftly removed two of the food bowls from the greedy plunging of many unimportant hands. She refilled the bowls with choice meat and placed them within easy reach of Twisted Wolf and Yellow Bear. She may be a *notae* from another tribe but she knew an opportunity for influence when she saw one.

Chapter Eight
---- o o o ----

Shining Horse and See the Dark knelt in the treeline and watched the white man walk out of the river bed with a dead rabbit in one hand and a shotgun in the other.

"We should kill him and take his rifle." said Shining Horse. Dark looked up at his friend and shook his head.

"No, this is not our country; it belongs to the Lakota. If we kill him here, the white soldiers will come and take revenge on the Sioux."

"Well, what then? Shall we just leave him in peace to kill our game and ride about as he pleases?" Shining Horse's questions were tinged with sarcasm. He stood up and took up his pony's bridle.

"We are not at war with the whites. We should find out what he is doing here" replied Dark.

Shining Horse turned to his friend, tetchy with impatience:

"And how will we do that?"

'We'll ride down and ask him."

Shining Horse staggered back against his pony, shocked that his friend could suggest such a stupid course of action against someone as unreliable as a *veho*.

"You may not have noticed but he is the one with the rifle. We only have our hunting bows and you are the worst shot in the whole Cheyenne nation…"

Though the younger man, Dark cuffed his friend across the ear. He spoke steadily, trying to calm Shining Horse who was rattled by the blow.

"That trapper who used to come into our village taught me some of the *veho* words. I'll talk to this one and find out his business then report it to the Lakota – they can decide what to do with him."

Shining Horse sulked; he knew See the Dark's plan was the better one. It had wisdom and thought – two things that Shining Horse lacked. He only ever chose the warrior's way. He had his doubts though about his friend's ability to speak the tongue of the whites.

"Two Talks is the one who speaks the white man's language, not you. It must be a new skill that you've learned instead of being good with your bow." It was an unkind remark from Shining Horse but Dark knew he was just fighting back as best he could after being hit.

"Well, Two Talks isn't here." They both knew that Two Talks was named not just for being able to speak in the white man's tongue but because he would use many words where only one was needed. He could be boring at the council fire.

Dark had mounted his pony and draped his bow over the horse's neck; it would be a sign that they came in peace. Shining Horse did the same; his friend's plan was fraught with danger against an armed white man but he would never let him face it alone. With wildly beating hearts, the two Cheyenne rode out of the trees and down the slope towards the river.

Dietrich Hagen was not a frontiersman but the previous squeamishness he had when gutting and skinning game had long since disappeared – hunger had hardened his city sensibilities. He flopped the rabbit onto its back and began to skin it on the ground after the European fashion. He had seen American Westerners spread-eagle rabbits from branches and deftly remove the fur like a winter overcoat, leaving the mottled red carcasses swinging like dead babies. It made his ordered German mind uncomfortable.

Even so, with the rabbit lying on its back, paws in the air and a breeze ruffling its pale, fine belly fur, he could not help thinking about his Aunt Giesela's cat back in Berlin. That useless animal had never caught its own food in its life; it just lay back waiting to be fed slivers of chicken. He had once stayed with his aunt in her fine house in Charlottenburg and she ensured the cat had eaten better than her nephew.

He smiled grimly to himself as he focused back on the rabbit, carefully slitting the furry outer skin from neck to tail with his sharp pocket-knife. Leaving the pale blue membrane covering the intestines until last, he pinched it between his thumb and forefinger inserted the blade and ran it upwards towards the chest cavity. With a swift flip he turned the rabbit onto its belly and removed the fallen guts. A red kite watched the proceedings with interest from a nearby tree. He carefully removed the rest of the skin.

The rabbit was big, probably enough for two meals. This pleased the German as it would save effort in getting dinner tomorrow. He idly glanced at his clasp knife blade as he gently eased the skin from the carcass. The blade was smeared in blood but he could make out the name 'Solingen' etched into the bright steel. It reminded him of home and gave him some comfort to handle something that was reassuringly well made. He wiped the blade on his pants.

Scooping the rank intestines into the discarded skin, he carried the bundle down to the river, walked halfway out and threw it onto a sandbar. Maybe a wolf would come down to take a drink and investigate the rabbit remains; he could shoot it and have a fine pelt – a travelling man could never tell when it would be of use. He could trade it or offer it as a sweetener to his other enterprises.

Dietrich was out to trade. He looked across at his pack animals; his investments were in those large canvas sacks – high quality German iron and steel goods. He had brought enough to excite the interest of his prospective customers, the Indians. A few well-placed gifts amongst the villages would soon have them clamouring for more at his new trading post near the fort. In return he would take all the pelts, skins and buffalo robes he could get – there was a ready market back east. He had not met any of his potential customers yet but he'd heard that the Indians were simple souls; the smell of unlimited profit was in the air. The German chuckled to himself.

He walked back down to the river with the rabbit carcass and crouched, washing it carefully in the cool water. A piping from the red kite made him glance up. He had expected the kite to swoop onto the rabbit fur but instead it was circling higher and higher away from the river, the piping call growing fainter. He wondered why it was flying off.

A rippling chill of fear swiftly replaced his puzzlement as instinct told him he was not alone. Still crouching, he turned his head. A sudden light breeze drove the front brim of his hat over his eyes – all he could see were his horse and mules moving into a position to watch something coming down the hill behind them. He stood up and pushed the hat to the back of his head. His animals still obscured his view so he stepped to one side, peering up the shallow slope into the heat haze. The whole hill looked alive with movement as bushes and grass clumps shimmered. Then he saw them, flicking into cohesive shapes – two Indians on ponies moving slowly down the hill towards him. Both stood high off their ponies' backs on rawhide stirrups, watchful and coming closer.

Dieter Hagen was in a quandary. He had come to show these people his trade goods, to tempt them to come to his new trading post outside the fort; he knew that a rash move towards his rifle or shotgun could sour the relationship before it even got started. It could also get him killed.

At a loss for a more peaceable gesture, he took off his hat, held it by the crown over his heart and let his left hand stay by his side. He had seen Americans do this on sentimental occasions; he hoped the Indians would interpret his lack of malice correctly. He watched them ride closer – they were silent but did not seem menacing. They were still sitting bolt upright on their saddle blankets, necks straining to keep him in sight as the folds of the escarpment altered the level of their vision.

The German stood stock still, blood thudding in his temples and his mouth getting progressively drier. For some unaccountable reason he held on to a vision of another civilisation – the horse drawn trams on the Kantstrasse in Berlin where he had been an apprentice for a while. He longed for the feel of stone paving, warm coffee shops and brick buildings. The Indians didn't look hostile but you could never tell… his trading career could come to an abrupt halt on this lush riverbank, five days ride from any white settlement. They could take his animals and trade goods and have his scalp hanging from their lodgepoles before nightfall. He wished he'd left his hat on; his distinctive yellow blonde scalp may be tempting to these people.

The Indians halted their ponies some thirty paces from the nervous white man. One, who seemed slightly younger than his companion and wearing a bandage over his left eye, cleared his throat. He pointed to the ground and spoke:

'Down, down'

Dieter's English was poor but he recognised the words. So they *did* intend to kill him. He dropped to his knees and prayed it would be quick.

See the Dark was startled by the white man's actions; he was merely being polite in asking if he and Shining Horse could dismount. It was bad manners to get off your pony at a stranger's campfire without being asked. Shining Horse clicked his tongue in impatience.

Did he understand your words?'

'Of course. He's a white man, I spoke in his tongue'

'Then why is he on his knees?'

'It's probably a greeting. Let's get down'.

With fluid ease, both young men dismounted and led their ponies past the strange white man down to the river to drink. The sorrel and the hobbled mules skittered nervously to one side as they caught the wild scent of the Indian ponies. It was not the friendly smell of hay and barns but of bear-greased manes and desolate places.

Hagen opened his eyes. He had seen the Indians leap down from their horses and come towards him. He had squeezed his eyes shut as he waited for the tomahawk blow or thrust of an arrow. Instead he was still alive and both Indians were drinking in the river with their ponies.

When the ponies had drunk their fill, Shining Horse turned to the white man, still on his knees on the bank. He motioned him to stand and Dieter understood. He stood awkwardly facing the two young warriors, his hat still in his hand.

Shining Horse pointed to himself and, extending the forefinger of his left hand, made sharp, cutting motions across it with his right forefinger - the cut finger sign for a medicine or striped arrow, which indicated 'Cheyenne'. The white man looked on unhappily, incomprehension in his eyes. Perhaps they wanted to cut his fingers off.

He began to apologise:

"*Es tut mir leid aber ich kann nicht….*" His voice tailed away as he watched as the older of the two walk over to the packs of trade goods that he had uncinched from his mules. The Indian opened the flaps of the canvas bags and took out an iron skillet, then kitchen knives and a pair of tailor's scissors. The knives seemed to interest him as he tested the edges on his thumb and seemed pleased by their ability to cut well.

See the Dark felt ignored. He had let Shining Horse play the lead role so far in case it had degenerated into battle but the white man seemed harmless enough even though they had seen, on closing with the *veho* camp, that the he had two rifles.

Dark tried to question the white man further about the reason for him being in Lakota country but was embarrassed that he was unable to remember any more of the trapper's words; he had stopped abruptly and walked away. Shining Horse would, of course, remind him of his boasting when they got home.

Shining Horse was already bored; he wanted to leave the white man's camp. There were only things for women here. He admired some of the knives but had nothing to trade. He brought his pony from the bank and waited whilst See the Dark also examined the trade goods. His friend was hefting a large meat cleaver in his hand and embedding it into a tree bole to test its edge. The white man looked unhappy about it but did nothing. He saw the butt of the second rifle sticking out of the white man's saddle bucket. Leading his pony across, he drew out the rifle and looked at it. It was shiny, heavy and well-oiled. Shining Horse had never seen one like it before and wanted to know how it worked. He gestured to the white man and called out to Dark to join them. He dropped his pony's bridle and it ambled back to the water and grass.

Dietrich had been starting to relax when it looked as though the Indians were moving off and leaving him with his scalp, stock and goods. Now the older Indian had his brand new Sharps rifle in his hand, perhaps he wanted to take it. It had been expensive at the fort, almost $75, and that was without the ammunition. The Indian, however, gave him the rifle and seemed to want him to fire it. The shaking German understood and pointed to a live oak across the river. He was reassured by the weight of the weapon in his hand, now he was on equal terms with these savages and felt less afraid.

Shining Horse watched the *veho* closely. Dark had wandered up behind them and stepped to one side as the white man swung the strange rifle up into the aim. Dieter knew he was no marksman but his Sharps rifle was simple to load and easy to fire. The first round crashed out into the still air. The Indian ponies jerked up from their drinking and sought a quieter spot down river, the white man's hobbled horse and mules crow-hopped sideways in alarm. The bullet whacked satisfyingly into the tree, a spurt of dusty bark erupting where it buried itself in the trunk.

Then, as a demonstration of the new technology, Dieter cranked the loading lever downwards with his right hand and, after he had replaced the linen cartridge and percussion cap, fired once more into the tree. He loaded again and pointed to a distant fallen log on a ridge. Shining Horse knew this was well out of range of a normal trade gun and wondered why the white man had pointed to it. He fired. Though he missed the log there was creditable splash of red earth next to it. The German reloaded quickly before the Indians got over their surprise. He held the rifle across his chest and waited.

Shining Horse was very impressed. The gun reached out a great distance. See the Dark was impressed too but he had been happy with the demonstration and walked to retrieve his pony. Shining Horse gestured to the white man to give him the rifle so he could try it out. The German shook his head and wrapped his fingers round the stock more tightly; no need to point it at the Indian yet but it would be an easy matter if he had to. The Indian gestured again with his left hand, sharply beckoning with his extended fingers. Dieter stood firm. Shining Horse looked at him coldly, his thoughts churning.

It was a warrior's dilemma. Shining Horse wanted the rifle but his main killing weapons were on his pony, now grazing over quarter of a mile away. He also remembered Dark's advice about not killing the white man in Lakota country and how such a death would probably bring the white soldiers down onto their camp. Fighting back his instincts he shrugged and walked to join his friend.

The German breathed a sigh of relief and pleasure; it had been his first real test against savages and he had seen them off without a drop of blood, especially his own, being spilt. The Sharps rifle had been his saviour; he would always keep it loaded and by him from now on. Those Indians had never seen one like it that was for sure; he would need to be cautious in future about displaying it when he went into their villages.

The two young Cheyenne rode past the *veho* without a glance at him or a farewell. See the Dark mused on the information they had found out - the soldier societies would be interested in the new and lethal rifle and the Lakota would be happy to give them food in return for news of the white man on their land.

Shining Horse hoped they would kill him.

Chapter Nine

---- o o o ----

Viajero still rode slowly north out of Mexico following the direction that the horned lizard had shown him. His string of accompanying ponies had now increased to three. The *vaquero's* horse he had been using as a pack animal had developed a split hoof and rapidly became a burden, dragging on the head rope. Its working life was over.
He had led it to a small canyon and stuck his knife in its neck, standing clear as the horse subsided with a rattling gurgle onto its side, blood gushing from the wound, hoofs thrashing feebly. He butchered the animal. He ate some then cut the best meat from the carcass and draped it over the saddle of his own pony. He left quickly as the buzzards began to circle, betraying his position.

He had stolen the other three ponies from a small ranch some days ago. He had not attacked their owners, a Mexican family. His recent dreams and talks with his spirits had not contained any instructions to make him resume killing or plundering. This had surprised and worried him slightly; spiritual and physical power had always been present during the raiding times. The smell of smoke, of gunpowder, of ponies and of blood had once made his heart race. Then, he had felt alive and taut, like a well-strung bow. He hoped the lack of fire in his belly now was just a passing thing and that he was not witnessing his own descent into old age.

The Mexican ranch was a rundown place with some scrawny cattle grazing on the poor grass, chickens scuffing the dust and the three horses in a small corral. A rickety buckboard, its shafts resting in the dirt, stood behind the house. Viajero could tell by the wear on the horses' coats that only one was a saddle mount whilst the other two were used for pulling the wagon. The family consisted of a man, a half-breed Zuni woman and two small boys running around barefoot in ragged cotton trousers. He had watched them from a clump of mesquite bushes near their boundary fence. He was waiting for any sign within him – a rush of energy or surge of desire for action – which would make him resume his old ways. There was none – no urge to kill the Mexican, no desire for the woman – nothing. Instead he waited until the moon slid behind a cloud and led the horses away one by one, his hand clamped over their nostrils.

The theft of the horses gave him some pleasure. He had used his warrior's skills of patience and silence to get what he wanted but the burning ache to exact his usual quota of blood and terror seemed to be missing. He would watch himself closely over the next few days. He would speak to Usen again and look for omens that would give him a better understanding of what was happening to him. It was a strange and worrying time.

Practical matters forced him back to reality. Not wishing to be tracked as a horse thief he had laid a false trail to the south before looping back north to resume his journey. Mexicans, if any followed, would soon tire of the pursuit, especially when they found that his real trail was days old and headed into the land of the Americans.

Riding further north, Viajero suddenly got lonely. On a pure whim, though he would never admit to himself that he craved company, he had veered east and into the lands of the Mescalero. Viajero smiled grimly to himself; he hoped Usen could see he was trying to be more human though, even as he rode into the closest Mescalero camp, he knew it was just pretence.

It had not been a friendly meeting. They had been suspicious of him at first – a lone warrior from another Apache band riding into their camp was a strange thing. He could easily be a spy for the hated white eyes, gathering information about their location and strength. Mexicans, and before them the Spanish, had been known to employ renegade Apache scouts. He had been questioned closely, though this took some time because of the differences in their languages. Viajero had told them he was on a quest though he could not describe why or where he was going. In truth, he did not know himself but he was sure that a sign would tell him when he had arrived and what he should be doing. Mescalero suspicion relaxed after a few days and Viajero's skill as a hunter with an additional rifle was looked on favourably. Filling the pot was a sure way to make friends.

He had quickly attracted the attentions of a young Mescalero woman who sat near him at the campfire and made sure he had the choicest morsels of food. She had not been forward with her affections but something drew her to him. Her grandfather was her sole surviving relative and he had not protested at her behaviour. Nor would he, she was already of age and knew her own mind. For his part, Viajero appreciated the attentions of the young woman but, for now, kept her in a separate part of his mind. He had been this way with his wife in their good times. Then, her well-being and that of his son had been his major concern when he was with them but he shut them away from his thoughts when he was raiding. It did not pay to let his concentration wander when there was killing to be done.

Viajero had not lain with a woman in comfort for many months. Lying with his wife before her murder was just a dim memory now. He had, of course, casually raped American and Mexican women before killing them as part of his warrior's reward on raids but it was relaxing to couple with this woman without the screaming or the blood. Because of the shortage of marriageable warriors in any tribal group close to hand, the young woman had not yet taken a husband.

Viajero never mentioned marriage or even staying with the Mescaleros and nor did the woman. She was happy in the moment and the welcome change the Westerner brought to her life. He was different to the Mescalero men that she had encountered up to now. He was not considerate, spiritual or inclined to speak much but he did exude a raw power that she liked; to be Viajero's friend would be a great thing but to be his enemy would be fatal. She thought of him as her *Coyotero*.

The young woman smiled to herself as she felt her heart and feelings race ahead like an unbroken pony. Although she knew that the *Coyotero* had little affection for her at the moment, she felt that she could fill the gap in his life. She knew he was just passing through, driven by some invisible force to find something, as yet unnamed, on his life's trail. She did think, though, that she might go with him when he left. She thought it best not to tell this to anyone, especially Viajero.

After some days, Viajero was already restless, eager to be gone. He had relished the company of the Mescaleros who were not so different from his own White Mountain band but the trail called and he could not refuse it. He began making his preparations to leave. The woman noticed this and, secretly, began making hers.

He had climbed to a nearby rocky hill to take his last turn as night guard as the sun was still a hand's breadth above the western horizon. He always did this to accustom his eyes to the gathering darkness. Sitting down with his back to a well-worn spot on the rock, he checked his rifle and settled down to watch over the sleeping encampment of the ever-cautious Mescaleros.

The moon came out, a huge silver disc pulsating with light. Viajero smiled when he saw it. It was the Raiding Moon, beloved of the Comanches far off on the Staked Plains of Texas. Viajero had sometimes met the Comanche to trade horses. They were the best horsemen he had ever seen. Their mounts were desired by many tribes, their breeding stock was the envy of the other horsed nations. The Comanches had told him of the Moon and its significance in lighting their way down ancient war trails from the Llano Estacado, far south into Mexico. Viajero briefly envied them the brotherhood of the war trail and hoped the moon was a good omen for his own, more indistinct, trail.

A brief pattering of crumbling rock behind him made him start. He recovered in an instant with his rifle fully cocked and pointing at a dark figure approaching up the hillside. It was the woman, she had brought food and a gourd of water. He relaxed the hammer of the rifle back onto the percussion cap and led her by the arm to the summit. They both sat back against the sentry rock overlooking the silvered hills and ate in silence. Like many Apaches, Viajero did not encourage conversation. Silence was a respected discipline on the hunt or in war. The babbling of Mexicans or Americans, even during tense moments before battles, had often surprised him. Their uncontrolled tongues had led him to them and had resulted in their deaths. He knew the woman had something to say but he would not help her say it.

He did not know the woman's name and had not asked; she had not asked his. He had been grateful for the slight language differences that had developed into a mutually respectful quietness. There had been words, of course, but only so he could give instructions or ask for something. Now, she was on the verge of telling him something and he realised that he was afraid of what it might be.

"You are leaving soon?" she asked.

Viajero nodded in the darkness.

"I will go with you" she announced simply.

"No" he replied; his voice flat as he could make it. He did not want to fling Mescalero hospitality back in their faces; they had been good to him. *She* had been good to him. He did not want to provoke tribal anger.

She remained calm and dignified and did not respond. Instead she pulled a small bag tied to a leather thong from around her neck and put it over Viajero's head.

"Carry this memory of the Mescalero country with you and return here when you have finished what you have to do."

She did not plead or ask. It was just a simple statement of what he should do in the future. Viajero now had a home if he wanted one though he had had no sign from Usen that this Mescalero camp was his final destination. He felt the soft deerskin pouch. There was a hard round object inside; he attempted to pull open the drawstring and see what it was but she stopped him.

"Wait until daybreak before you take a proper look. It is not a charm or a magic potion, just a piece our land to remind you to come back."

With that she got up and carefully made her way back down the hill to her *wickiup* in the tribal circle.

After his spell as night sentry, Viajero slept only a few hours into mid-morning of the next day. The woman had not come to his wickiup and he did not feel it was right to ask where she was. When he had eaten and was alone, he opened the deerskin pouch and pulled out a spherical black stone, polished until smooth and glossy. He had seen them before whilst out hunting with his Mescalero companions, scattered on the ground like black beads. Turning the globe over to admire its sheen, he noticed a small etching into the surface. It was an antelope. He knew the woman had scratched the image into the stone, perhaps her name was Antelope. He would remember her too. He put the stone back in the pouch. It was a good reminder of the Mescalero land; he would keep it.

He saddled his pony, now well rested after grazing with the Mescalero mounts. He made a quick decision and transferred the provision bags from one of his string of ponies to his own Mexican saddle, stolen from the young, tortured *vaquero*. The silver platework was tarnished but the saddle still rode well. The boy would just be a pile of white bones now, picked clean and scattered by turkey vultures and coyotes.

Viajero slung his bow, now unstrung in its case of bobcat fur, across his back and put his freshly loaded rifle in the saddle bucket. His precious supplies of powder and ball were wrapped carefully in a rawhide pouch and placed securely in one of the saddlebags. The Apache slung his powder horn over his head and across his left shoulder; it would hang there ready for use. Twenty lead bullets were to hand in a skin bag hanging from the saddle pommel. With food in the other saddlebag, he finished his preparations.

His heart lifted as he welcomed shedding his responsibilities to the Mescaleros and to the woman. Viajero did not need much, even the spare horses. He would travel even faster without the *remuda* jerking the lead rope behind him all day. His pony danced a little as it felt the weight of the saddle and the provisions; both rider and horse knew it was time to go.

Viajero walked through the small encampment to the wickiup of the Mescalero leader and stood respectfully outside with the three spare horses. The old man eventually came out and Viajero gave him two of the ponies. It was a good gift and the elderly Mescalero was satisfied, nodding his dark and wrinkled head enthusiastically. Viajero asked that the other pony be given to the girl; the older man nodded and said it would be done. It was unusual to give a horse to a woman but the man from the White Mountain was the gift-giver and it was his business how he divided his wealth.

"Where will you go?" asked the old man.

"A horned lizard pointed me north so I will keep to that path for now" replied Viajero and mounted his pony. The saddle creaked at the unaccustomed weight.

"That is good", said the old man, "horned lizards know things. They know how to live in a hard land without water just like the People. They are wise and tough; it is a suitable sign to follow."

Viajero nodded in acknowledgement and trotted his pony towards the colder lands of the north.

One night later, the young woman led her newly acquired pony out of the *wickiup* circle for the last time to follow her chosen one. Her grandfather watched but did not stop her. Bright Antelope Woman of the Mescalero Apache was setting off on her own quest.

Chapter Ten

---- o o o ----

Shining Horse and See the Dark had been silent with each other after they had left the white man's camp. Shining Horse had fumed about not taking the powerful new rifle from the puny *veho*. He had wanted to go back to kill the white man and steal the rifle. Dark's wisdom had prevailed but only just. They had been friends since they were boys but, for now, the disagreement cut deep.

Their visit to the nearest Lakota encampment to report their findings had been poorly timed. The village that they found, home to a small band of Minniconjou Sioux, was in the process of moving. Instead of the polite hearing that they hoped for, as well as some welcome hot food, there was a bustle of urgent activity. No one had the time to discuss the white man and his rifle.

Shining Horse looked around where the tribal circle was rapidly being dismantled. This was not the usual relaxed breaking of a camp in late summer. Something was wrong. Fires were hurriedly put out, the pony herd was on the move, jerked meat was quickly gathered from drying frames outside tipis and children rounded up from their play. Women were stripping the buffalo hide covers from their lodges, packing *parfleches* with food and clothing and piling their goods onto travois lashed to their ponies. The soldier societies were out in a protective screen around their people. It had the feel of a sudden war move. The presence of a single white man in Lakota country, new rifle or not, now seemed unimportant.

Impotent amongst the preparations, Shining Horse and See the Dark looked for someone they knew to tell them what was going on. Both young men's knowledge of the Lakota tongue was poor though Shining Horse was the better at it. Asking the women and the old men using hand sign had not provided many facts other than there had been a clash with soldiers near the fort on the big river. Some had been killed. The village was moving before any retaliation came.

Leaving the centre of the village, by now reduced to flattened circles of grass where the lodges had stood, the two Cheyennes rode further out. A warrior on a bay mustang, rifle butt resting on his hip, rode out of a clump of bushes and challenged them. Again using hand sign to overcome their language differences, they said that they were Cheyenne hunters passing through. The warrior relaxed when he saw the cut finger sign and recognised them as friends. He beckoned to them to approach him and the two younger men complied.

The Minniconjou warrior was wearing his full battle paint. His face was painted black divided by a bright, white line from scalp line to chin. Three white bars were slashed across each cheek, two nocked eagle feathers were fixed into the hair at the rear of the man's head. His confident eyes blazed out from the paint mask. He was ready for war. Shining Horse and See the Dark were impressed but put on an outward show of cool normality as their ponies picked their way over the stony ground.

As they got closer, Shining Horse recognised the warrior as Bitter Heart. They had met before when Bitter Heart paid a visit to one of his relatives who had married a Cheyenne woman of Shining Horse's band. They had eaten together once.

Bitter Heart was glad to see them but made it clear that he was on important tribal duty, protecting the village from any approaching column of the white soldiers. Shining Horse asked him why he thought the soldiers would come, what had the Minniconjou done wrong?

"Nothing, "said the Lakota. "But one of our young men, staying with our Burnt Thigh cousins up near the Platte, killed a cow belonging to a white traveller with a wagon train. Soldiers from the fort came to arrest the one who shot the arrows. They brought some of the big iron guns with them. The chief there offered to pay the *wasichu* in horses for the cow but the soldier chief would not listen and still wanted to take the cow killer to the fort…"

"Horses should have been a good payment for just a cow. The soldier chief must have been crazy," Dark interrupted rudely.

Shining Horse slapped his friend across the shoulder and silenced him; it was impolite to break into another man's story, especially when that man was fully armed and aching for the war trail. But he did fall silent. Shining Horse could tell by the warrior's face that there was worse to come.

Bitter Heart nodded approvingly at Shining Horse's rebuke of his younger companion and then continued:

"The soldier chief was young and a hothead but the Brule chief would not give up the warrior who had killed the cow. The soldiers then turned their iron gun on the village and fired at the lodges – the chief was killed. Of course, the Brule people then turned on the soldiers and killed them all – they took about thirty scalps."

Bitter Heart paused to let this sink in.

"The soldiers from the fort will come soon for vengeance, we have to be ready."

"Why would the soldiers seek out the Minniconjou if they have done no wrong?" asked Shining Horse.

The warrior looked at the two younger men in exasperation and answered icily:

"Do you think the *wasichu* know the difference or even care? They will seek us out and kill any of us they find. To them we are like the buffalo – we all look alike; we are just another animal to be hunted when it suits them."

He put the rifle across the cantle of his saddle and leaned forward to emphasise his words:

"Tell your people about this. Make them heed my warning. Our Brule cousins have not asked for our aid and we would be foolish to seek war with the whites. We will move now but we will fight if we are found. Your people should do the same."

Bitter Heart's pony reared slightly as a gust of wind caught the bushes and lashed branches across its rump. The Sioux warrior, with years of experience on the backs of nervous ponies, merely shifted his body position to compensate, pointed his rifle to the darkening sky and sang a song of bravery that his father had taught him. He made a fine sight that both young Cheyennes would remember for a long time. With a final flourish of the rifle, Bitter Heart turned his pony and rode off to protect his people.

Shining Horse and Dark returned to their village just in time. The Cheyenne band was also about to move. The killing of the white soldiers up on the Tallow River had already been reported to Twisted Wolf and he had held a council to discuss the idea of breaking camp. The war chiefs agreed that the village should move.

Twisted Wolf had counselled Smoke and Broken Knife that their young men should be restrained and not released to fight alongside the Lakota – so far no injury had been done to any Cheyenne band. Getting hotheads involved in any joint raids would only make them targets for the *vehoe*. The war leaders promised to do their best though their control of young warriors was not total – any man could seek out battle if he so wished. They would try and persuade them for the greater good of their small, mixed band.

One of the elders suggested going to the soldier fort further west on the Tallow; this would serve two purposes, they could collect their allowance of rations for the winter and see what preparations the soldiers were making. Smoke on the Moon thought that the plan had some merit and said so. He had been surprised when the camp chief spoke sharply:

"We have never relied on the whites for our food even though we are entitled to these gifts after we signed the treaty at Fort Laramie three summers past. We should not start now – those who take scraps from *vehoe* hands are no more than dogs…."

Smoke butted in:

"Everyone else does it – the Lakota, Arapaho, Crow and Shoshonis - many great tribes who are not dogs, including some of our own people. These gifts from the *vehoe* are to reward us for keeping to the words of the Big Treaty."

Twisted Wolf would not be swayed though he had little actual authority over the final actions of members of his band. He was, however, influential. His words carried wisdom and the band relied on his skills to lead them to their many campsites where there would always be game, grass, timber and water. A man of around fifty with a slightly withered arm, he was still a formidable opponent in a debate. He turned to Smoke on the Moon:

"You remember taking your son to see the wagon train pass through our country some years ago? Well, at that time that is what the *vehoe* did, they just passed through and didn't stop. Now they stop to build roads. Their farms and towns will come next. Those white soldier forts are there to protect their own when they need more land. Already our buffalo are harder to find. The whites are like ants crawling over your skin – when they are few they are easy to forget or brush off but when more come you have to kill them to make them stop. The Lakota who rubbed out those soldiers have shown they can be overcome. We should set our face against the *vehoe* to show they are not welcome."

Smoke was not convinced but Broken Knife seemed to support Twisted Wolf. His words had the ring of truth that even Smoke could not deny. The whites seemed to increase in numbers year on year; Smoke himself had been almost twenty years old before he met his first white man - a lone trapper that came to the village to trade. Now, in the *vehoe* travelling season, the dust from their wagons formed an almost continuous signal cloud throughout the entire summer. Their fat, lumbering cattle took the grazing meant for buffalo and this sometimes forced the sacred beasts to wander from their accustomed feeding grounds and away from the sharp arrows and hungry mouths of the Cheyennes.

Perhaps Twisted Wolf was right; only war with the whites would halt them in their tracks. For now though, the need was to avoid the whites if at all possible and watch what happened to the Lakota.

Shining Horse's report of the move of the Lakota village only served to confirm their fears. Nervousness of reprisals by white soldiers, sentiments that had been echoed by Bitter Heart of the Minniconjou, settled the issue. The Moon of Falling Leaves was fast approaching, they would soon need to find winter quarters anyway. They would leave at daybreak. Criers rode through the camp to proclaim the decision.

Shining Horse and See the Dark had listened to the heated debate with interest but eventually rejoined their families and ate a decent, if hurried, meal. The hunting trip into Lakota country had reminded them that they were friends but the man/boy gulf returned within their own village. Shining Horse was being encouraged to train with the war bands of the soldier societies; Dark was not.

Both young men met down by the river in the twilight to discuss what they would do if it came to a fight. Even Shining Horse had not yet gone out on a raid or war party and he was a year older than Dark. Despite training with the soldier societies, he was worried that he wouldn't be chosen to fight.

Dark's gloom, absent when he was busy, returned now he had time to think:

"Things will go well for you. You are good with a bow and always have been, even when we were much younger. You will be welcome in either of our soldier societies. My father has always spoken of your skill. I keep practising but never seem to get any better. Unless I get a chance to prove myself, I'll always be seen as a boy rather than a man."

Shining Horse, glowing from the unexpected tribute from Smoke on the Moon, tried to console his friend:

"Well, Broken Knife seemed impressed by your bearing in your time of pain…"

"Women bear pain in childbirth – it's not enough. I won't be trusted to fight."

He was careful now about his remaining eye. A deerskin band covered his empty socket to keep out the dust; it gave him a slightly lopsided appearance as the left-hand side of his face had started to droop slightly. Muscles he had once used to turn his eyeball in its socket and blink were wasting away. Any irritation in his healthy eye now rendered him temporarily blind, or at least it limited his sight.

The lack of an eye brought its own peculiar disabilities. He constantly had to turn his head and much of his upper body if people approached him on his blind side. His judgement of space was also affected; once, he had tried pouring water from a skin pouch into a pot and missed. His good eye throbbed with the effort of double the work.

However, See the Dark clung to a gleam of hope. The war leaders still included him in all the tuition on battle skills with the other youths. The youths were all younger than him and it was, at first, an embarrassment to be seen with them. For their part, all knew that he had been given his man's name without any of the tests of manhood being passed. Some occasionally muttered 'Otter' just to see what reaction it would provoke. Dark acted as though he hadn't heard and the ribbing faded away.

It had seemed odd at first to be practising war skills without Shining Horse or Thorn. Thorn still lived in his father's lodge but his dogged resistance to trying for another vision to point out his life's trail did not sit well with his parents. The boy just practised alone with his bow and now scarcely spoke to anyone. There was bad blood there and it made See the Dark uncomfortable. The few words that he exchanged with his boyhood friend had now grown strained and tense. Thorn had admitted that he heard voices in his head but he refused to say what they said. He spurned any help that Dark offered and set his face against their previous friendship. Dark despaired and, after a while, left Thorn alone to communicate with his spirits in his own way.

Eventually, Dark decided just to keep busy and join in with the youths under training. He was a good rider and he had reared his pony well. It had grown into a swift, well-trained horse with good wind and stamina; an asset to any aspiring hunter and warrior.
He excelled at precise riding and could manoeuvre his pony closely alongside other mounts to accomplish any task given him by the war leaders, even during practices carried out at breakneck speeds. Here his pony showed another virtue; it did not shy away from streaming war bonnets or flapping blankets, introduced by the instructors to replicate the confusion of battle. The horse ran where Dark told it to go.

He had been teamed up with a youth called Bear Runs. They had unexpectedly forged a close bond, each anticipating the moves of the other during the mounted battle drills. They were particularly good at rescues of other warriors stranded, unhorsed or wounded on the battlefield. Their eagerness and skill brought nods of approval from the war leaders.

See the Dark also shone in other ways. His thinking times during his recovery now seemed to have prepared him for this; he found that he could remember a great deal of vital information. Remembering the different types of tracks of the game animals he pursued had been relatively easy. But now the quarry was far more deadly; enemies, raised with the same discipline and war skills as themselves. He had to look at various types of moccasin prints and be able to tell the tribe that made them in order to discern friend from foe. Even many experienced warriors could not do this accurately but Dark could, more often than not, recognise the footprints of their main enemies the Pawnees and the Crow. The war leaders, of course, wanted more – was the man walking or running, was he walking backwards to try and fool them, was he wounded? There was much to learn.

See the Dark's confidence gradually returned like a pot being slowly filled with water as he absorbed all the detailed knowledge he needed to prove himself fit for the war trail – how to remember landmarks, find water, which plants to eat. The bow and arrow remained a weakness but it did not seem such an obstacle as before. Even his father seemed more optimistic about the future.

And yet, it sometimes seemed as though he would never get to apply his hard-learned lessons in action. Though he had offered himself for duty on horse raids and war parties, all the leaders were reluctant to take him. He could see their point – the lives of valuable fighting braves could rest on his skill with his weapons and his ability to see.

Bear Runs had already been out on his first raid and excitedly told Dark about it. He had carried out the usual duties of a raiding novice – carrying the water, food, clothes and other baggage. He had helped build brush shelters for overnight camps, guarded the horses and stayed behind when the main party of twelve warriors went into a Pawnee camp at night and led twenty horses away. They had escaped unscathed and undetected until daylight. They had swung back to collect Bear Runs and their gear before making a two day hard, continuous ride that put them out of reach of enemy pursuers. Bear Runs had not killed an enemy or counted coup or had even claimed a stolen horse. It was his first experience of enemy country and he was exultant with the thrill of it. He yelled his triumph when returning to the village. See the Dark's morale plunged again.

Smoke on the Moon was aware of his son's despair. And Badlands Walking Woman would not allow him to overlook it. She had led her husband to a nearby grove of alder to discuss the matter.

In the bright moonlight around them, the People were restless. Some were making preparations for the next day in the silvery light, picketing ponies outside lodges, lashing travois poles and packing food parfleches. There was a low hum of activity, a sense of anticipation and fear. Badlands Walking Woman, though, was surprisingly cheerful; she had an idea. She just needed to convince Smoke on the Moon to try it.

Smoke recognised the signs that a difficult conversation was coming – his wife's hand was on his arm as she looked up at him, a half gourd of tasty meat in her other hand. He sighed; he knew that he was like a willing animal going into a trap. He could not deny, though, that his wife was a relaxing presence that overcame his tensions about the possible trials to come in the morning. He waited for her to begin. Her black eyes, reflecting the moonlight, looked like cold pools of spring water and he was vaguely unsettled.

She had been a difficult choice as a wife, not that Smoke did not love her – but that had to come later. She was seen as an outsider and not to be involved in breeding future Cheyenne warriors.

When the young captive had arrived in his village, the tribe's medicine man at that time was old and without a wife. As a prisoner, she was made to share his lodge and work to earn her keep. Smoke remembered that she made a reluctant guest, refusing to help the women with camp chores even though she was beaten many times. She would stand at scream at them to keep their distance. They, of course, couldn't understand what she said as she spoke a different language to them, but they knew what she meant. The men steered clear of her and thought her possessed.

Her saving grace, and great skill, lay in her knowledge of medicinal plants. She had spent many hours watching her mother collecting herbs and preparing poultices, liniments and drinks to ease the pain of wounds or illnesses of her people. Here, on the northern plains, some plants were different but her interest was renewed in their use. She helped the old medicine man in his forays to collect his specimens, patiently watching how to use them and when. For his part, he was flattered by her interest and impressed by her understanding of the healing properties of his plants. They spoke and understood each other more; she would speak the Kiowa Apache word for an object and he would say the same word in Cheyenne.

During one particularly harsh winter, the old man died. No other men came forward immediately to take his place so she, almost by accident, became the dispenser of medicine. She continued to live in the increasingly run down tipi of the old medicine man. Usually, on his death, it would have been burned along with all his possessions. She begged the tribal elders to let her keep it in return for her medicinal skills to benefit the tribe. They agreed.

Gradually she became accepted. She had joined the rest of the women in their chatter about suitable and available husbands as they washed skins in the river.

Most of her companions were soon married but no-one seemed to want a former slave. She accepted this for now, controlling her desires and her loneliness. Summers were always a time of plenty and she could fend for herself. She could bring down a wild turkey with a well-aimed rock or catch fish in the fast-flowing rivers. Winter was a harder time, small gifts of food in return for her potions was not a reliable source to fill her belly. It was never said, but she knew that a particularly harsh winter without a food provider in her lodge would mean starvation. No warriors courted her, put off by memories of her erratic behaviour in earlier years. They wanted wives from a more conventional mould; marrying Badlands Walking Woman would only bring trouble. Smoke on the Moon's proposal that they marry had been as welcomed as it was unexpected. Jokingly, he had later told her that he only married her as she scared off all his enemies; he would be able to have a relaxing life away from the war trail with her by his side.

"My husband, our son's heart is heavy because he cannot be a warrior. Not one of the war leaders wants him on the war trail with them. I know that his skill with the bow is not yet good enough and his one eye is seen as a weakness but if he is not allowed to be a man soon then I fear for him."

She rested the gourd in the forked branch of a tree; Smoke picked out a piece of buffalo tongue and chewed it in silence.

"I am just a *notae*. I cannot hope to have your wisdom and good judgement. I often forget or ignore the tribal ways of the People. But this is just because I am an ignorant outsider…"

Smoke knew that this was not the only reason. Badlands Walking Woman would always sweep aside tribal customs if she needed to get things done. She gave an outward appearance of a good Cheyenne wife and had merged into the society of women, accepting her place as an equal. She could sew and cook well, set up and break camp efficiently and organise a comfortable lodge. She was still a pleasure to couple with under a buffalo robe on a cold night. But she was different. She had an iron will and would not hesitate to display it if she needed to better her family.

"Our son's war skills are improving every day. But they will never be tested if he does not face the trial of manhood against our enemies. He is caught like an eagle in a trap – he wishes to soar but cannot because he is held back."

She was pleased with the eagle trap comparison. She had seen how warriors who wanted an eagle feather for their warbonnet would dig a shallow ditch, cover it with lattice boughs and lie in it, some fresh meat as bait on top. When the eagle landed to eat the bait, they would grab its legs from beneath and pluck its tail feathers.

Smoke watched her, a half smile on his face; he wondered if she had practised the eagle trap part of her speech. His wife now spoke fluent Cheyenne but her Kiowa Apache past was always etched into her accent when she was excited or had something important to say. He recalled when they were first married; she only ever spoke to him with her eyes averted, as was the custom of the dark skinned peoples from the south. It was almost as though she was looking for threats beyond his vision. She used her hands a lot. Her right hand, fingers outstretched into an axe shape, constantly chopped into her left palm, movements that sliced away at superfluous words. Not for the first time did he realise that his wife was a formidable woman.

Then, just as he relaxed into the affectionate reverie, the verbal ambush came.

"I want you to take our son with you if there is a fight. You are the leader of the Striking Snakes soldiers, they will understand and accept him if you say so. He would never ask this for himself. As his mother, this would not be my choice for him but he needs to test himself as the other young men do. Without this he will turn into a camp dog, fit only to skulk amongst the lodges and fill his belly when he can."

It was an uncomfortable image and Badlands knew it. Smoke angrily spat out the piece of buffalo tongue and grabbed her by both arms.

"You ask too much woman," he said forcibly and loudly. "The Striking Snakes are not some women's society for making buffalo robes, where anyone with a sewing awl can join in. There are sacred rituals and preparations; soldiers trust me to lead them to the enemy so that they can show their courage. I am the pipeholder, their leader. I will not force an untested boy on them."

Smoke put his hand over his wife's mouth as a warning to keep silent. He dashed the gourd out of the tree, the meat rolling into the dust. His marriage was one of equals but he would not accept any interference in his war duties. He stalked off to cool down. Others making early preparations for the move at daybreak, looked at the squabbling couple but got on with their business.

Badlands Walking Woman had, though, only suffered a minor defeat. She had even guessed the outcome of this, her first sally. A rangy yellow dog rapidly sniffed out the meat on the ground and began wolfing it down. She kicked it in the ribs, making it yelp. She hurried after her husband and found him sitting on the riverbank, throwing pebbles into the moonlit water. It was time for him to know the other part of her idea.

The next day at sunup, the People broke camp and moved. It was an orderly affair. They were to move south and west, looking for hills to circle them against the coming chill winds and snows of winter. They would need plenty of timber for fires, some with all-year leaves to feed the pony herd if grazing became scarce and of course, good water. As the main camp chief, it was Twisted Wolf's job to know these things as he set out in front of his people just as the sun was beginning to warm the ground. He rode ahead with Yellow Bear, the spirit diviner. Together they would seek signs and omens to confirm their choice of campsite.

It was not a hurried departure like the Minniconjou several days before but there was a subdued air of tension amongst the moving village. Scouts from both the Thunder Bear and the Striking Snakes societies rode far out on the flanks to warn of any approaching bluecoat soldiers.

One of the scouts was See the Dark. He rode proud and alert, pleased to be of service to his people at last. He had not asked permission of the Thunder Bear soldiers but had ridden out with them in their file anyway; he did not wish to embarrass his father by trying to link up with the Striking Snakes.

He knew it was common practice for young men on the up to sneak off with war parties and tag along in the hope of proving themselves. They could be sent back by the pipeholder as the young bloods were not always the steadiest of companions. But occasionally, if they were obedient to the war leader, they were allowed to stay in some menial capacity.

This had been the other part of his mother's idea. This move was not a war party. When the tribe itself was in danger all able-bodied men were expected to help defend it, there would be no time for choosing who was good with the bow or not.

She had counselled him that it would be better to avoid riding with his father's soldiers for now. If he acquitted himself well on the march, it could count in his favour and he would gain experience. Smoke had not taken this solution well when she had mentioned it the previous night on the riverbank but he too had been at a loss to know how to bring on his prized son. At least, this way, See the Dark was doing what he had always wished and following the warrior's path. He would not stand in his son's way of finding glory and honour in battle; living to an old age was frowned upon anyway. Better the war trail and die young.

See the Dark was excited and his mind a flurry of thoughts as he rode his bay pony out on the periphery of the moving column of his people. He had decided not to use paint yet, he had no accomplishments to mark on his body or his horse. No, he would wait for things to happen on the march or later and would only adorn himself sparingly when the time came. He had not yet been on his vision quest so his links to the spirits that would guide him in later life were weak. No matter, he reasoned, that time would come when the visions and dreams would be ready to be revealed to him. His patience would be rewarded.

It was whilst he was in this thinking time, mulling over these important things, that a wolf's head appeared momentarily over the crest of a nearby hill. The Pawnee scout under the pelt, withdrew quickly from view and wondered why the young unpainted Cheyenne below had not spotted him. See the Dark, unaware of the danger on his blind side, rode on, deep in thought.

Chapter Eleven

---- o o o ----

Viajero knew the woman was following. He had been trailed many times by enemies but this was different. It felt strange. Enemy pursuit usually had only two results – Viajero evaded them or killed them. The woman, of course, was not a threat. Not to his life anyway. The Apache was more disturbed by the dogged and calm way that the Mescalero woman tracked him.

He was puzzled by this unexpected turn of events. The woman had been a pleasant companion in the wickiup and at the campfire but he had not bargained on her being so independent. Perhaps she had read more meaning into his gift of the pony than he had intended. He had wanted to give gifts to the Mescalero for their hospitality but he had also been happy to offload the spare horses with the tribal elder and the girl rather than take the string of ponies along with him.

His practical warrior's brain was defeated by the woman's presence on his trail. Why was she here? The female line of the Apaches was a strong part of their tribal life – the women from Viajero's family had not been not chattels or slaves. This Mescalero woman would have her own thoughts and opinions; she may have spoken to her spirit counsel. Perhaps, she too was following the path of her own horned lizard. He just wished it wasn't so close to his.

When he first rode out of the Mescalero camp, Bright Antelope Woman had kept well back from the *Coyotero*, following his sign; the pine and white oak forests and deep canyons concealing her from him. As Viajero's journey went on, he had become vaguely aware of a presence behind him, an insistent prickling at the back of his scalp. Viajero would not ignore these signals; they had kept him alive more than once in the past.

On a rocky flat he had ridden round in a half circle to cut the trail of his pursuer and lain in wait. He had been startled to see her. She was leading her pony by the reins, eyes carefully scanning the ground for a bruised grass stem or chipped stone which would confirm where Viajero had gone. She moved slowly and took her time. The wind ruffled her cloth skirt and fanned out her dark hair. Her soft moccasins, long in the leg in the Apache fashion, moved silently over the rocks. From time to time she stood up and tugged at her deerskin shirt as it became uncomfortable from crouching too long; she had a long hunting knife in her belt. There were leather food pouches across the saddle pommel of her pony.

The mount was very distinctive; even from a distance he could recognise the white blazes on its legs. It was the saddle horse from the trio he had stolen from the Mexican family; he had given the two wagon horses to the old Mescalero. Viajero wondered what made him give her the best of the three horses – had he wanted her to be well mounted so she could follow him?

He watched as she occasionally stopped and stood completely still, listening and sifting the sounds and scents on the wind like an animal. Viajero smiled to himself - she was making sure that no-one was following her! She was a true Apache.

He was angry at first. He had assumed his new life trail would only include himself. He had limitless land to roam over, he could survive well and in some comfort in this easier climate – what was this woman doing? Viajero was not a charitable man but he quelled his rising irritation and made himself become calm. The reason for her being here would no doubt be revealed to him. Perhaps he should take it as a good sign from Usen.

Now that he had crossed into the land of the Americans, he would sometimes double back to see where she was. As the country flattened out from sharp edged mesa and rocky arroyos into semi-arid grassland, she became easier to spot. He smiled as he watched her patient progress, her eyes constantly scanning the ground for sign of the Coyotero. She was a good tracker and read sign well. Whilst still in the rocky country far to the south, he had considered losing her on ground where neither he nor his pony would leave tracks. It was too late now though, it would require considerable effort to evade her watchful eye in this rolling grass country.

On a whim, he had stopped where the dust would leave good tracks. He had chosen the place so he could watch from a far ridge and then ride off without being detected. Laughing to himself, he had walked backwards in a wide circle around a hill, then mounted and ridden off. Later in the day, the woman immediately spotted the track and was about to follow it round when she stooped and looked more closely. Viajero watched as she brushed her long hair from her face with her right hand and stood up. She had noticed the difference in tracks that a man makes walking backwards; the deeper imprint of the heel being driven into the ground as the weight of a man's body made an opposite image of a forward track. The woman did not bother with the trail any more, instead he watched her cast around for the spoor of his ponies unshod hooves. Though she was some way off, Viajero was sure she was smiling.

He never considered stopping to let her overhaul him; he had not asked her to follow and he told himself that he did not seek her company. Whatever her reasons were for following him was not a matter of concern to Viajero; perhaps she would tire of the pursuit and go home. He fingered the deerskin pouch around his neck, feeling the hard smoothness of the black stone. Maybe he would leave it in a prominent place so she could find it and take it as a sign to go back to her Mescalero family. He decided against it. Giving back a gift would be rude and her people had shown him hospitality. He just continued to feel mildly disturbed by her constant trailing presence. Though he would not approach her directly, he had taken to lying out at night just to watch her campfire. She made no effort to close the gap during the day; it was as though she was content just to find comfort in the sign he had left.

Viajero had stopped using his rifle as he moved onto the southern plains and reverted to his bow and arrows for hunting. He was being cautious – he still had plenty of powder and ball in his pouches but this was unknown country. A shot could warn others of his presence. Getting into a fight with some of the grassland people could deplete his ammunition stock with little chance of finding more. There were no Mexicans or whites to steal it from; some of the roaming tribal bands he had seen did not appear to have many guns. Powder and lead would be hard to replace so he would conserve them.

He was also careful now about his movements. Whilst he still rode generally northwards during the day, he kept off sky lines, taking the more tortuous routes around hills and ridges so as not to be silhouetted against the bright blue canopy. At nights he only lit a small fire and then, after he had eaten, slept away from his campsite in the darkness. He was not afraid of any living man but his quest still remained without an objective; it would be a pity to die by another's arrow before he had eased his mind.

One night, he wondered where the woman was. The nights were getting chill and the days shorter. Soon the bitter weather would come and he would need to find a refuge for the winter. He had not seen the woman during this particular day as he had been pre-occupied getting meat. He crept to the top of a hill and there, not far off, was the light of her fire. This woman was very persistent. He made up his mind - he would go to her tomorrow and ask her what she was doing.

He returned to his campfire, now just a circle of glowing embers. It gave him some heat but would not cast light as he had screened the fire with stones. A prairie dog, skewered onto a green twig, grilled gently over the red-hot mound. Viajero took the small carcass and stripped the flesh with his fingers, eating thoughtfully and thinking about the woman. He could not yet tell whether she was to be part of this new trail in life or whether she had just intruded onto it as an unwanted visitor. Life's twists and turns were often mysteries that only Usen could divine. Tomorrow would bring an answer.

Chapter Twelve

---- o o o ----

The Pawnee raid had come out of nowhere. Stone Turtle, their war chief, had observed the move of the Cheyenne village but, wisely, chose not to attack at that time. The Cheyenne band was not invincible but the presence of ready mounted, alert and, armed Cheyenne warriors out on the flanks deterred them. His Pawnees would have been extremely foolhardy to try to run off horses or kill enemies at that time. The Cheyenne soldier societies would have made them pay dearly for an unprovoked attack on their families. The killing would wait until the time was right.

Stone Turtle had decided that the best time to attack would be a few days after the new Cheyenne camp had been set. They would keep watch on their despised enemies whilst sending for reinforcements. He knew that Cheyenne vigilance would relax slightly if they reached their destination without disruption, the number of guards would be lessened gradually and some normality would return.

The Cheyenne weakness would be in their lack of detailed knowledge of the land around their new campsite. They would be busy settling the pony herd onto new grazing, looking for fresh game trails and filling their lodges with food for the approaching winter. Stone Turtle instructed his forward scouts not to leave the slightest trace that they were in the area. The scouts were ordered to wear Cheyenne moccasins. He wanted regular reports on their enemies, especially on their state of alertness.

The seasoned war chief moved the main group of his warriors some two days ride from the Cheyenne camp. They were not yet strong enough to carry any attack through to victory. The move had a calming effect on the hot-blooded, younger ones who wanted to kill the Cheyenne immediately. They would need to learn patience.

He sent back two swift riders to summon a larger war party to join him. Stone Turtle was ferocious, almost demented, in battle but he wasn't crazy – he wanted to win the coming fight and the odds needed to favour his people. His chance of slaughtering a full band of Cheyenne, to diminish their malign influence on his beloved tribe could just be at hand. He would take their horses as well as their women and children; he would kill the rest.

The Pawnee war chief rested on a trade blanket in a moonlit hollow and spoke to his war leaders and opened his heart:

"I said before we set out that this coming battle with the Medicine Arrow people would be different."

His men stirred uneasily – how could it be different? The Cut Fingers were the enemy, all men of the war party would try and kill as many as they could and plunder the village.

"For once," Stone Turtle paused and took a deep breath, "we need to hold back on individual warriors seeking glory only for themselves. We need to use the weight of our numbers to make sure of victory…"

It was a blow to the traditional way of fighting and could only end badly. The shock of the soldier leaders was plain and deep:

"Nonsense! Glory and showing courage are the reasons why we go to war. Our numbers will make sure we win anyway – we already outnumber them two to one."

"How can we paint our ponies and war shirts telling of our bravery if we are just in a crowd of others? I'm ashamed."

Some stood up as if to leave but hesitated. Stone Turtle let the dissent die down and then stood up to speak. The standing warriors resumed their seats in the grassy bowl:

"Some of you know this already but my brother acts as a scout for the white soldiers…"

"Yes, we know, leading the whites against more of our enemies is a good thing. But what has this got to do with fighting the Cheyenne?"

"Let me explain…he has seen the white men go into battle against the Sioux. They always plan everything before they fight – how best to approach a village, how to overcome their sentries, how best to use those on horses and those on foot…"

Impatient voices cut in: "Yes, Yes – we do that too – we're doing it now with the Medicine Arrow camp…"

"Well, the whites don't allow their soldiers to fight as individuals – they bring together their strength at the point of attack to have the best chance of success; they attack at slightly different times and different places to catch the enemy off- guard; they use their guns at the same time to kill more enemy at once…all the things we don't usually do. Look, the Cheyenne are a brave enemy but we can only defeat them if we don't fight in the expected way."

The warriors lapsed into sullen murmurings; their talks with their guiding war spirits had not foretold this. Stone Turtle stood to one side and let them talk. Eventually a spokesman, Hair Shirt came forward:

"You are our war leader and we won't desert you but we need to know two things – what omens does our spirit diviner see and what do you want us to do on the field of battle."

Stone Turtle smiled in the twilight; he had already paid Runs Red, the shaman, to support his plan for the battle. Now he would convince the doubters, by drawing that plan in the dust.

After ten days, Stone Turtle's battle preparations were complete. Hidden in a gully behind a distant hill, the flower of Pawnee military might had assembled. They had ridden in silent columns, mainly at night to prevent observation by Cheyenne scouts or their Arapaho allies.

This was deep in enemy country for the Pawnee; the thrill of impending battle was in the air. At dusk that day, Stone Turtle's scouts had come in to make a final report. Stone Turtle instructed each scout to make his report twice, pinching him hard after the first time to make sure he was telling the truth. Runs Red agreed with the scouts – all would be well. A dark cloud hid the moon, prompting an outbreak of howling from a nearby family of thin coyotes. Stone Turtle smiled grimly in the gloom and rode out. Soon the Striped Arrow people would also wail as they mourned their dead.

Two sunrises later, See the Dark was up early, unpicketing his pony from outside Smoke's lodge. He wanted to use the breaking dawn as time to travel and then make best use of the daylight to hunt. Some days earlier, he and Bear Runs had found a buffalo wallow. It had been used recently and they planned to lie up and watch it, killing any animals they saw.

They had not seen a buffalo herd for some time now and Twisted Wolf's legendary powers of finding them seemed a bit slow this year. Meat was dwindling in all the lodges. The presence of a herd would be a valuable asset but confirmation would be needed before they made hopes rise in the village. The wallow was a good sign but the tracks around it pointed to just a few beasts so far, perhaps an ageing bull or two cast out or unable to keep up with the main group. Still, it would mean welcome supplies for the two families.

Bear Runs walked his pony across to meet Dark and both young men mounted and trotted out of camp. They turned their ponies towards a wooded hill and entered the tree line, following the shortcut they had found. Rabbits bounded out of their way, a dozing owl back from a night raid of its own, awoke hurriedly and glided out of the riders' path. See the Dark rode ahead along the narrow wooded trail.

A thud behind him made him turn round. Bear Runs sat beside his pony, grunting and gurgling. See the Dark was about to chide him for falling off his horse when he saw the blood. Bear Runs had an arrow through his neck. He fell to one side, feet kicking the soil, gouts of dark red blood spurting between his fingers.

His father had always told him what would happen when he was in battle for the first time. And it was true – See the Dark froze.

A piercing war shriek cleared his head. He caught a glimpse of two Pawnees crashing through the bushes to tear him from his pony. An arrow swished past his head as he ducked into the neck of his horse and tried to make a small target. More screaming and yelling erupted.

Whirling his pony back round to the village, he kicked his heels into its flanks and thundered towards his friend. Bear Runs saw him coming and weakly raised an arm. They had tried this in practice but now it was the real thing. Dark shouted to him to remember the battle drills.

The hooves of Dark's pony churned up the soil, spattering Bear Runs with dirt. The prostrate youth was weakened but made a last effort to grab See the Dark's wrist and succeeded. Bear Run's body was whipped around by the forward momentum of his friend's horse and he was unceremoniously dragged back out of the trees and towards the village. See the Dark heard himself screaming that the Pawnee were coming. Sleepy Cheyennes tumbled out of their *tipis* fumbling with their weapons.

"Honehetaneo!" the assembling Cheyennes took up the cry, warning of the Pawnee raid. Some sang their death songs; many regretted the lack of time to make their sacred rituals before battle or to put on their war shirts.

Whilst rushing to the scene of the fighting, Smoke on the Moon was intercepted by Raven Heart, one of his Striking Snake soldiers. Raven Heart told him that his wife had just entered her monthly bleeding cycle the previous night; she had not known this until after she had fed her husband from a tin ladle. Raven Heart was now contaminated; he would surely die that day. Smoke on the Moon understood and left the decision to Raven Heart whether to fight or not. There was no dishonour in protecting yourself if the spirits were against you. The two men stood, surrounded by the growing clamour of battle and looked at each other, Raven Heart close to tears. Eventually, Smoke ran off into battle. Raven Heart hesitated for only a moment before announcing to all that it was a good day to die then ran to join his comrades.

He was just in time. A group of Pawnees burst out of the tree line on foot and pounded towards the village, yelling and shooting arrows into the assembling Cheyenne. A mounted group, singing a war song, now rounded the crest of a hill and split up, one party heading into the pony herd to run it off whilst the other came to add numbers to those on foot. Many of the mounted Pawnees had rifles and a volley of shots was now added to the screaming tumult of the battle. Bullets zipped through lodge skins and thumped into human flesh as the surprise attack gained momentum. Then, as more Cheyenne joined the fray at the edge of the village, a third group of screeching Pawnees attacked the opposite edge of the tribal circle and rode down the escaping women and children.

Yellow Bear was herding the children behind a nearby hill when he saw them coming. There was nothing that Yellow Bear could do but put himself between the children and the riders. Yellow Bear sang his death song and faced the oncoming riders. A piebald pony ridden by a yelling Pawnee brave crashed into the thinly framed medicine man, flinging him into the dirt. He lay motionless.

Other Pawnee warriors, sensing a weak point, rode up and began snatching at the smaller children, especially the boys. The thin arms and legs of the children flailed against their captors as they struggled not to be abducted. Boys screamed in defiance but writhed in vain as the wiry muscles of their enemies quelled any escapes. Some had run with their small bows and arrows and they turned these on their attackers. But the arrows were small and the bows not powerful enough to do any real damage; they could kill a sand grouse but not a grown man. Still, some of the leading Pawnees found themselves with more than one of the frail shafts in their arms and legs. These they ripped out, laughing in admiration at the fighting nature of the Cheyenne boys. Defiance among the young though turned to wails of terror as the realisation dawned that they were being ripped from their families forever.

One boy, slightly taller than the rest, managed to free one of his pinioned arms, drew his small hunting knife and slashed at the face of his Pawnee kidnapper. Blood spurted down the warrior's cheek and he let go of the wriggling body in order to clamp his hand over his wound. The boy fell from the horse into the dust but he immediately sprang up and ran after another Pawnee pony. Here he doggedly held onto the slim wrists of his younger brother, struggling to pull him from the enemy's grasp. A blow from a war club knocked him to the ground where he lay silent.

Now the Pawnees wanted the women. Badlands Walking Woman was in front of this group. She was pulling some of the shrieking, terrified younger women along to try and escape. An enemy group rode through them, breaking her grip and trampling one of the girls. Two of the women were hoisted, kicking and screaming, up into the saddles; their captors rode away whooping in triumph.

A third warrior had spotted White Rain Woman; even in the heat of battle he could see she was very beautiful and would make a good prize. If he didn't keep her himself she would command a high price in ponies from other men when they got home. He charged towards her, yelling a full war cry. In his hurry to close with the woman, the Pawnee had failed to see she was carrying a sharpened stick that she had grabbed from amongst the drying racks when the attack started. The warrior's full cry ended in a bloody gurgle as she let him run onto the fire-hardened point; his pony carried him off still in the saddle but with a stake in his throat. White Rain yelled her triumph. Her fear was gone, she just felt elated.

Another warrior came for Badlands and, leaning low from the saddle, grabbed her deerskin shift and used the forward motion of his pony to sweep her off balance. With a grunting effort, the warrior managed to drape her across his pommel and he tried to ride off.

She yelled at the indignity but quickly recovered. She took her bone sewing awl from its sheath on her belt and jabbed it deep into the warrior's leg, removed his foot from the left stirrup and heaved him out of the saddle. The Pawnee slid, hands scrabbling to get a grip, over the rump of his horse. She regained the flapping bridle and mounted properly. The Pawnee lay on the ground, winded by his fall; Badlands trampled him to death with his own pony.

From her new mount she watched the progress of the battle. The sun had now risen and the pre-dawn gloom had lifted. Cheyenne and Pawnee closed with each other on foot. A couple of the quick-thinking guards on the Cheyenne pony herd, knowing that their warriors would need to be mounted, drove a part of the herd towards the village. Some of the ponies, terrified by the gunfire and shouts, dashed between the opposing groups fighting on foot, creating a pause. Some others ran into the village where some of the older Cheyenne men and remaining boys caught them and took them back to the soldiers fighting on foot. That day, many rode ponies that did not belong to them but the dire need of the People came first. She couldn't see her husband in the confusion of bodies and dust below; he hadn't had time to put on all his war gear at the lodge when the attack began. Smoke had dragged her out of the tipi, told her to run then dashed off to find the enemy. She hadn't seen See the Dark since he set off hunting at dawn.

Smoke on the Moon was in the thick of it, charging into the Pawnee again and again. He was without his battle paint but it mattered little. When his arrows ran out, he used his lance and hatchet to deadly effect. This was no time to count coup, this was a time for slaughter and to stem the Pawnee tide.

See the Dark had dropped Bear Runs outside the young man's family lodge; the boy did not rise. See the Dark glanced at him once then, nocking an arrow onto his bowstring charged his pony back to join his father. His kinfolk streamed all around him, boys and men running towards the fight and the old men shepherding the women and small children away from the carnage. The Pawnee were not going away. Their warriors seemed to be everywhere, determined to cause as much destruction and death as they could. Rifle balls and arrows ripped through lodge skins and seemed to fall out of the air from all angles.

As he neared the edge of the village, a heavy calibre bullet hit See the Dark's bay. The pony staggered and crashed to one side, Dark managing to throw himself out from under its body before it pinned him to the ground. His bow with the nocked arrow was still in his hand as he rolled to his feet. It was just as well – out of the rising dust charged a stocky Pawnee youth. His face was painted in alternate red and black lines with other red lines curling round his arms. He carried a heavy war hatchet raised above his head and was leaping broken branches and small bushes to get to the young Cheyenne. His eyes were on fire; his face, already terrible with the paint, was a snarling mask of hate.

See the Dark knelt quickly and loosed off his arrow at the rapidly approaching warrior. The arrow was true, even Dark couldn't miss at that range. The shaft buried itself deep in the youth's chest cavity. The Pawnee promptly fell onto his face and lay grunting with pain, the force of his fall pushing the shaft through his body. The bloody arrowhead burst through the back of his ribcage. Light bubbles of blood dribbled from his mouth, his lungs had been punctured. See the Dark leapt onto the downed warrior and jerked him onto his back by pulling his hair to one side. The Pawnee screeched as the protruding arrow tip broke off under him. Dark pulled his hunting knife and sat on the chest of his enemy; the boy seemed to be younger than him. The Pawnee spat words at him that he didn't understand. The Pawnee's chest heaved beneath him with exertion; it was time to end it.

See the Dark rammed the blade of his big hunting knife deep into the Pawnee's breast, where he judged the heart should be. The youth writhed as he pushed it in to the hilt, pinning him into submission with his body. It seemed to take a long time for a man to die. Blood spurted from the wound and the Pawnee's head thrashed from side to side. Eventually, a gurgling rasp came from his throat as his spirit left him and his frame went limp.

Dark pulled out the knife, kneeling against the dead man's chest to release the blade from the suction that held it. Then, making a rough incision around the Pawnee's scalplock, carved off the long, greased tuft with the skin still attached and pulled it away from the bloody skull.

Standing astride the body he held the dripping forelock in the air and yelled to anyone who had time to listen. No longer would he be left at home when there was fighting to be done, horses to be stolen or enemies to be slain. He was See the Dark of the fighting Cheyenne. He looked down at the first man he had killed, then at the dripping scalp lock. The scent of newly spilt blood and warm, newly-dead bodies washed over him and Dark threw up.

Chapter Thirteen

---- o o o ----

The commotion woke Viajero early. He looked carefully out of the dried streambed where he had slept wrapped in his blanket. His fire was out, no smoke came from the grey pile of ashes; his pony was still picketed further up the coulee but its head was up, paused in its grazing. The clamour came from just over the crest of the hill. It came from the direction of the woman's campfire. There was yelling and wild screeching in a language he couldn't understand; they seemed to be celebrating something. There was a thudding of pony hooves and the occasional shot. They were not his people but he recognised the exulting tone of a blood raid.

Whoever these warriors were, Viajero had no quarrel with them but he knew that in the joyous time following a successful spree of killing and plunder, wildness took charge. The smell of their enemies' blood would still be in their nostrils and they would feel invincible. They would not hesitate to attack anyone not of their own kind.

Viajero's own survival now depended on his caution and stealth. He gathered his few belongings, quickly scattered the ashes of his fire and saddled his pony. Using the head high banks of the dried streambed as shelter, he led his mount to the foot of the hill. The pony snickered slightly, catching the scent of the hard-ridden horses beyond the crest. Viajero took the time to stroke the long nose of his pony, breathing his own scent over its velvet muzzle. After a few moments, the horse became quiet. Tying the reins firmly to a branch, the Apache carefully crept up the hill and slid into a small pocket of sage, using the fragrant silvery stems as cover so he could watch undisturbed.

The war party was big, with dozens of warriors. They were obviously on their way back from a raid; captive women and children were tied behind mounted braves who whooped and yelled, jerking them along with rawhide ropes. The wounded were lashed to pony travois and led by younger men. A cloud of dust behind a nearby hill confirmed the presence of the stolen horse herd. The main body of the war party was exultant and sang songs of victory. They brandished their weapons and chanted in an unknown tongue.

Viajero could not see the woman, he hoped she had seen or heard them coming and hidden. A victorious war party was not the sort of company she would need at her campfire. He did not know which tribe the warriors came from, all the grasslands people looked very much alike to him. They were not Comanches, he was certain of that, their hair and clothes were different. Whoever they were, they made a fearsome sight and Viajero was happy to remain unobserved and alive.

Dust screened the passage of the raiders and Viajero could not see any sign of the woman; perhaps she had evaded them after all. She had surely heard them coming. He had persuaded himself that this was so when several painted warriors emerged from a clump of alder scrub. One was leading a pony with distinctive white flashes on its legs. It was the horse that Viajero had given to the woman.

The group mounted their tethered horses and rode off to join their companions, the pony on a head rope tied behind a young brave. Viajero felt a sudden stab of anger and it surprised him. That pony was his gift to her, though, he remembered, he had actually delivered the gift through her grandfather. The woman was probably dead now; he had not seen her coloured linen skirt and long moccasins among the captives. Her body must be down there somewhere.

The Apache waited a long time for the war party to move on. He did not want to expose his position to any rearguard. Sometimes on his own raids, a small party would deliberately ride behind the main group in order to round up stray horses and warn of any pursuers. Viajero was too experienced to be caught in the open. Eventually, around midday, he rode round the side of the hill and headed into the alder scrub where the raiders had been.

He dismounted and looked into the undergrowth but could see nothing. Keeping the reins in one hand he searched for sign in the confused tracks in the dirt. Then, he saw it – a definite print of a Mescalero moccasin with the blurred edge of the upturned toe, then another print; then another. It looked bad; her signs were on top of the war party prints. She had been with them. Next, he found scuffed marks where she had kicked out and struggled, then channels in the dirt where she had been dragged. She had fought them but they had been too many. There were drops of blood here.

He found her in the dried coulee, roughly thrown aside after the repeated rapes. Her deerskin shirt was ripped to the waist, bloody chunks bitten from her flesh, the coloured calico skirt bundled above her thighs. She lay on her side, one arm draped over a rock. She was white with dust, black lines of blood around her mouth and smeared onto her cheeks. He stood over her, confused by what he felt. She meant little to him but it was hard to see one of his people treated so badly with no revenge taker to spill the blood of those responsible.

His hand automatically went to touch the deerskin pouch around his neck. It still contained the black stone from the Mescalero country that this woman had given as a gift. A stab of guilt cut inside him. He should take care of her last needs then leave.

The old deep fears of his people would not let him touch her body but he walked back to his pony to fetch his blanket. He would wrap her in it and bury her in the coulee. Rocks would keep the wolves and the carrion eaters away. In the rains, sweet water would scour the grave and carry her bones to a better resting-place. They would be washed clean of the violation she had suffered here. His debt would be paid.

He was walking back with the blanket when the woman lifted her arm.

Chapter Fourteen

---- o o o ----

Smoke on the Moon and Broken Knife listened to the reports from their badly shaken people. The Cheyenne village had suffered badly though the raiders had not escaped unscathed. Seven Pawnee warriors had died in the fight. Two more had been discovered, badly wounded but alive, amongst the bodies left on the field. The Pawnee had not bothered to try and rescue them, their days as warriors were over. The two captives were turned over to the Cheyenne women and tortured. Those newly widowed or whose children had been carried off took a leading part in making sure that the captives' journey to the next life was not undertaken without considerable pain. The badly mutilated pair welcomed death when it eventually came.

The remaining members of the soldier societies tallied the horses. Over three hundred mounts had been run off from the Cheyenne herd, many of them war and hunting ponies; prime stock that had been carefully tended and trained. Many more were scattered into the hills – it would take days to get them back.

Broken Knife and Smoke listened grim faced to the tally of human casualties. The losses were a crushing blow; keening wails and grief songs of the remaining anguished women dominated the smoking encampment in the days following the raid. Many were widows now and starvation loomed with the first winter chills. Men too were in tears – some grieved the deaths of wives and children slain by flying bullets or arrows. Others shouted for vengeance on the Pawnees that had taken their families into slavery.

Sixteen men of fighting age had died in the battle, Bear Runs, Shining Horse, Raven Heart and Twisted Wolf among them. Three more had later died of wounds and twelve women and children had been captured and carried off. The lodges which housed See the Dark's band were much reduced, burned to the ground by the Pawnee mounted group that took the Cheyenne families. A sense of shock and bewilderment hung about the village, the smell of smoke and death adding to the desolation.

Bear Runs had died from the arrow in his neck. The shaft had struck true and deep, his blood had pooled black and glossy on the dirt once Dark had dropped him. His mother found him unconscious outside their family lodge as she was preparing to join the others in fleeing the camp. She could not revive him. Bear Runs never awoke and her own life was in danger. In tears, she reluctantly left him on the ground, his body half inside the *tipi* flap.

Shining Horse had been shot in the head at close range by a ball from a rusty trade rifle but his body had been immediately recovered by Broken Knife to deny the Pawnee more glory for counting coup. There was still honour to be had from just touching the body of a fallen enemy during a fight. Broken Knife had been wounded in this incident but had continued fighting ferociously alongside his Thunder Bear soldiers, blood flowing freely from two arrows in his thigh. Shining Horse's face was unmarked except for the round hole where the ball had crashed through the bone but a terrible star-shaped wound at the back of his skull had blown grey gobbets of his brains down his back.

Raven Heart had known that he would die that day and Smoke had suspected that he would. His contamination, brought about by his wife's bleeding time, was now known throughout the camp. His guardian spirits could not possibly protect him after this and his fellow warriors accepted his fate as a matter of course. But Badlands heard how the women muttered to themselves and blamed his wife. Raven Heart's wife had, at first, ritually gashed her legs and arms after his death but, after the whisperings crept to the surface, cut off a finger on each hand to atone for her carelessness as well as to appease her critics. Smoke on the Moon had seen Raven Heart fall during the fighting but had been powerless to prevent him being scalped and mutilated by the swooping Pawnee. Raven Heart's eyes had been cut out and his legs and arms deeply hacked with war hatchets to prevent him firing a bow or mounting a pony in the next life.

Stampeding Cheyenne ponies had run down Twisted Wolf; his battered and crushed body was not found for a while. His lifeless form had been kicked aside into a small ravine and lay partially covered with dust and fallen rock. A horse with a broken leg had landed on top of him and had churned up the ground and the chief's flesh trying to get back on its feet. The animal's screaming had eventually led the People to find their leader.

The loss of the women and children was a disgrace deeply felt. Yellow Bear, with several cracked ribs after being hit by the Pawnee pony, blamed himself for not getting them to safety sooner but everyone knew that the Pawnee raid had been well-planned and carried out.

It had been a different sort of attack that even Smoke on the Moon understood. His soldier society only ever fought as single warriors once battle had commenced, there was little unity and no organisation. They would take enormous risks to reap the rewards of their individual bravery. Now Smoke had suffered the reverses brought on by a planned attack; it would be a lesson well learnt. The Pawnee normally fought has haphazardly as the Cheyenne but on this occasion they had listened to instructions and it had brought victory. Whoever the war chief of the Pawnee was, his judgement had been faultless that day.

See the Dark's band was slumped in defeat but Dark himself was quietly jubilant. His family had survived, their lodge was intact and, in the heat of battle, no-one had questioned his lost eye or now saw it as an obstacle to being a warrior. Now he was an accepted part of the tribal fighting strength; he had proved the doubters wrong. He had tried to tell all this to his mother but she had rounded on him for his smugness, hissing at him in her anger:

"Keep your boasting to yourself! We have too many dead to be happy that your vanity has been satisfied. Killing is the easy part, re-building this village will be much harder."

Dark, stung by his mother's words, stalked off back to the tipi and lay on his bed and seethed at the injustices meted out by parents. He didn't do this for long as his mother followed him, tipped him off his buffalo robe and told him to move further to the curved wall.

"Other people will be living with us soon. Winter is coming and we'll all have to share with those who have nothing."

Dark had sighed audibly and, with an air of long-suffering, moved his bedding over. Badlands noticed the display of ill-grace and grabbed her son by the hair; it was an extreme insult but she *was* his mother:

"Don't act like a child. Being in the service of the People isn't just about arrows and war hatchets. You'll need kindness and consideration in the coming months, life will be hard for all of us. Make sure you don't let us down."

As if in contrition, she stroked the side of his face but her petulant son turned away and walked outside to gather his thoughts.

Smoke and Broken Knife took command of the devastated tribal group as they added up the losses. Around a third of their fighting strength was gone, horses for hunting or packing were scattered or stolen and replacement shelter and food for the oncoming winter was at a desperate level. The Spirits had deserted them and both felt tribal confidence waning.

Despite their warnings to the hot bloods, desire for revenge put fire in the bellies of the younger ones and several rode out to try and avenge the deaths of their friends and rescue their families. The Pawnee had anticipated this and had laid a strong ambush on their back trail; two of the reckless ones paid for this with their lives and the rest had barely escaped. Stone Turtle's cunning in battle would be much praised back in his own country.

Smoke ordered the burials and these went ahead with solemn ritual. Timber scaffolds were erected and platforms were built into tree branches to hold the remains of those who had died protecting the village. Personal possessions and weapons were laid with their dead owners on the scaffolds, ready to be of service to them in the next life. Bodies were wrapped in buffalo robes, bound with an occasional rawhide rope to keep the worst of the weather out. On a whim, all were left with their faces uncovered, sightless eyes staring towards the sky. They had often looked to the heavens during life to seek inspiration or direction. Now, in death, that same vast canopy would be the roof of their tomb.

Broken Knife, not known for his sensitivity or following religious rites, stopped the ritual slaughter of dead warriors' ponies at the funeral scaffolds, arguing that they did not now have enough horses to waste in that way. Older men and women took against him and complained publicly at his sweeping aside of ancient traditions. He was happy for Smoke's support and the horses were saved.

Yellow Bear led all the ceremonies, his heart heavy with his own guilt. He had failed to stop the Pawnee taking the families and would bear this burden until his dying day. Some of the surviving warriors had blamed him for losing their loved ones. They snubbed him at the council fire and, without Twisted Wolf's mature words to balance any arguments, called for him to be replaced and banished.

Smoke on the Moon and Broken Knife did their best to calm things down, especially when it came to forbidding any revenge raids until the tribe had recovered and could put a strong war party into the field. They did not replace Twisted Wolf but the loyalty and strength of their two soldier societies brought some semblance of unity to the badly shocked Cheyenne. Both were practical men. Traditions would have to be laid aside. Revenge would eventually be meted out to the Pawnee but at a time and place to suit the Medicine Arrow people.

For now, families needed lodges, food and horses – the village would move again, closer to their Arapaho friends. They could not stay in this graveyard and prosper.

Chapter Fifteen

---- o o o ----

Viajero rigged a travois for the woman and lashed it to his own pony. It had only been when he lifted her up that he realised she had been badly wounded as well as raped. The unknown warriors had stabbed her with knives and lances; not deep enough to kill but enough to drain her strength. They had intentionally left her alive and then abandoned her so that she could testify to their greatness in battle. She had been allowed to live as a scarred trophy.

Somewhere, deep inside the White Mountain Apache's spirit, a spark of revenge was fanned into a small flame. The woman was not his, nor even of his people; but blood spilt called for a blood reckoning. But the heat of the flame was only momentary and went almost unnoticed as the warrior wallowed in self-pity at the new burden.

The journey on the travois was not easy; pain, from the jarring ride as the shafts slewed over rocks and lumpy ground, lanced into Bright Antelope. Though, as an Apache woman, she was determined to show none of it. She would make sure that her *Coyotero* would be proud of her.

Viajero walked alongside the pony with bitterness in his heart. It was not just the horse that was burdened now; he too was weighed down by the presence of this woman. Usen surely had not meant her to be on the trail with him. The One-Above was testing him in some way. It would be much better if the woman died and released him from the ties of her need.

It was hard to remember that he had been a much-feared warrior in his own country. Once, the talks with his spirits had been powerful; Usen had guided and protected him on many raids and had given him the strength to kill his enemies. Now the warrior smells in his nostrils had gone. Now he only smelled the woman and her sickness. He was reduced to tending to her - chores that did not suit a fighting man. He had hoped that Usen would give him back his appetite for blood and vengeance. He had set out on his quest north to seek a return to his powers but God seemed to have other plans for him.

Still, despite his seething anger, Viajero had fed and comforted the Mescalero woman as best he could. But she was getting weaker, he would need to find a village of the grassland people and leave her there. Either that or end her suffering himself. Food had been short since he had found her. The pony was now used only for dragging the travois; Viajero couldn't range after the bigger game that they needed for nourishment to stay alive.

The horse, trained only to the saddle and carrying the lightly equipped warrior for raiding, was not accustomed to dragging heavy loads and had quickly gone out of condition. Despite wrapping the travois poles in soft moss and grass, sores appeared on the horse's shoulders and caused it discomfort. It occasionally stood still to alleviate the pain and only a beating from Viajero got it moving again. If he used the horse for hunting as well, it would probably wear out quicker and die, leaving them on foot. There had been no sign of other people since the war party had passed many days ago. Viajero knew that disaster was close. Usen had deserted him.

The Apache suddenly stopped and sniffed the air. There was a recognisable tang on the light breeze. He let the pony's head rope fall and walked quickly up a nearby slope. A thin wisp of wood smoke beckoned beyond a tree-covered hill. The mountains off to the west were covered in a light snow and the air was chill with the onset of an early winter. Following his life trail northwards would have to wait until the spring. Usen seemed silent on what he had to do, so the Apache headed towards the smoke.

But it wasn't a village or even a single lodge. It was a sod and timber cabin set in a clearing by a fast flowing river. The smoke was coming from a vent hole in the roof. Two well-fed saddle mounts trotted round a split rail corral and a white man was dragging buffalo hides into a pile by the house. There were piles of cordwood neatly stacked in a small lean-to and a shirt hung on a line to dry in the wind.

Viajero weighed up the challenge; two horses probably meant two whites, both possibly well-armed. The house looked permanent and, oddly, many trails were etched into the soil leading to the place. People came here many times from different directions for some reason. This was not just a dwelling house of the *indaa* – there was a reason for the trails. Viajero thought about them for a while, trying to guess their significance. Then, with a rare smile, remembered similar places he had seen. It was a trading post. The trails were those of trappers or others that came to trade for goods or gold. He would scout the post after dark and decide his next move.

He led the pony and travois back into the tree-line on the hill, wrapped the woman in the thin blanket and laid her on the ground. It was too near the post to light a fire but at least he was a safe distance from the many small trails that led to the hut. They troubled him – he could not watch them all; a threat could come down any one of them. He would check the tracks and sign in daylight and see which ones were most used.

The Apache unlashed the travois from his long suffering war pony and watched the animal shiver and twitch as flying insects found the fresh blood on the exposed sores. Scraping some wet dirt and moss from a tree bole, Viajero plastered this onto the pony's blisters. It seemed to soothe and cool; at least it barred the way for the biting flies. It was a simple act that surprised the Apache. He was never usually this caring about his stock. In normal times, a horse was a useful way in and out of battle. He would ride one until it dropped, kick it back onto its feet and then ride some more. If it lay down again, he lit fires under it until it stood up and resumed its journey. If it didn't get up, he killed and ate it. His treatment of the pony's wounds was merely another step on the trail to survival.

The woman stirred and asked for water and he untied the water pouch from the horse's neck. Viajero ripped a strip of leftover meat into small pieces and fed them to her, giving her sips of water to help her swallow. She was thin and had a fever; her eyes were round and luminous, like the Comanche Raiding Moon. She would not last long without shelter and hot food. To his shame, he found he was tempted to let her die; to be released from his obligations so he and his pony could winter somewhere and he could resume his quest. He had not told her about the cabin and she hadn't questioned why they had stopped, their mutual silences a natural barrier to any shared desire to live.

As darkness fell, Viajero slipped from the timber, crawled through the brushwood surrounding the trading post and silently stood in the shadows at one end of the cabin. He peered round the corner, keeping his head at ground height, and was surprised to see a man sitting out on the front verandah smoking a pipe. The man was white, probably the one who had been carrying the buffalo hides. The *indaa* was wrapped in a brightly coloured blanket, only his head and pipe jutted out of the top. It was impossible to see if he was armed.

Viajero jumped slightly as the door creaked open behind the man and an Indian woman joined him, dragging another chair alongside; she too smoked a pipe. The curling tobacco smoke carried to the nostrils of the Apache. It had been a long time since he had smoked. The man and woman carried on a stilted conversation in a language unknown to Viajero.

From inside the cabin, the Apache heard another noise, just on the other side of the timber wall from his head. It was the sound of claws clicking on wooden floorboards – a dog, coming out to join its master. Viajero didn't like dogs, except to eat. He crept swiftly back through the scrub and into the forest.

Viajero's morale had risen – the trading post meant survival. He explained what he had found to the woman and she forced herself to sit up and talk about what they would now do. She didn't trust the *indaa* any more than he did. As for the Indian woman down there, she must be a slave or an outcast from her own people. The best course would be to avoid the trading post altogether and find a tribal band they could trust. She would then rest and recover and her *Coyotero* could complete his journey.

Viajero could not argue with her logic but the trading post drew him. These places had stocks of all the things they needed to stay alive.

He had been inside one before, near his own land. He had been hesitant about going in at first – the Mexicans who ran these places could never be trusted. But his wife's brother had persuaded him. They had not raided for a while so the countryside was quiet; the Mexicans had ceased to be vigilant. Both men had dressed in clothing stolen from the villages they had plundered. His wife's brother spoke a little Spanish; they had posed as Navajos with stock to trade. They had traded two mules for gunpowder, ball, percussion caps, flour, coffee and hardtack bread. The mules had been high grade so the trader had even thrown in some strange, round metal boxes for them to enjoy with the hardtack. It had taken Viajero two days to work out that there was food inside the cans; an irritated stab with his hunting knife had pierced the metal shell and covered him in peach juice. Viajero and his brother in law had roared with laughter and delight at the bounty. They laughed even harder as they remembered that they had traded for all these goods with two stolen mules. Cunning was valued amongst the N'de as much as courage. An Apache would always make a better trader than a Mexican.

The memory brought a glow of pleasure to Viajero and a stab of anticipation. He wanted to do it again. He returned to the woman and told her he intended to attack the *indaa* and his woman; he would take everything to ensure their survival, including the fresh horses. Viajero was excited by the prospect and spoke rapidly. Usen seemed to have entered his heart again. Bright Antelope strained to keep up with his words. She understood much of what he was saying but the plan seemed flawed. She waited for a pause and then spoke:

"My brother…" She always called him this; it was an intimacy one step removed. She now knew his name but, as was the formal custom, avoided its use in conversation. Her heart belonged to him but she guessed that this was not returned; she would wait until the time was right to announce her true feelings. For now, they both had to stay alive.

"Your plan is that of a warrior. It is simple and you have the courage to make it work. But it is the plan of a warrior in his own country and when he is not weighed down by a weak woman; you are neither of those things."

She watched the Apache's eyes narrow and glare at her. He was not used to being criticised.

"The trading post has a white man there; other *indaa* will probably visit it using the many trails you saw. We do not know when they will come or from which direction. Killing the white eyes will bring pursuit from others. We cannot hope to find rest with a village of the grassland people if we are being followed – it will be dangerous for us as well as them. But we need that food in the trading post. I have a way to do it."

Viajero choked back his resentment and listened to her plan. Some of the things she suggested would not work and he told her this. She, in turn, listened and made concessions. He became more enthusiastic as the strands of their cunning knitted together. The Mescalero woman was clever and thought beyond the immediate bloodletting. She got Viajero to think and see like an *indaa*. If he did this, then he could outwit them.

In the end, the plan seemed as though it might work. Now they just needed *Usen* to bring them good fortune to get things started.

Chapter Sixteen

---- o o o ----

The dismantling of See the Dark's village had not taken long; there were few enough remaining lodges to fold and pack. The scattered horse herd was gathered up though many ponies had run off, never to return. The smell of smoke and death was still in the air. Packs of wolves, emboldened by human lethargy, skulked around the camp fringes, waiting. A stray colt or unguarded child was an opportunity not to be missed.

Bad Elk, urged on by Smoke on the Moon, had scouted another campsite some two days ride away. Bad Elk was pleased to be of such service. He was not a member of either soldier society and his brother's request had given him some extra standing with the People. It was a great honour to be chosen in this way. Bad Elk was much respected as a hunter; his prowess with the rifle was already well known but the importance of finding a camping ground for the winter was a great challenge. He had undertaken the task with thoroughness, trying to imagine what Twisted Wolf would have looked for. Bad Elk knew, during his scout, that the survival of the People now depended on the choice he made for winter quarters.

The death of the much-respected camp chief had left a yawning gap in this basic survival knowledge of the People. Twisted Wolf had known all this instinctively; he knew where his band should camp for both the summer and winter months. He had known the buffalo trails and the best combinations of game, timber, grass and water. The People had left it to him; they trusted him and he had never let them down. Now he was gone and Bad Elk was being tested with an heavy responsibility. This small band of Cheyenne could die out in the coming months if he got it wrong.

Smoke's brother had fought well during the battle with the Pawnee. He had bitterly resented the mocking departure of the raiders, singing their songs of triumph on the skyline above the old village. Bad Elk had not had much time to use his rifle during the raid as reloading took time and, anyway, it was an impractical weapon for the close and bitter personal fighting. However, he had sensed that the Pawnee thought they were safe on the hill and he wanted to strike the final blow.

He had unslung the rifle from his back and poured black powder down the barrel from his horn flask. He had added an extra measure to make up for the distance and height that the ball would have to travel and then rammed the lead bullet down hard on top of it. Cocking the hammer, he placed a percussion cap on the iron nipple under it and took aim, resting the barrel on the shoulder of a fellow warrior to steady the weapon.

Bad Elk did not know which Pawnee in the line of riders was the war chief but lined up the sights on the leading warrior. The rifle boomed, startling the exhausted Cheyenne, and smoke belched from the barrel. A smoke ring followed and hung on the still air, indicating that the ball had not been seated properly. No matter, it had been a good parting shot. The heavy bullet had slammed into the shoulder of the Pawnee warrior's pony and brought it tumbling down the slope, its rider trapped beneath it with a broken neck. It had been a small gesture of hope during the ignominy of defeat. The Cheyenne raised their cracked voices in delight. Bad Elk had done well.

His scouting mission had also been productive. The omens for the new village had been good, helping to restore the faith of the Cheyenne. When Bad Elk had returned to his chosen site, with the exhausted tribal band strung out behind him, a small group of skunks had watched them from behind a fallen tree.

Elders in the band had spotted the skunks and had been delighted. They sang the old songs of hunting the fat little creatures in past times when the leaves were about to fall. Skunks were generally solitary in their habits but this group seemed to reassure the exhausted Cheyenne that food was here. Bad Elk generously ascribed this omen to the power of Yellow Bear's communication with the Spirits. Bad Elk's standing rose and Yellow Bear's reputation, scarred after the loss of the women and children, regained a little ground.

See the Dark's good heart had brought him round from the spat with his mother, mainly because he knew she was right. He was impressed by the recent behaviour of his blood kin. His father had, as expected, fought well during the Pawnee battle but also, with Broken Knife, had brought order and discipline out of the shock and confusion of defeat. Smoke on the Moon now had a leading role in the future of the tribe though he himself had not sought it. The success of his brother in securing a well-found winter camp now brought an added dimension to the influence of See the Dark's family.

Dark's mother had survived her battle ordeal well and was highly thought of for her killing of the Pawnee; she had kept his pony and his scalp as war trophies. When her humour had returned she would flap the scalp in Dark's face and say she was now qualified to be a warrior like her son. Her skills had been much in demand in helping the wounded. Typically, contrary to popular opinion and against Smoke's advice, she had helped put healing poultices onto the finger stumps of Raven Heart's wife. The woman had been grateful but had later torn off the dressings and allowed herself to bleed to death in woods close to the old village. Badlands Walking Woman blamed the gossiping women, shrilly censuring them for the death. It had been an awkward time.

See the Dark was now in his seventeenth year and an accepted warrior by virtue of his actions during the battle. His lack of an eye had not bothered him during the fighting, though he did have to remember to constantly sweep his head from side to side to spot approaching enemies. In addition to the plump Pawnee youth that had been his first victim, he had killed twice more during the fighting, though he had only two scalps to show for it. The third Pawnee had kept his hair but had been unsaddled by a blow from See the Dark's hatchet and dragged away by his pony, one foot caught in his stirrup ring. See the Dark, the red heat of killing on him, had recklessly chased the pony back into the wood, repeatedly smashing the face of his opponent whenever he caught up. Smoke had to order him back to prevent him being cut off by the remaining Pawnees. See the Dark had been unscathed by the fighting; light bruises on his arm where he had grappled with the enemy and a scrape on his leg where his pony had fallen with him were the only physical reminders. His mother made much of this, especially to those who had forecast a dim future for her one-eyed son.

Rebuilding the camp to its former, comfortable circle of lodges in time for the winter would not be possible. Some surviving warriors had lost their entire families; wives and children had either been carried off or killed. They did not have the will to make a fresh shelter just for themselves; relatives could help some of them. A few lucky ones had lost only their lodges but the families remained intact. But the pressing majority were widows and children without food providers – some had lodges that were undamaged but others were totally destitute. Bad Elk and Smoke on the Moon had convened the whole village to plan what to do.

Making a new lodge was not a man's work nor, as their wives had reminded them in the carefree past, did the men have the skills to do it. The village lodge maker, an ancient and toothless woman called Sings Loud, had always presided at such communal gatherings where women, skilled with awl and sinew thread, could stitch and fit a new tipi over its pine poles in a day or so. Sings Loud had always been well rewarded with soft foods for her work. Occasionally, a wealthier woman had given her a colt or a blanket as well. The husband of Sings Loud had died of disease long before the Pawnee raid. The old crone's skills would now be much in demand.

Before the village had gathered around the council fire, Bad Elk had consulted with Smoke, Broken Knife, Yellow Bear and some of the surviving elders. They agreed a plan to be put to the People. Some of the things that needed to be done would upset traditions, many would waver and try and cling to the old ways and familiar rituals. But Smoke had learned much from the Pawnee raid. The Pawnee war leader had not stuck to the old ways in battle and had won; Smoke's depleted Cheyenne band would someday have their revenge but first needed to survive the winter. Bad Elk would put these ideas to the People; they would decide.

So, in the gathering twilight and far from their own land, the sad remnants of the mixed band of Twisted Wolf's people gathered around a crackling fire in the centre of their newly erected camp. Wisps of exhaled breath gleamed silver in the chilly air; a hungry baby cried out but was silenced. Bad Elk rose and wrapped his buffalo robe around him; it would be a difficult speech.

"You all know me; I am the son of Great Horse and brother of Smoke on the Moon. You also know that I am not your chief…"

There was a low murmur of acknowledgement; the spirit of Twisted Wolf would always be close and strong.

"I ask only that you listen to what I have to say at this council fire. When I am done, then you can decide if my words are worth anything. I am not a prophet or a holy man; I am only a servant of our People."

There was a general nodding of assent and approval of Bad Elk's modesty.

"The fight with the Pawnees cost us dear. Some of our best men now sleep on their funeral scaffolds at the battleground and many of our loved ones are held as slaves in the Pawnee camp. These things will be avenged…"

A young man jumped up, his greased skin glistening in the firelight. He was carrying a war hatchet and pointed this accusingly at Bad Elk. He shouted sharply and loudly:
"When will we be avenged? While we sit here and talk, coyotes take the bones of our dead, our enemies ravage our women and our children are being raised as Pawnees. Let's mount up and find them before the snows come!"

It was a disrespectful interruption and some old women told him to sit down. Other youths, galvanised by the remarks also made to stand up. The meeting was already in danger of breaking up without a decision being made. Out of the darkness on the fringe of the huddle of people, two soldiers of the Thunder Bear Society leapt at the young man, kicked his legs out from under him and forced him to sit down. Bad Elk looked at Broken Knife who stared impassively into the flames. It seemed harsh to put down dissent even from hot heads. He continued:

"As I said, these things will be avenged but in our own time…"

Young voices still growled in opposition but there was no further demonstration.

"We are weak from that fight. We need to rebuild our strength and spirits before we seek out the Pawnee. Many horses are gone, our lodges are few, food is scarce and winter is almost here. Our biggest fight is coming soon - it will be against the north wind and the snows. If we lose this fight, then none of us will be able to draw a bow against the Pawnee in the future."

Making the coming struggle with winter sound like a battle was a subtle turn in Bad Elk's speech. It would channel the energies of the young and rekindle the courage of the old to face a common adversity. Yellow Bear and Smoke grunted in approval.

"In this first battle against winter, all of you, old and young alike, will be warriors. The People need shelter – we do not have time to find and kill enough buffalo to use their hides for our lodges. So we will do something different – we will go back to the old ways, to the time before our grandfathers when the animals could talk to us. We will build lodges out of timber and earth like our ancestors – we cannot build one for each person or family but a few such dwellings can house a group such as bachelors or widows…"

Bad Elk's words were drowned out by the rising hubbub of voices in his audience. The People were divided on the wisdom of this new, old way. An excitement bubbled amongst them as discussion overtook good manners. Interruptions and questions came. The Thunder Bear soldiers looked ready to intervene again but Broken Knife shook his head.

"I will only live with my fellow warriors in the Thunder Bear Society" a thin faced man announced and nodded his head once as a final, emphatic flourish.

"You are a married man and your family will want you in your own lodge which is one of the few that still stands, "replied Broken Knife sarcastically. "This is not a chance to leave your wife and live as a bachelor"

The audience hooted with pleasure at the humour and a relaxed atmosphere reigned for a while. The wife of the thin-faced man glared at him. Some of the questions, though, required a more serious response. A chubby young woman brought the gathering back to reality on a practical note:

"It is a long time since this type of lodge was built – does anyone still know how to do it?"

Silence fell as people looked to the old ones for guidance but most shrugged their shoulders and shook their heads. To everyone's surprise, the question was shouted again to someone out of the firelight; Crow Star was venerable but deaf. The ancient one shuffled forward and nodded his head, saliva dripped from his mouth on the down stroke. His voice was as dry as rustling leaves:

"When I was a boy, my grandfather once built me a model of one of these old houses out of sticks and mud. I can remember what it looked like. Of course, he was too young himself to have lived in a timber lodge but building one cannot be too difficult."

There was a cautious acceptance of Crow Star's expertise, though there was a difference in seeing a pile of twigs and mud many years ago and building the real thing out of heavy logs. However, there was no other choice and could be no dissent, Crow Star became the sole expert on timber lodges.

The chatter subsided and Bad Elk continued:

"The lodges that still stand will need to house as many neighbours as possible. The warriors without families will live in a large timber lodge that we will build. The Striking Snakes will live at one end, the Thunder Bears at the other; this will give space for the sacred rituals. Those who do not belong to either will live in the centre of the lodge. Women without men who have no lodges will live in another timber house; they will cook the food for the single warriors. We will build a separate small lodge for women to live in during their bleeding time"

His audience nodded in assent; the communal use of the timber lodges seemed sensible. The separate lodge for menstruating women was absolutely necessary; no-one had forgotten what had happened to Raven Heart when this basic precaution had been ignored.

Bad Elk pressed on with his plan for winter survival – children would help in adding to the food store; they could fish, kill birds and rabbits and trap skunks. Mens' hunting parties would be kept small to ensure that the maximum number of warriors would be available to guard the village. Unblooded braves would be sent to find horses – they were to be rounded up from the wild and not stolen; the People were not strong enough to repel a retaliatory attack. Crow Star and other old men would be in charge of felling timber for the new lodges; older youths would help drag it and erect the frames. Sings Loud would be kept supplied with buffalo hides as these were found; she and her group of women would slowly rebuild the skin tipis. A supply of lodge poles was to be found and cut....

Crow Star struggled to his feet again, helped up by eager hands; he had a question:

"Lodge poles are easily cut or broken when they are green. However, you now wish us to fell heavy trees – how will we do this? Many of our hatchets are of the *veho* iron but they are too small and light to get a big tree down quickly; hollowing out trunks and setting fire inside to topple them takes time. The snows will be here before we have a single log on the ground."

It was a question for which Bad Elk had no answer. But Broken Knife did

"The *vehoe* have many things that can be of use to us – they have bigger axes, specially made for cutting down trees. They also have an iron blade that has small teeth like a coyote; these too cut trees. On their wagons, they have a cloth that keeps out rain, these would help in making our lodges tight against the snows. The *vehoe* are to blame for making us move from our land. We should take these things from them so that our people can live"

Broken Knife remained standing, a tall, austere presence in front of a cowed group of refugees. The People were silent; they knew the whites hadn't forced them to move from their land, the Pawnee had done that. Everyone did know though that the white soldiers would soon take to the war trail to avenge themselves against the Sioux, perhaps they had already done it, no-one knew. Perhaps the whites would then want to come after the Cheyenne. Perhaps their misfortunes were building up like rain clouds; it was difficult to make a decision.

One thing was only too clear. Raids on the whites would only bring destruction and death in return and now Broken Knife wanted to put them at risk. Elders shook their heads but did not speak up – Broken Knife had been one of the saviours of the tribe both during and after the Pawnee battle. The younger hot bloods began to murmur amongst themselves – at last, the chance for war! Two stood up, as if in solidarity with the Thunder Bear leader but he motioned them to sit down; they obeyed.

Smoke knew it was time to act and stood up alongside his warrior companion. He had never spoken much at council fires before the Pawnee battle; he had always been content to leave the speeches to men older and wiser than himself. But since the defeat, he had gained much experience in speaking his thoughts. He used a comradely tone:

"The leader of the Thunder Bears is right; the *vehoe* have been part of our misfortune…"

Heads turned to one another in disbelief, surely Smoke on the Moon was not going to agree with Broken Knife and take them to war in their current weakened state?

"But, like the Pawnee just now, the whites will be hard to find. Even though, as we all know, the *vehoe* are crazy, they are not so crazy as to cross our country during winter. This is the time when their wagons have passed. They will wait until Spring before they come again. We can find them then."

Broken Knife looked at Smoke with narrowed eyes, as though he had been tricked. But after a moment's thought, he sat down without a word. Smoke had bought some time. There was a low hum of approval from the audience.

Smoke continued:

"As for logs, look closely in the woods for trees already fallen – they will save work. Some are on the point of falling now, tie a rope to a horse and bring them down. We must use all our cunning and skills to help each other. We start tomorrow."

Slowly, the villagers dispersed back to their lodges. Most *tipis* were full to bursting point, taboos and rituals forgotten for now as practical survival skills surfaced. Single men wrapped themselves in their blankets and buffalo robes and stretched out around the fire. They would not be able to sleep outside for much longer; the earth was chill and heavy. A bitter wind whistled through the trees and into the encampment. All had much to think about and went to their beds to consider their fate.

Only Yellow Bear returned to an empty lodge. As the tribe's spirit diviner much of what he did in his sacred rituals was not for outsiders to see and so he was usually alone. But since the battle, many still blamed him for the loss of the families. No-one wanted to openly support him by sharing his lodge, even at a time as critical as this. The gaunt, angular medicine man now seemed to minister to a divided people, his powers gone and reputation badly dented.

Seeing the skunks had been a good omen but in his heart he knew he had not prophesied this. Bad Elk had been courteous in giving him the benefit.

He lit a sheaf of sweet grass and, with a cupped hand, pulled the smoke over himself to purify and expunge. He held his medicine bundle high and prayed. The small deerskin parcel contained all his talismen and amulets, chosen by and known only to him. It was the very essence of his being as a Cheyenne. On a nearby hill, a wolf howled, the dying, chilling notes blending perfectly with the sorrow of the medicine man. Deep in despair, Yellow Bear wept.

As if in sympathy, the first soft snowflakes began to land on the small Cheyenne camp.

Chapter Seventeen

---- o o o ----

The snow also fell on Dietrich Hagen as he made his dispirited way to the trading post near the south fork of the Solomon River. He just hoped he was on the right trail. *Gott sei Dank,* he had called in there only a few days before to rest a lame mule – the post must be around here somewhere.

He peered through the thick, wet flakes and trusted to luck. He rode, hat tilted against the white flurries, and cursed his misfortune. God alone knew why he had thought that a personal tour of Indian villages would be more profitable than letting the red savages come to him in the comfort of his own trading stall up on the Platte wagon road.

Hagen was on the right trail. Some three miles ahead, Caleb Grimes strode around his cabin with a lantern hoping to catch sight of the stocky German. It was just turned noon but the snow had turned dimmed the daylight into a grey gloom. The hills seemed to close in; darker and more hostile. It reminded him of a painting he had seen once, hanging in a saloon in Independence showing the glowering hills and desolate crags around a place called Glencoe in Scotland. Murdo MacDonald, the saloon owner said it was a picture of his homeland; no wonder the bastard was so miserable.

Grimes had warned Hagen about the coming weather and advised him to stay at the cabin when he brought in his limping mule. The German thanked him but said that he wanted to avoid going home broke; he would ride out north for a day or two, find a big village and try to turn a profit. It was a lame plan and Grimes, in his usual forthright way, told him so. Profit, he argued, lay up on the Platte where passing homesteaders would be more inclined to buy the household tools. Theirs would have worn out or have been lost on the trek west. Cash money was better than stinking hides.

Hagen had bristled at the criticism but his native stubborn streak would not let him back down. Grimes told him not to stay out too long but head back to the Solomon when the weather closed in. He could stay until Spring and help with the winter trading; Grimes would be glad of the company. His Arapaho wife was fine but had limited conversation; even Hagen's poor English was better than her gabbling.

Caleb Grimes rarely regretted leaving his life as a wagon train captain. His last trip had been in 1850, only two years after he had first ridden along the newly blazed Mormon trail on the Platte. In the wake of the gold strike in California, the trails had, almost overnight, become clogged with people and wagons. Greed had taken over from venturesome spirit. His beloved, once-empty grasslands had become a Goddamn main street. Hundreds of rigs now queued at river ferry crossings, taking days to re-assemble on the far bank; wagon companies often charged past each other on the trail, vying for water and grass; richer pioneers now took one wagon to live in and others to carry their baggage and freight. It was a different life and he was tired of it.

Riding back alone from Oregon after his last trip, he had called into the Mormon settlement by the Great Salt Lake to look for a pretty woman that he had once met and spoken to in Council Bluffs. He had helped her load supplies into her wagon and she had rewarded him with a gift of an embroidered handkerchief. As usual, Grimes had put more stock in the gift than the young woman. It had turned out she was already married, one of a trio of Mormon wives closely guarded by her solemn and miserable spouse. Grimes had hoped that her old goat of a husband would be pushing up daisies by now. He still had the handkerchief with the embroidered honeybee on it, though it had not been washed well.

Of course, he had not found the woman. And no wonder, the Latter Day Saints' desert community had swollen to thousands. The burgeoning city had streets full of stores, eating-houses, assay offices and lawyers. The valley was full of cultivated fields – all the trappings of civilisation were tearing great chunks out of the wilderness. It had unnerved him and he had ridden swiftly away.

He had reached home, if his flea-ridden Missouri cabin could be called that, in the Spring of 1852 after short stopovers to find paid work in Fort Laramie. He had been there for the signing of the peace treaty with the Plains tribes on Horse Creek.

Caleb Grimes was not impressed by much but the sight of almost 10,000 Indians in one place had struck a chord. They were colourful, quarrelsome and as handsome a sight as he had ever seen. God alone knew if the treaty was worth anything but Grimes saw the gathering as a possible business opportunity. No more hard days in the saddle, poor food and whining settlers; no, now that the Indians were friendly, he could live close to them and trade. He could build a house, find a wife and live in comfort.

Women had always been his blind spot; he loved their shape, their smell and even some of their foibles. They, unfortunately, had found him short, coarse and generally undesirable. Of course, that was just the white women; Indian squaws were much less fussy.

He had seen a slim Arapaho girl coming into the adobe walls of the fort during the treaty signing; she came with her companions to giggle and stare at the soldiers. Grimes quickly decided that she was the one after exchanging only sly glances. Beads, mirrors and blandishments had won her interest if not her heart and, for two good horses and an illicit jug of corn whiskey, Grimes had bought her from her dissolute father.

Once married, they had both scouted out the best site for the trading post. She told him her Arapaho name but he insisted that she be called 'Mary'; he made her repeat it until he was satisfied. She had helped him build their cabin on the Solomon and was a useful channel for communicating with the Indians, mainly Cheyenne that came to trade. Yes, she had been a bargain at first – a comfort at night and help with the business. Somehow though, she seemed to have got fat and cranky quickly. Taking a rifle ramrod to her back had quelled her a little but pleasure seemed to have been replaced by sullen acceptance of each other. Grimes always welcomed white visitors – they ensured that he didn't need to talk to his wife.

The snow lifted around three in the afternoon and Grimes heard his dog yapping outside. It strained at its leather leash tied to the rickety steps; the dog looked at the hill and barked again. Black against the surrounding snow, Grimes watched the ungainly German pick his way down the hillside, his horse slithering from time to time on snow-covered rocks. He was leading his mules on head ropes and they brayed with anxiety at the slippery path.

Grimes could see that the packs were still full of those damn heavy trade goods – the German had no more business sense than his mules. He waved the lantern in welcome and the rider waved back. The trader went back into the cabin and told his wife to put more wood on the fire and reheat the stew. He took a bottle of whisky from his wooden chest near the fire and dusted out two glasses. The German would be frozen to the marrow, a glass or two of his precious drinking liquor would help thaw cold bones and flesh. The braying of the mules got louder and the dog was still barking. Grimes went outside to shut it up.

" Tess, hold yer tongue you damn fool bitch. Can't you see we have company?"

He turned to the rider.

"And as fer you, ye dumb bastard , didn't I tell you that business wouldn't be.."

Grimes was flung backwards as the heavy calibre bullet of the Sharps rifle boomed from the muzzle. The lead missile smashed into his breastbone, punching deep through the chest cavity, stopping his heart with the shock wave. The Arapaho woman shrieked from inside the cabin but came running out onto the front stoop, meat cleaver in hand. A bullet from a heavy revolver exploded through her cheek, sending teeth fragments and pink flesh flying. She sat down in a surprised heap, leaning against a post, dark red blood gushing from the ugly wound. A second ball crashed into the bridge of her nose and out of the back of her head. Timber flakes flew off the wood. She gurgled, vomited up more dark red clods of blood and was silent.

Viajero thrust the smoking pistol back into its holster and dismounted gingerly. He walked around to the bulging panniers carried by the mules and carefully unfastened a large canvas bag on one. Inside, the Mescalero woman was almost frozen to the bone and very pale. He helped her out and onto his shoulder; she needed a fire and food quickly. He carried her into the cabin, past the snarling dog peering from between the wooden steps, its leash caught tight around its throat. The Apache laid the woman down on a buffalo robe bed and pulled her close to the crackling flames of the cabin fire. He left her there to ease heat into her thin flesh. She would live now.

Back outside, he led the other loaded mule around the side of the cabin and, removing logs from the store pile, created a large hole. He pulled the mule closer to the stacked timber and then unfastened the large pack from across the saddle crosstrees. Carefully he lifted the heavy load and laid it in the hole, still in its canvas covering. Viajero then re-stacked the logs around the bag. The dead white man with the yellow hair would rest well there until he was needed again.

Viajero walked back into the cabin, noting with satisfaction the distinctive prints of the white man's boots that he left behind him. The heavy leather high boots were difficult to wear but it was important that the tracks he made here were not that of an Apache. The plan was working. The woman had thought things through; Viajero was impressed.

Back inside, Bright Antelope had stirred and was sitting up facing the flames. She put another log on the fire and looked round for cooking utensils but there were none that she could recognise. She could smell some food though from the back of the cabin; she told Viajero this as he came back in. He went into the lean-to at the rear of the cabin and found the iron pot containing the all-in stew that the *indaa* had been about to eat. He carried this back into the main room and, after some moments trying to balance the pot on the pile of blazing logs, worked out that a blackened iron pole with a hook on the end could be swung out across the flames and the pot suspended from it. Pleased with himself, he hooked up the pot and walked around the cabin, hobbling occasionally in the white man's boots.

The trading post was similar to the one he had been inside in Mexico. There was one main room with a long, waist high trestle table on which goods could be laid out for inspection and money counted. The fire was in the centre of one wall, set in a stone hearth, an iron flue led to the smoke vent in the roof. A large bed was by the side of the hearth; it was a hollow plank box roughly cut from logs and filled with springy pine boughs covered by a red trade blanket. Bear and buffalo robes were the bedding covers. The Mescalero woman sat with these around her shoulders as she stirred the stew. Behind the table, in a dark part of the room, was a set of low shelves containing trade goods, Viajero would examine them later. He hoped there were more peaches in the round iron boxes.

He went out into the small lean- to which was separated from the main room by a heavy canvas curtain to keep out the draughts. A smaller bed was out here; vegetables and meat portions hung from nails hammered into the roof beams. He went back into the main room and pulled the curtain behind him. The cabin had only one window, looking out to the front porch. Through the coarse glass he could see the stiffening bodies of the trading post owner and the squaw. He would need to cover them up so they couldn't be seen by anyone approaching the cabin. The dog, still barking fitfully from under the raised planks of the stoop, would need to be dealt with too.

With light now fading fast, the Apache dragged a body to either side of the doorway and covered each one with a buffalo hide taken from a pile at the back of the cabin. He kept the trader's pipe; he would look for some tobacco later and enjoy a smoke. With his booted foot, he swept the fragments of flesh and bone from the trader and his squaw down through the gaps in the porch planks. The dog ate them and whined for more. Viajero went back inside and closed the door. More snow began to fall.

The woman sat on the bed, her back to the wall oblivious to the hot food bubbling in the iron pot. She snored slightly in a deep sleep. Viajero sniffed the stew and tasted it from the ladle – he had eaten worse. He remembered the advice of the woman and walked to the shelves, took a tin plate and two horn spoons from a pile and came back to the bed. The woman stirred and asked for water. He dragged a water cask over to the bed and dipped the chained metal cup into it and gave her a drink. Ladling out the stew onto the plate, they ate in silence, rapidly shovelling the greasy mess into their mouths. It felt good to be warm and well fed but they couldn't linger long.

"Your plan seems to be working…" Bright Antelope Woman suddenly announced. "We have food, fire and shelter. "

Viajero knew that the plan was not his and he gave her credit for her

ideas.

"Your thoughts have much power and cunning. Here I am leaving the tracks of a white man, eating like a white man and wearing his clothes. We have killed the trader and his squaw with a white man's new gun and when we go we will leave only the iron shoe tracks of the *indaa* horses. Anyone who comes to trade will find the bodies but only discover sign belonging to whites. They will try to hunt down a white thief and find the trails lead to nowhere. It's a good plan."

The Mescalero woman bowed her head at the praise. The dog outside howled and Viajero leapt to the window. Darkness had fallen but the snow reflected enough light to see; no-one was there. Some wandering animal must have disturbed it. Taking out his hunting knife, Viajero told the woman that he would kill the dog; they could eat it tomorrow.

"No!" Her tone was sharp and shrill. He paused and closed the door and looked across at her, angry at being thwarted. Her skin looked a better colour; the food had helped. She dropped her eyes, aware that she had spoken harshly; if they had been married he would probably have beaten her with a mesquite branch. She tried to be conciliatory:

"It is a small thing, but could raise questions in the mind of those who will discover the bodies. The *indaa* don't kill and eat their dogs like our people. We should leave the dog alive; it will be one more sign that only whites were here."

Viajero sighed heavily in defeat; was there nothing that this woman hadn't figured out? Still, he looked forward to their departure. Then, his part of the plan would be put into action. He comforted himself with the thought and smiled at his own cleverness. The corpse of the *indaa* with yellow hair would help lay more false trails.

The woman curled up under the bear robe and tried to sleep. She would have to choose her words more carefully in future to try and avoid upsetting her *Coyotero*. It would not do to make him so mad that he would leave her forever. She heard the flames crackle into life as Viajero added more wood. Peering out from under the fur robe, she watched for a while as he examined the workings of the new rifle he had taken from the *indaa* with the yellow hair. It would become deadly in his hands, she was sure of it. Sleep came suddenly as before, her body relaxing in the unaccustomed warmth of the cabin.

Viajero checked the rear of the cabin. Outside, wrapped in a dark grey canvas shroud, the body of the white man with yellow hair stiffened in his timber tomb. The single knife wound to his throat stopped bleeding as temperatures dropped. Two opportunist rats tore at the flesh of his eyelids. The *indaa* still had more deceptions to perform and the Apache smiled.

Chapter Eighteen

---- o o o ----

Winter had been hard for the impoverished remnants of See the Dark's village; their plan to build earth lodges had worked, though only after a fashion – at least no-one now slept in the open. Crow Star, the elderly expert on these homes of their ancestors, had done well though not without some mishaps. It had been difficult to work out how the timber and earth sods were to be placed in order to make the structures strong and tight against the cold. The first one fell down after two days, narrowly missing women cooking inside it.

Crow Star was very old and his authority was quickly eroded. The youths, assigned to him to move the heavy timbers, rapidly became bored with the menial work and drifted off to hunt and fill their bellies. Only the threat of strict discipline from the soldier societies brought them back. One who refused to work for the common good was savagely beaten by two Thunder Bear soldiers on the orders of Broken Knife. Momentum and peace were restored but grumblings were only just below the surface. Snow had fallen before the work had even started and it fell intermittently during the building time. The new lodges were finished off during a blizzard which ripped through the tattered tipis and clothing like cold knife thrusts.

Crow Star was pleased with the earth lodges, the two strange buildings had been completed in three weeks; one housing the single women and widows with children and the other shared between the two soldier bands and those single men without a family lodge. They were not exactly as Crow Star had planned but he took advice from others who had seen Mandan earth and timber houses up on the Missouri. They would have to suffice, though some elders said that they looked like houses that only the *vehoe* would live in.

Yellow Bear had given ceremonial blessings to the new lodges, wafting sage and sweet grass smoke into all dark places, shaking his turtle shell rattle to expel any bad spirits. He called on *Maheo*, the Sacred One, to recognise these traditional dwellings, saying that those who lived in them would not be any less Cheyenne than those who didn't.

See the Dark ventured inside one; he was glad that his family lodge still stood. The warriors and women who had to occupy them told him that they had found it strange at first; the smell of damp earth was strong and remained so until many fires had caked this hard on the inside walls. They were uneasy away from the familiar curving walls of a skin lodge; people likened it to living like a badger or a prairie dog. Bark and insects fell from the roof and annoyed the sleeping residents but they were glad of any shelter when the real storms came. Swiftly, the days became black with overcast skies and snow fell continuously. The winds howled like packs of wolves, temperatures fell and even the clear, running water of the river froze over with a crisp carapace of dirty ice.

See the Dark had organised the older children into hunting parties to fill communal pots. Before the snows, everything that could be eaten was collected and shared out. Skunks, rabbits, badgers and other small game were snared on every trail where they had left sign. Birds of all varieties were shot with arrows, netted or knocked over with rocks, fish were hauled from streams and the deer population quickly vanished after a few fell prey to the first arrows or rifle shots. Even beaver were hauled out of flooded creeks and added to the total. Most of the precious food was eaten daily, just to sustain life and movement. Some was dried and kept against the harder days to come.

 Bad Elk's standing improved after he noticed movement in a gully near the camp. A small group of fifteen buffalo, seeking shelter themselves in the warmer clefts of hills, were cornered and wiped out by See the Dark's people; their meat quickly eaten or smoked to preserve it. Nothing was wasted. Scraps of meat shaved from dressing skins, normally cast aside or given to camp dogs in times of plenty, produced a broth and sustained them for a while. Marrowbones were cracked open and the fatty sludge eaten with enjoyment. Every last morsel of fat and meat removed during the hides was collected and cooked. Camp dogs prowled hopefully by cooking fires but were given nothing.

Sings Loud, the ancient skin lodge maker, welcomed the few new buffalo hides but they were barely enough to make just one lodge. To avoid confrontation as to who would occupy the lodge, Bad Elk, with increasing wisdom suggested at the council fire that the lodge should be for menstruating women. It would save the effort of having to build a third timber lodge.

Over six hundred buffalo would be needed to complete the much-needed new tipis. It would be an impossible task in the winter as the buffalo, like the People, split into small groups just to survive. Sings Loud had been widowed many years before and her son had been killed during the fight with the Pawnee. Gifts of food were vital to her if she was to live to complete her task to rebuild the village.

Yellow Bear had sought spiritual guidance to find more food but accurate visions now seemed beyond him. No-one openly blamed him now for losing their women and children as captives to the Pawnee but many still thought it. Yellow Bear's fall from grace removed a spiritual focus from the small band and the religious ceremonies that were a mainstay of Cheyenne life had dwindled to the bare minimum. He still presided at funerals and attended sickbeds but he was a man isolated. His skinny frame became leaner and more malnourished as gifts of food for treating the sick were few and far between. Only Badlands Walking Woman, acting as usual against the advice of her husband, fed the lonely spirit diviner when she could spare it. Smoke on the Moon, Bad Elk and Broken Knife had held the small band together but it had been a struggle. Even they, as practical fighting men, could sense the aura of spiritual decline in the lodges. There was an element of disrespect and dissension in the air. Spring seemed a long way off.

Bad Elk and the soldier societies made sure that food collection dominated the entire winter. When the last of the dogs had been killed and eaten and the stews of roots and bark gave out, the People started the slaughter of the horse herd. This had already been much reduced after the Pawnee attack and few of those running loose following the raid had been recaptured. Care had to be taken not to leave the tribal group completely immobile. The better mounts were spared and allowed hunters to range further afield if the weather permitted.

See the Dark helped tend the horse herd and watched them as they foraged as best they could, nuzzling at poor grass under the snow. He told the children to strip tree bark and feed the ponies to give some respite. The beasts were shaggy-coated now in winter; all their reserves of toughness and resilience from their mustang forebears were now needed. They stood in blizzards, rumps to the wind, and either lived or died. The deepening snow, however, gradually stopped all pony movement and the village slumped into a trancelike inactivity as hunger and cold took a double toll on the People.

Quarrels amongst those forced to share the few precious skin lodges were not uncommon. Traits tolerated in one family were seen as unbecoming in another. Men quarrelled about sleeping space and who did the biggest share of hunting; women quarrelled about cooking and how much each other's family ate. Bad Elk sighed as the warmth and politeness of Cheyenne society hardened and cooled with the earth.

The threat of starvation had not improved See the Dark's skills with his bow but it had increased his patience and skill as a hunter and tracker as he knew he had to get much closer to game before he could release an arrow capable of killing it. This was not a bad thing and Smoke said so. Dark was learning to live with his limitations though when he looked at his reflection in the creek, the collapsed side of his face repulsed him. The few remaining young women in the village did not directly avoid him but did not seek him out as they had done before. His mother had said that this was not because of the way he looked but that they had other more urgent responsibilities at the moment than looking for husbands. Dark was not convinced.

A small pinprick of light and warmth had occurred though. He had taken to walking around the campsite, checking on the children and their catches of small game; ensuring that all families shared equally in the available food. There wasn't much to go round but he felt it was important to try.

Though he had known of her before, White Rain Woman sometimes now spoke to him if she was outside the women's lodge. She had been married to Spotted Buffalo, one of the warriors killed in the Pawnee raid. She was around three years older than Dark and seemed impressed by his efforts to feed the village. Whenever Dark spoke to her he shuffled round nervously in a circle so that she could only see the unwounded side of his face. She was pretty and laughed at his embarrassment:

"You needn't try to hide your face from me, I've seen worse than that. I had to wrap up my husband for the scaffold after the Pawnee fight."

Dark mumbled something in reply. She didn't seem that sad about the loss of her husband though she had ritually gashed her legs and arms at the time; the scars were healing well.

"Your family will be proud of the way that you are helping the village. Were you hurt in the battle?"

Dark was about to say that he hadn't been injured when he changed his mind:

"Not really wounded but my pony fell on top of me and a Pawnee almost killed me with his hatchet. He sliced me a couple of times before I killed him…"

Dark pointed to his arms and was glad he was wearing a winter buckskin shirt with long sleeves. He blushed in his story-telling. The woman had cocked her head to one side and stared at him. Dark wasn't sure if she had sensed his boyish lie but she said nothing.

The woman now moved closer to him and looked at him directly. Dark felt his remaining eye grow wider and more uncomfortable as she held her stare. Eventually, she placed her hand on his sleeve, her dark brown eyes gazing at his crumpled face:

"I will dress those wounds for you if your mother is too busy."

Dark nodded, unable to speak. He was old enough to know that he had made some form of connection with the woman, just not what it meant.

At night in his family lodge, now shared with six additional people, he sought sleep but couldn't find it. His coming together with the young widow seemed strange and preyed on his mind. He thought about her a lot though was at a loss as what to do about it. He didn't confide this to his mother or father; they had enough to think about during the winter. But thinking of White Rain Woman made him happy; he would let Maheo decide where it would all end.

Chapter Nineteen

---- o o o ----

Lieutenant Henry Armstrong of the 2nd United States Dragoons stared down at the body, though there wasn't much left to see. Snow had covered the desiccated shell over the winter and it was only now, as the first warming fingers of spring pushed into the air, that the remains could be seen. And 'remains' accurately described the scattered pile of bones and ripped clothing. It had once been a man, probably white to judge from the rough tweed coat and heavy drill pants, though hungry wolves and coyotes had eaten much of soft tissue during the hard winter months. Eye sockets, picked clean by small animals, stared blackly at the overhanging trees. Tufts of yellow blonde hair were still attached to the skull.

Armstrong ordered his patrol to dismount and draped his bridle over the cantle of his saddle. He tied the animal to a tree by its head rope. His horse pawed at the hard ground and nibbled at a patch of moss as Armstrong walked across to where the body lay. His Troop Sergeant, a tall Missourian named Peck, followed him. The scout, Baptiste Clauville, a gaunt and tetchy Crow breed, rode back along the trail and rejoined the patrol:

"Nuthin' up ahead. This was done during the snows, no tracks left now." He spoke with the slight French accent he had inherited from his father.

"Thank you Mr Clauville. Come over and look at this poor unfortunate and see if you can tell us anything else" replied Armstrong, turning some of the bones over with the toe of his riding boot. Clauville smirked at the officer's English accent but lowered his head to hide the knowing smile.

"I wonder if he had a happy Christmas" offered Peck wryly, inclining his head at the corpse. "Ain't enough here to put in a decent parcel to his relatives, Lootenant." He sucked on a curved pipe, glad of the respite and chance for a smoke.

Armstrong nodded, wishing for the thousandth time that Americans would pronounce Lieutenant properly, in the English way. Life on this wild frontier produced coarse people.

The corpse lay partially concealed in sodden black undergrowth at the side of the trail some twenty miles from Grimes' trading post on the south fork of the Solomon River. Rusted tins from the trader's shelf stock lay deeper in the brush. Armstrong's patrol had found the bodies of Grimes and his squaw murdered on their own front porch after a trapper had gone there for supplies and raised the alarm.

Armstrong estimated that some three or four months had passed since the time Grimes had been killed. The trail was as cold as the dead man's bones. His troop was wasting its time here.

"What do you think Mr Clauville?"

The scout squatted on his haunches and poked around in the brush with his long hunting knife, turning over clumps of wet twigs and dead leaves, shifting smaller body parts as he formed a picture of what the sign told him.

"Hard to say but my money is on this guy being the killer of Grimes and his squaw. Remember we found those boot prints in the unmelted snow in the corner of the porch? Well, the leather on the right heel was worn just here. This boot made the mark."

He pointed to a definite semicircle of wear on the remnants of leather encasing the dead man's feet.

"Not much of the uppers left now, critters ate the soft bits during the winter, but the heel is the same."

"Well?" Armstrong prompted impatiently.

"My guess is that old Mr Stone Cold here, killed them, robbed their store and then got set upon hisself, Indians probably. He's been scalped. Odd though.."

"Well?" repeated Armstrong.

"Ain't enough of him left to tell a full story. Hard to tell how he died. There's a possible knife wound here in the neck."

Clauville pointed to a slit in the grey remnants of skin. Peck looked over, still pulling on his pipe. Armstrong pretended that he had seen it. Clauville continued:

"No arrows, no crushed skull, no other tribal signs that I can see. My guess is that he was killed by just one man, maybe ambushed and robbed of the stuff he'd taken from the trader."

Peck blew out a thin stream of blue grey smoke.

"Why would this white man kill Caleb Grimes, Frenchy? He seems well set up to me – good coat, good boots – what's left of 'em anyway. Don't make sense."

Clauville bristled and stood up, pushing away the braids of his long black hair behind his neck.

Like many in the troop, Peck held that only Indians were to blame for any evil overcoming a white man out here. He would never lack for company in that view. Peck looked on his own people as nation-builders, harnessing their courage and skill to settle the empty vastness of the continent. Peck's own kin had moved across the Alleghenies, down the Ohio and pushed back the impenetrable frontier to the Missouri River. Now he was helping police the expanding nation west of that great muddy waterway. Indians could not expect to be tolerated or trusted while they kept to their old tribal ways. Their day was long gone and belonged in the past with Egyptian mummies and Roman chariots. Whether the Indian problem was solved by treaty or by bullet and sabre was immaterial to Peck.

Baptiste Clauville was the son of a French trapper father and a Crow mother. However 'white' he might become in his speech or attitude, there would always be people like Peck to remind him of his bloodline. Clauville pointed the knife at Peck's face; not threatening but emphasising.

"Not only Indians are murderers and thieves, Peck. Grimes was robbed and killed because all men can get greedy. The prospect of dyin' during a hard winter just plain takes away that civilised feelin' that you white folk always bleat about. Robbin' that trader was an easy way to stay alive for someone. "

The sergeant looked coolly at the blade and smiled. He was about to reply when Armstrong interrupted.

"That's enough. Sergeant Peck, get a couple of troopers to gather together all the pieces they can find and bury him. Tell the men to stand down for coffee, we'll noon here. Put a picket on the horses, there may still be some Indians around. We'll rest for thirty minutes then push on back to the post. We've done all we can here."

Henry Armstrong was excited; he had come to America to find adventure and now it was in his grasp. Not this irrelevant little episode at Grimes' cabin but a full-scale march against the Sioux was in the offing and he was keen to be part of it with his troop of Dragoons. Provided he could get back to Fort Kearney in time.

That damned trapper who had found the murdered couple had forced this distraction on him when he should have been getting to know his regiment before the imminent campaign. Well, at least he had seen what his own troop was like on the march and he wasn't impressed. He felt sorry of course that a white man had been murdered, even if he had been a squaw man. As for the killer lying in scattered pieces by the trail, well he had got his comeuppance. Justice had been served there, even if some ignorant red savage had done it.

Yes, Armstrong felt had done the best he could under the trying circumstances and now he would lead his men back to the fort and prepare for the arrival of Colonel Harney, their new Commander. He could report that the death of the trader was not a sign of further trouble with other Plains tribes. No, Grimes and his savage wife had just been unlucky when a criminal came along. Colonel Harney could concentrate on punishing the Sioux for the massacre of young Grattan and his detachment last year. That was the real business of soldiering.

Armstrong walked back to his horse and gave it a small feed of oats from the leather satchel tied onto the cantle of his saddle. The animal grunted in appreciation.

Unlike his men, Henry Armstrong was pleased to be out on the Plains. The patrol to the Solomon was not only a change from the boredom of Army post life in Fort Kearny but also it put him three thousand miles of ocean away from bloody awful London and his previous life as an English cavalry officer.

He had been a slovenly recruit to British Army paperwork, lacking the brains, commitment or grasp of detail to make a success of it. There was no excitement, no glorious sabre charges or indeed, anything that smacked of real soldiering. The soirees and parties in Knightsbridge were no substitute for being in the saddle. He knew that his father despaired of him and he suspected that his secondment to the 2nd United States Dragoons had come about as a favour to his influential family and their links to the current US high command.

Some of Henry's people had settled the trans-Appalachian West; struggling through the Cumberland Gap to Kentucky and Missouri. His blood kin, the Armstrongs, and Scotts on his mother's side, had been here for over a hundred years. Still, Henry didn't care what strings had been pulled to get him to America – he was here in this brand new country as it spread its wings westward. And he was riding with an Army that still had an enemy, even if they were painted savages.

There was only one small pang of regret. From a rare newspaper on the post, he had learned his English regiment of Hussars had been sent to a fly-blown country called the Crimea. God knows where that was but it didn't sound pleasant. Even worse, the English were allied with the French against the Russians. He shook his head in disgust. It just wouldn't do – fighting some agricultural oafs from the Steppes whilst trying to be civilised to the Frogs. It didn't bear thinking about. Thank God to America for rescuing him from all that. There did not seem to be any remnants of the unpleasantness of 1776 or 1812; he was happy and settled here. The pursuit of the Sioux would be glorious fun and would make excellent after-dinner stories on his estate back home in Cumberland.

Tin mess kettles were brought out of saddlebags as fires were lit and the coffee prepared. Dragoons squatted around the blossoming flames, their ponchos trailing on the muddy ground. Not many of them were natural horsemen and a break was always welcome. It was a long way from Fort Kearney up on the Platte. Getting saddle sore, cold and stiff seemed a heavy inconvenience just to bury a dead trader and his squaw. A warm barracks was hard to leave in the winter to follow damn fool officers, especially some chinless John Bull who kept them in the saddle too long.

Armstrong knew his men disliked him; he knew that they thought of him as an English fop. Not that any one of these damned mounted ploughboys would recognise a real fop if they saw one – fops were probably pretty scarce amongst the sod hut hovels that these drunkards called home.

His Dragoons had no sympathy with his views on Indians either. To most, Indians were godless, Stone Age savages who needed to be eliminated so America could be settled, tamed and turned to profit. Armstrong, back in the bachelor officers' quarters at Kearney had openly praised the Plains tribes - their free way of life, their passion for war, their superiority in the saddle. Of course, they would always be red Barbarians but they deserved a grudging respect. His brother officers had howled him down and his unpopular opinions had spread to the soldiers. The men muttered and grumbled in private. They did not want to be led by some milk-of-human-kindness Momma's boy who might stay his sabre or pistol bullet when it mattered. Indians needed to be killed not admired.

His fop image had not lasted long. Peck and his cronies had been surprised that Armstrong could stay in the saddle, let alone lead a long, hard ride down to the Solomon. Armstrong smiled grimly; he would push them hard again back up to the post, just to see what they were made of. He needed to prove to his American superiors that he was capable of command so he could take his rightful place in the column marching against the Sioux. Leadership of men was a difficult quality to prove – every opportunity had to be taken to show that he had it. Even leading American ruffians who wouldn't last five minutes in an English regiment.

Trooper Bennett, Armstrong's striker, brought him a tin mug of coffee as the young troop commander stayed in the trees, maintaining the required, discreet social distance from his men. The American Army was much like the British in that respect. It was a useful divide; it never paid to get too deeply attached to men that may have to die for you. Armstrong thought little about it – social division came naturally to the British. The Americans, despite their protestations about freedom and equality, had to work at it.

Clauville wandered into the treeline and, without asking permission tucked a mouldy bear robe under him and sat down opposite Armstrong. The young English officer bridled slightly at the intrusion on his privacy but said nothing. The scout looked across at him, his dark brown eyes boring into Armstrong's face. A single scalp dangled from a beadwork armband around the scout's bicep. He saw Armstrong looking at it.

"Ain't from an Injun, Lootenant. Took it from a white trapper that raped my mother up on the Stinking Water River some years back." He had a rasping voice and did not waste words.

Armstrong nodded but did not choose to pursue the conversation; Clauville, however, did:

"I know your secret Lootenant. I know why you're here and why you're different to them." He gestured with his chin towards the small huddles of Dragoons around their coffee fires.

"And it worries me. Plain fact is you like Indians. Ain't never met a white man that did, you're the first."

Armstrong was about to protest when Clauville spoke again:" You told me once that your family were mounted raiders back in your own country…"

"That was over three centuries ago, Mr Clauville," countered Armstrong, wondering when he had ever let his social guard down and deigned to speak to this half-wild, man scalper. It was true; his ancestors had raided into Scotland as part of the bloody conflict between the two countries in the Sixteenth Century.

"Well, three centuries is a long time I guess but the fact is, it's in your blood. No wonder you like the Sioux and Cheyenne, you're almost kin. Mounted raids, stealing stock, killin' – hell, you could've been an Injun."

Armstrong was appalled at the comparison between an English gentleman, though admittedly not out of the top drawer, and an ignorant Redskin. He was about to reply when Clauville, sensing the bristling anger, stood up:

"You know, the Ojibway word for Sioux translates out as 'Treacherous Snakes', don't you forget that when we close with them. Just make sure you don't stay your hand when you have to kill one."

Armstrong sprang to his feet and threw his coffee at the scout, spitting out his words as his blood and voice rose:

"Don't bloody well tell me how to conduct my business, Clauville, you bastard French oaf! Keep a civil tongue in your head or I'll cut it out and feed it to my hounds and use your filthy scalp to wipe my arse."

Clauville grinned at the fuming officer insolently. The scout seemed satisfied with his baiting:

"Just checkin' how heavily civilisation sits on your shoulder Lootenant. I'm glad to see it don't."

Sergeant Peck tamped down his pipe to save his precious tobacco, stood up and smiled at his red-faced officer :

"Shall I mount the troop, Sir?" he said, flourishing an unnecessary salute.

---- o 0 o ----

Book Two

Chapter Twenty

---- o o o ----

See the Dark's pony scented them first and turned its head sharply, its rider following suit. The young warrior had been lost in thought again; once more a potential threat had loomed on his blind side and he had missed it.

Two riders approached slowly up a deep ravine that still sheltered drifted snow, as yet unmelted in the weak sunshine of the new year. Dark's hand went to his bow case but he relaxed as he saw they were not Pawnee.

The pair rode slowly up the incline, their thin ponies out of condition after winter grazing. See the Dark's mount was in no better shape; the last of the stripped cottonwood boughs surrounding his people's lodges had gone weeks ago to sustain what was left of the undernourished herd. Moss, tree bark and rank river grasses were poor substitutes.

They came closer; a mature warrior rode ahead followed by a woman astride a piebald. The man carried a well-cared for rifle resting vertically on his right thigh, another rifle was in the saddle bucket; it was a white man's saddle. The man seemed impatient with his wheezing pony and constantly kicked into its ribs to spur it to greater effort in getting up the hill. In contrast, the woman, wrapped in a large buffalo robe with only her head protruding, seemed content to let her mount pick a weary path to the top.

See the Dark rode to where both riders could see him and stopped. Once on the crest of the ravine, the approaching pair did the same. It didn't occur to See the Dark to speak – he merely signed that he saw them and was peaceful. He gave the Cut Finger sign of his people.

The man wore a grey coat cut from an old trade blanket; he wore no feathers but had a buffalo skin hat over a red bandana on his head. He had dark skin and looked fierce. The woman was impassive, a high cheek-boned, dark face staring out from the thick brown robe. See the Dark thought she looked like his mother.

The man spoke a few words of a language that Dark did not know but then resorted to signs.

They were from the country far to the south. He and the woman had wintered with the Osage as the woman had been sick. The Osage chief had wanted the man's rifle in exchange for looking after them; the man had refused and the pair had ridden off at night; the Osage had not pursued them. They needed food and shelter.

Dark asked what people they were from and the man answered in his own tongue as well as with a sign that Dark could not recognise. The man repeated it:

"N'de, N'de"

It was a guttural sigh, not unlike his mother's own language. Perhaps she would be able to speak to them better. He would ask his father's advice about letting them stay.

He signed that they should follow him to his village to eat. The young Cheyenne reined his pony in a semicircle and walked it back along the path through the damp, dark woods. The other two riders fell into single file behind him. Sunlight ceased once they were in the tree cover of the tall pines; melting snow occasionally slid off overloaded branches and slopped onto the dank trail. The ponies skittered at each sound. As they rode, Dark ruminated on the wisdom of leading two strangers back to his village. Still, he was sure that the two riders behind him were not Pawnee. He just hoped that there was some food to give his two guests when he got home.

During the winter, the young Cheyenne warrior kept a band of rabbit fur across his empty eye socket, with a stronger deerskin bandage over the top to stop it slipping. Occasionally, the fur would ride up and a needle of icy air would enter the cavity and make him wince. The bandage was an encumbrance and he wished for summer so that he could remove it and lie alone on some hilltop; just to let the sun's rays warm the hole inside of his head where his eye had once been.

The first signs of spring had been welcomed by all. Some bears came out of hibernation early and fell to the hungry Cheyenne, bringing much needed fat to the skimpy diet. The sizzles of roasting bear meat and the tang of woodsmoke announced a rebirth. The river ice melted and fishing resumed, returning birds of passage were killed on the grassland and on the water. And slowly, very slowly, the margin between hunger and starvation, life and death, widened as more bellies were filled. Hope and optimism rose with the first green points of new grass. The shattered Cheyenne band was coming back to life.

Dark had sought out White Rain occasionally as she went to the river for water or wandered through the woods collecting kindling. They talked a little but Dark was not sure how to court an older woman. He was not even sure he was actually courting. Younger girls, in better times, could be wooed by playing eagle bone flutes outside their tipis; they could respond by walking under a robe with a boy while they discussed their futures. There was no common ground now, all the tribal customs had been abandoned while they concentrated on surviving the winter.

Once, under protest from Dark, White Rain had washed out his eye socket with clean water and applied a balm she had made herself. It had worked better than his mother's poultices – he decided not to mention this to Badlands. Women got irrationally jealous.

See the Dark was jerked out of his thoughts as a shot crashed through the trees behind him. This was followed by an exultant whoop, not unlike the sounds made by the Pawnee during their attack. His pony bucked in surprise and almost pitched him onto the track. Whirling round, he galloped a short way back down the trail to find the stranger levering another linen cartridge into his powerful rifle. Blue smoke curled up from the muzzle. The woman was rapidly dismounting from her piebald and running into the trees, her earth-streaked cloth skirt riding above her knees as she leapt over fallen boughs. He reached for his bow but the dark faced one pointed through the slender tree boles and put the butt-plate of the rifle back onto his thigh. The warrior did not dismount but rode up and down the track singing a song in his own tongue. He seemed pleased with himself.

The young Cheyenne looked through the trees and saw the woman cutting the throat of a large elk that had fallen to the bullet of the Sharps rifle. Blood spilled out, rich and red onto the pine needle litter of the forest floor. The animal's legs twitched in their last spasm as the light behind its eyes went out.

It was a big elk; too big to be hoisted onto any of the skinny ponies. The warrior rode up to the woman and threw a sinew rope to her. She tied off the rear legs of the elk, lashing the other end to her own hide saddle. She did not remount but led her horse by the bridle, the dead weight of the dragging elk making the pony slither for a foothold in the shallow mud. All could see that the weakened pony would never manage the load alone. Besides, the journey to the village would scrape off much meat as the heavy animal was dragged over the hard earth outside the timber.

The warrior signed to See the Dark that they would need a travois and both men dismounted to find the poles to make one. The warrior called Dark over to a patch of smooth mud and, with a mix of signs and drawing on the slick, black surface, explained what he wanted. The travois would need to be pulled by two ponies if they were ever to get the precious food to Dark's village. The young Cheyenne understood and both men walked into the wood to seek the slender timber needed to make it.

They had not been at the task long when they heard the high pitched yells and felt the thudding of hoofs from the direction of the Cheyenne village. Bad Elk's people had heard the shot from the warrior's big rifle. Dark raced back to the trail to find the woman surrounded by screaming Striking Snake soldiers. She was crouched low astride the elk, pointing her hunting knife at the circling, yelling riders.

Dark crashed out of the tangled underbrush and shouted at them to stop. The soldiers, hearing only the hot blood thudding in their temples, whirled on this new threat and spurred their ponies to charge him down. Dark stood and watched as a Cheyenne soldier bore down on him. He was at a loss as to how to make the man break out of his blood trance and recognise him.

The mounted warrior was Thorn, his friend since childhood but now oblivious to who Dark was. He raised his war hatchet and slashed hard at Dark's head. The young Cheyenne threw himself to one side, shouting both their names. The mounted warrior's pony slithered into the trees and almost lost its footing on the slippery black earth. Thorn, deaf to Dark's shouts, wrenched the horse around and steadied it before he charged again. In that momentary pause, the heavy boom of the Sharps rifle echoed from the other side of the track and the lead bullet smashed into the tree trunk near Thorn's head. Shattered twigs flew. The pony reared and threw Thorn into the mud. At the shot, the other Striking Snakes looked at the opposite side of the trail and saw a dark faced man kneeling by a tree bole reloading a rifle. They were about to charge him when Dark's shouts penetrated through the red killing mist that had clouded their eyes. Thorn's voice now joined in and calm, of a sort, fell over the small, nervous group.

To Dark's surprise, Smoke on the Moon was one of the riders surrounding the woman; Dark had not recognised him during the melee. The woman still crouched over the dead elk, hissing and pointing her knife at anyone who came near.

Dark walked over to him:

"Father, they are friends. They were bringing a good gift of food." He pointed to the elk. Smoke said nothing but looked across at Thorn, now smeared in wet mud but back in the saddle.

"These new warriors must learn to distinguish friends from enemies," he said loudly. Thorn looked away in embarrassment. Smoke watched as the strange dark-faced one casually walked across to his pony and remounted, his rifle resting, as before, on his right thigh. The man did not seem afraid, even though the Cheyenne soldiers outnumbered him.

Dark explained as much as he knew about the strangers; his father nodding occasionally. When the youth had finished, Smoke backed up his pony and turned to his soldiers:

"Let us help this man," he said, pointing to the mounted stranger," he has brought us food and we need a travois to carry it." The Striking Snakes dismounted and went into the timber for the poles.

Dark remounted and rode beside his father back to the village. Behind them rode the woman and the stranger with the rifle. Bringing up the rear, the soldiers wrestled with the heavy elk on its travois, a thin trail of blood falling from its open mouth and onto the trail.

Smoke turned in the saddle and glanced behind at the woman. She glared back at him defiantly. Smoke looked away quickly and then spoke to his son:

"She reminds me of your mother," he said quietly.

Viajero and Bright Antelope Woman rode into to the Cheyenne camp and they weren't impressed. Viajero had met the Cut Finger people before whilst trading with the Comanche for horses. They had seemed fine warriors - prosperous, handsome and aloof. Then, they had been dressed in their finest clothes; soft, supple deerskin shirts with porcupine quill chest plates and leggings decorated with intricate beadwork. This ragged circle of lodges and the two strange timber houses did not seem to do them justice; perhaps these were just poor relations of the same tribe.

Several young men ran at them, shouting in an unintelligible tongue. Viajero just barged them aside with his pony; Bright Antelope did the same. They moved aside after these ritual displays of showing no fear. The Cut Fingers seemed weak and without purpose. Their leader, riding in front, forced a passage through the gathering crowd.

Viajero was not afraid of these grassland people but he was vigilant in case he and the woman had to break out and ride away. The people in the village now looked on silently as the strange little procession made its way to the centre; they were eyeing the elk hungrily. The older leader of the Cut Finger people halted his pony in front of a small group of determined looking men who stood wrapped in blankets and buffalo robes and stared impassively at the newcomers. The leader said something to the people and then pointed at Viajero; there was a triumphant shout shout and shrill yelling. A team of women, knives drawn, dragged the elk from its travois and expertly butchered the carcass.

Viajero remembered a similar reception from the Osage at the beginning of winter. Then, with all the valuable items that he had taken from the trading post hidden in leather pouches and canvas packs, he and the woman had ridden boldly into the Osage camp carrying a bear as an offering of food. The Osage were not great hunters and the fat grizzly bear carcass showed that Viajero had used courage as well as skill to put food in the pot. Viajero was lucky to have spotted the bear as she had made her way, late, to her hibernation den. The Osage seemed pleased.

The Mescalero woman's plan for the trading post had been a good one and had worked well. The white man with yellow hair and powerful rifle could only have been going to the post to wait for the snowstorm to stop. He had been easy to kill. Viajero had also agreed to kill his unshod war pony and hide it. It would not do to have their plan undermined by an obvious Indian mount close to the white man's cabin.

Faithful as ever, the pony had followed him wearily to the rimrock of a small canyon. Perhaps thinking of better times – of free running, good grass and without the festering sores on its shoulders, it had scarcely raised a sound as the Apache's hunting knife had punched into its throat. The animal had looked at him with a mixture of sorrow and relief as its legs buckled and it slipped down to its last resting-place in a rocky crevice. The steel and iron goods on the mule panniers were laid to rest in the same place.

They had only left traces of white men at the post – no-one would suspect that Indians had been involved in the killings of the trader and his squaw. Viajero had not liked dressing in the man's boots but it was part of the plan, though he wanted to keep the hat and the coat. The woman had persuaded him not to. The post had furnished them with all they needed though there were none of the same linen cartridges for the new rifle. Still, the dead *indaa* had plenty in his saddlebags and Viajero would husband those carefully.

Against better judgement they had stayed at the cabin for three whole days. It allowed the woman to break her fever and at least get back in the saddle. Viajero, nervous at remaining static after the killings, ranged out into the surrounding woods to check if others were coming but none came. Before setting out on the fourth day, they had eaten as much as they could and carried what the horses could bear. The better of the two mules resumed its duties and became the pack animal and the two fresh mounts from the trader's corral allowed both he and the woman to ride. They shot the horse of the yellow-haired indaa and his second mule – more animals would only slow them down. It also fitted well with the plan. The indaa were wasteful, slaughtering perfectly sound animals was what they would do.

Viajero had carried the body of the yellow-haired indaa, now reunited with his boots, hat and coat, across his saddle. After a two-day ride, he had dumped the body in some undergrowth in a small copse of box elder and cottonwood; Viajero then scalped him. He hung the scalp around his saddle horn, flung some tinned goods into the brush near the man's body and rode off. He hoped his part of the plan would work too.

Viajero had not liked living with the Osage, they were sly and seemed intent on stealing his precious supplies. They liked his rifle and constantly tried to trade for it – he was offered horses and women in exchange. The constant strain of trying to communicate using sign tired him and Viajero considered at one point that they may be better off alone out on the open prairie. But the snows came on heavily and the woman needed to rest. No Osage lodge opened to them so he laboriously built his own shelter, using a trade axe to fell saplings for lodge poles and stretching the trader's sheets of canvas around them until it resembled a skin tipi of the grassland people. There was a wary acceptance of their presence by the Osage but Viajero always carried his rifle ready and loaded at all times.

A chance shot at a distant solitary buffalo had made Viajero realise the power and range of his new weapon. He would never have attempted the shot with his old rifle; powder and ball would have been wasted. But he had been desperate. Several Osage warriors constantly followed him around when he went out hunting, begging to try the rifle out for themselves. Viajero would have none of it; he knew that once he had let the weapon fall into their grasp, they would have found a way to keep it or even kill him and the woman. The Osage needed a lesson in what the rifle could do.

The buffalo was an old bull, silhouetted black against the snow. It was pawing the ground to get to grass or moss; its flanks were torn where over-ambitious wolves had tried to pull it down. Even so, it could run off at any moment. A long stretch of smooth snow stretched between Viajero and the bull. He signalled for the chattering Osage to be quiet and checked the wind; they were downwind, the buffalo couldn't smell them and at this distance couldn't see them either. However, it could spot movement against the long rolling undulations of white and would be wary of any returning wolves.

Viajero sat down slowly and cocked the hammer on the Sharps, checking that the percussion cap was still in place. With his elbows resting on the inside of his knees, he steadied the weapon in the aim. Weak sunshine gleamed off the snow and made the animal appear as if dancing in front of the barrel.

The Osage knelt down and waited, mystified why the dark one was aiming his rifle at this long range; he would only scare the buffalo off. Viajero had looked through the sights down the long barrel, bringing the muzzle up until it was just forward of the animal's shoulder. He had learned how his other rifle shot at distances, the lead bullet often falling short, below the target. He would correct this today and aimed slightly higher than the buffalo's body. He squeezed the trigger.

Joyously the Osage had jumped up as the beast had slumped forward, then rolled sideways down a shallow slope, sliding to a stop in the compacted snow. Viajero watched them go to butcher the buffalo and reloaded quickly; they would be even more impressed with the rifle now and the power that he had whilst it was still in his hands. The Osage would now know that he could rub them out at a long distance if ever in future they chose to follow him. For now, he held sway but his advantage could not last long.

That night, some two months after Viajero and the woman had come into the Osage camp, the chief visited their canvas lodge. The Mescalero woman had cooked their share of the buffalo meat and was smoking the rest over the fire. The chief sat down and was alone. Outside though, Viajero's keen hearing picked out the sound of cautious footfalls in the crisp snow as others circled him in the darkness.

The chief had a whining voice and neither Viajero nor the woman could understand him. Through signs he said that he hoped that the woman was well after her sickness and that all his people admired the great hunting skills of the dark warrior from the south. Viajero stared at the chief with glittering black eyes and said nothing; he was listening for other sounds that the chief's companions were coming closer. The chief wore a thick red trade blanket wrapped around him against the bitter chill of the night. He did not remove it whilst he sat at Viajero's fire; the Apache thought he could be concealing a weapon. A bronze medal hung around the chief's neck on a piece of worn blue ribbon; it was an ornament from the *indaa*. The Osage could not be trusted if they were friends with the white eyes.

Viajero hoisted the rifle across his lap and listened to the chief speak. The woman was much better at interpreting signs and she kept him informed of what the man was saying.

The chief rambled on about Osage generosity even though his people were poor. He felt that it was time for the dark ones to pay their way during these hard months. The woman, to Viajero's surprise, butted in and told the Osage leader that her Coyotero had kept the Osage from starving by his skill with the rifle. Whilst she spoke in her own tongue, she used her hands to sign this, pointing to the rifle in Viajero's lap. The Apache started as she pointed to the Sharps; he had missed what she said, he was still listening for sounds outside the lodge.

The Osage adopted a more wheedling tone; if his people had such a gun then hunting would be much easier every winter. The numbers of elders and children who died from being undernourished would decline, all would be much happier. He wanted a gift as payment for their hospitality; he looked meaningfully at the rifle.

In past times, Viajero would have just killed him, trusting his own battle skills to extricate himself from this hostile place or die in the attempt. But now there was the woman to consider; it did not strike him as odd that he now did this automatically, without thinking or regret. Somehow, he and the woman had become one.

Viajero had been half expecting such a demand from the Osage and was prepared. He reached across behind the woman and opened a leather bag from his Mexican saddle. He drew out the pistol of the older vaquero that he had slaughtered all those weeks ago. He had managed to remove some of the rust and a slick of oil had loosened up the action. The chamber now revolved as it should, only sticking occasionally. A bright copper percussion cap decorated each chamber nipple.

He now handed the pistol to the chief who seemed at a loss for words – he had asked for a gift and had got one. The chief muttered something in a low voice and the soft footfalls could be heard, crunching away through the snow, not caring now to conceal their presence. The chief was in a dilemma; he could not refuse the gift but was unwilling to give up the chance of getting the rifle. Rudely, he offered the pistol in exchange for the Sharps - but only once. A sign from Viajero indicated that only death lay along this route if the chief persisted.

The chief pulled his blanket around him and got up as if to go. Suddenly he whirled around, cocking the hammer as he turned. The Osage pointed the pistol at Viajero's head and pulled the trigger. Viajero was surprised but did not flinch, the woman shrieked but then fell silent. Only the sharp, shallow cracks as the thin caps exploded could be heard as the panic stricken chief went through all six. Viajero stood and thrust the rifle barrel against the chief's head pinning it between the metal muzzle and a lodge pole. He said nothing and the chief turned and left, shaking, into the cold night.

Viajero smiled at the woman and spoke to her; he may have been generous with the pistol but he wasn't crazy enough to hand it over loaded. For the first time in many weeks, Bright Antelope Woman laughed out loud. They left the Osage encampment the next night, silently leading their laden ponies out into the darkness of the endless Plains.

The two Apaches were expecting nothing better from the Cheyenne. If anything they seemed poorer than the Osage. Something terrible had happened here, Viajero would again keep the rifle close.

Chapter Twenty One

---- o o o ----

Smoke on the Moon emerged from his crowded tipi and looked at the sky. At long last, spring was turning into summer and the Cheyenne village had moved. Warmth was back in the ground and the sun brought the People back to life. His brother had postponed the move several times; the weather on the great grasslands was unpredictable at the best of times. Only when the settled, warmer weather arrived had Bad Elk decided that they could risk leaving the timber and earth lodges that had saved them through the time of the snows. It was now warm enough to move out onto the rolling green and yellow vastness, away from the shelter of the higher hills. The homeless ones could survive in more makeshift tipis until enough buffalo had been killed to restore the skin lodges.

Smoke, like all his kinfolk, had been pleased to move. Their proximity to all the waste, human and animal, which had accumulated over the winter had been a trial. The cold weather froze and, at first, deadened the smell. But with the first signs of thaw came the flies and the stench. The timber lodges, though, were still needed and could not be abandoned yet; it was still too cold, even in early spring, to risk the People out on the Plains. So the Cheyenne stayed even longer in that one place and eked out a living during the muddy and wet months of a new year.

The criers that announced the long-wished for move were met with hoots of joy, people began to smile again and even the horses seemed relieved at the prospect of fresh grass. There was an initial stab of nervousness as the shelter and concealment of the hills were left behind. They were now out in the open and enemies could see how weak they were. The Pawnee would be unlikely to range this far south but any passing or ambitious tribe could see that the homes and horses of the Cheyenne were poorly protected. The next few months would be an anxious time.

Smoke looked across at the shabby canvas tipi built by the dark warrior from the south. The stranger and his woman were still with the Cheyenne and moved their canvas lodge with the main village. They lived just on the outskirts of the Cheyenne camp and became accepted, if quiet, companions.

The elk that the pair had brought on their arrival had been welcome; elk were notoriously difficult to kill and the dark stranger seemed to have a rifle that was up to the task. The man from the south had managed to earn his keep by using the longer range and deadly power of the Sharps to keep meat coming into camp. He took a share for himself and his woman but then always gave the rest to Bad Elk to divide up amongst those in need. It was a gesture that brought him respect from the Cheyenne.

Smoke's wife had told him that the southern woman had healed well; the wounds that she had received from the raiding party dried out and scabbed over quickly after Badlands Walking Woman's healing potions had been lathered onto her lacerated flesh.

Bright Antelope Woman was not ashamed of the knife and lance cuts though she was careful to conceal them as much as possible from Viajero; it would not help her own cause to remind him that she was already a scarred victim of many rapes. The Apache pair had begun to couple again and both found comfort in the act; binding them closer to each other in their new status as part of the Cheyenne village. The Cut Finger people, though, were different to the venal Osage. They seemed to genuinely accept the pair from the south as a permanent addition to their much-reduced tribal band.

Viajero had been initially shocked by the air of poverty and desolation but had gradually learned the reason. It seemed that both the Cut Fingers and the Mescalero woman now had cause for revenge against the Pawnee. The Apache felt a strange feeling enveloping him as he pondered these things – it was a sense of belonging and a glimmer of hope that he could now be useful. At last, Usen was showing him that his greatest skills would not be wasted. There was killing to be done.

Viajero himself was much more settled after Usen, the Life Giver, sent him a message. It was a sunny Spring day; Viajero had walked, rifle in hand, out onto the Plains to look for game. Whilst he was sitting on the crest of a dusty ridge, a horned lizard scurried out from beneath a stone, its flat and frilled circular body moving quickly on stubby legs. The creature scuttled up a small mound and turned to face the Coyotero. It spoke plainly though not loudly:

"It is here."

The animal then disappeared between clumps of greasewood. The Apache pondered this for a moment; not the fact that the lizard had spoken, just that it had spoken to him. Everyone knew that animals could speak; it is just that most chose not to or only spoke to a select few men who had rare powers. He was intrigued but slowly it dawned upon him.

Viajero knew that he was not a chosen one; he could not have long talks with animals like the medicine men or spirit diviners. No, the little creature had just been a messenger; it had completed its task and could not be questioned further. The Apache smiled grimly; a lizard's message had yet again secured his fate. First, all those months ago in Mexico, a horned lizard had set the direction for his journey and now this. It was obvious - Usen, the One Above, had sent it. It was the sign that Viajero's journey was over.

There had been surprisingly little contact between the Apaches and the Cheyenne of the village during the winter months. It was too cold to stay outside and no-one could spare enough food for them to be invited to a feast as guests in their tipis. But, as the weather developed into warm airs and blue skies, See the Dark and his mother had taken to visiting the Apache lodge on the outskirts of the encampment. The Cheyenne had assumed that the strangers were man and wife and so the *notae* Bright Antelope Woman, needed to be informed of how females were expected to behave in the village of the Medicine Arrow People.

Badlands Walking Woman's own tongue, though similar in some ways, differed enough from the languages of the Mescalero or White

Mountain bands to make conversation with Bright Antelope and Viajero difficult. However, it was not impossible. With the inbred patience of their people, they would sit in the summer sun and talk, using hand sign when words ran out.

At first, See the Dark sat slightly apart, as the Apache trio conversed earnestly. Sometimes his mother would turn round to him to ask him something and she would struggle to get back into Cheyenne speech. It made him laugh out loud; she would give him a good-natured swipe across his forearm and remind him to be more respectful to his parents. He would smile indulgently at her and Viajero noticed this closeness. During one conversation, Viajero had pointed to the deerskin wrapping that covered See the Dark's empty eye socket and Badlands Walking Woman had explained. Viajero nodded thoughtfully but moved the conversation on.

Just as Badlands Walking Woman had done when she had first come to the Cheyenne village, the Apache visitors memorised words of the strange new tongue. From time to time, they would try these out on See the Dark, normally when he wasn't expecting it. Taken by surprise at this garbling of his people's language, he would forget his good manners and hoot with laughter, rudely pointing at the newcomers. At first, Viajero had been greatly insulted but had been calmed by the restraining hand of Bright Antelope on his arm. Instead he sat and watched the antics of one of his hosts, his face immobile as stone. During one outburst, Badlands Walking Woman emptied a skin paunch of water over her son who was rolling on the ground in pretended mirth. She was sharp with him:

"A warrior of the *Tsis-tsis-tas* should be dignified and not act like a child. You should be grateful that these two N'de are learning your language as you certainly cannot speak a word of theirs. Perhaps they are better than you. Think on these things before you mock anyone again."

Viajero and Bright Antelope shifted uncomfortably and gazed into the far distance, ignoring the looming quarrel.

See the Dark had leapt to his feet, water dripping from his thick, black hair. He was about to remind his mother of his new-found status as a warrior and a killer of Pawnees and that he should not be humiliated in that way. Then he remembered that his mother too had killed a Pawnee brave; she wore the enemy scalp on the cougar claw necklace around her neck. Even now she stood defiantly in front of her tall son and glared at him. See the Dark hesitated. It would be an unseemly family squabble in front of two strangers; he said nothing but walked off in a huff. Badlands Walking Woman watched him go but then went back to her conversations.

Fuming, the young warrior walked down to the river and found the reflecting pool. He did not have a mirror like many other young men so he had started to come here when he needed to see how his hair looked or to try out a new way of painting his face or body. He also came to check how drawn his flesh looked as the atrophying fat and muscle were sucked back into his empty eye socket. It was not a bad disfigurement as these things went. It was not as bad as losing a limb or being scarred forever on the face by the white man's diseases. But it still made the young man sad.

His face however did not seem to deter White Rain Woman; she had become bold recently and he now let her routinely apply her balm to his wound. He was fairly sure his eye socket didn't need the medicine but he was happy to lie in the sun by the pool and let her minister to him. She would take off the deerskin wrap across his eye and scoop cold water into the black hole to clean out the dust, insects and plant fragments that often blew inside. She always tutted as she did this, as though Dark deliberately allowed such things in his wound.

During the winter, his father had carved him a wooden eyeball to put in the socket. The finely polished box elder root, greased with tallow, had worked for a time but the ball chafed the inside of his wound, then had dried out and split. It had been painful to remove and See the Dark had kept the socket empty since that time.

As he leant out over the pool, he was aware of the sunlight behind him being blotted out. He did not move but waited until the ripples smoothed out, back into the mirror-like surface. Slowly the image flickered into shape; it was the Apache.

Viajero stood and watched the young Cut Finger warrior washing out his eye socket in the river. The ripples faded and the Apache knew that the boy was looking at him in the still clearness of the reflecting pool. Viajero made no move to approach him, preferring to wait until the young man turned around; it would reassure him that the Coyotero posed no threat. He squatted down on his haunches and waited, enjoying the dappled shade of a cottonwood tree.

See the Dark stood up and slowly turned, tying the deerskin bandage behind his head. He was still self-conscious about letting strangers see his wound. Viajero stood at the same time and beckoned the young Cheyenne to follow him. The boy hesitated, fiddling with the sinew strings on his eye covering. Viajero noticed his reticence and walked back to him. He faced See the Dark and put a hand on the young man's shoulder in a friendly gesture. He spoke one of his newly acquired Cheyenne words:

"Come."

See the Dark now followed as Viajero led him through the busy village to his lodge. A string of wild horses was being run into a narrow, rocky defile up on a timbered bluff. Smoke on the Moon led the small herd to the mouth of the gap then reined his mount to one side as the excited ponies dashed past and into captivity. Dark watched as the other Cheyenne soldiers pulled logs and branches across the entrance to the ravine, penning the animals inside. The ponies would be useful as replacements for the ones stolen in the Pawnee raid. Smoke raised his hand in greeting as he saw his son walking across the village with the dark warrior. Dark acknowledged the greeting, breaking into a slight trot as the Apache quickly paced through the main throng of tipis towards his own grey canvas home.

Bright Antelope was still outside, talking to Badlands Walking Woman. Both women were seated and chatted as they cut meat and wild turnips for a meal. They looked up as the men approached but sensed that something important was about to happen and said nothing.

Viajero beckoned to the women that they should follow him inside the lodge and gestured that the young Cheyenne should do the same. As it was summer, the cooking fire was built outside, leaving more room in the centre of the lodge for guests. Apache heads of families, like the Cheyenne, sat facing the door of their homes. Viajero leant against his backrest of springy saplings whilst the others arranged themselves in a semicircle facing him. He had brought a burning twig into the lodge and rested this across his moccasin, a thin spiral of blue smoke ascending to the vent hole at the apex of the tipi.

The Apache warrior did not have a tribal or ceremonial pipe to smoke as he was not of the grassland people though he had seen and admired the finely decorated, red stone pipes of the Cheyenne men. Instead, he had the long-necked, straight briar pipe that he had taken from the dead indaa at the trading post. It was not as grand as a Cheyenne pipe, though the bowl did have a hinged silver cap. It would have to do.

He filled it with tobacco from a bulky leather pouch that had also belonged to the white man, tamping down the shredded leaves with his thumb into the polished bowl. When it was ready, he lit it with the smouldering twig, sucking hard on the stem to ignite the leaves. When the pipe was lit, the Apache flipped the cap back onto the mouth of the bowl and drew in air through the perforations in the lid. He breathed out a satisfying cloud of blue smoke.

Ignoring the women as they did not take part in ceremonies involving a pipe, he pointed the stem of the pipe to the sky as he had seen the Cheyenne do and passed it to See the Dark. The young Cheyenne took the pipe and put the end of the stem in his mouth and drew hard. This was a mistake; Dark was only used to the mild smoking concoction made from a mix of field tobacco leaves and sumac. He coughed and spluttered; his remaining eye watered badly and rendered him partially blind for a moment. He passed the pipe back to the Coyotero. Viajero looked almost apologetic and spoke rapidly to Badlands Walking Woman.

See the Dark's mother spoke to her son, translating Viajero's words into Cheyenne:
"The Traveller apologises that he did not warn you about the strength of the *veho* tobacco; he says it is best not to draw it into your body until you have grown used to it."

See the Dark coughed his thanks and realised that this was the first time that he had heard the Apache's name. Viajero now turned to the Mescalero woman and had a short conversation; if Badlands Walking knew what they were talking about, she did not enlighten her son. The N'de woman seemed to nod her assent to something that Viajero said and the Apache turned back to his guests. Speaking through Badlands Walking Woman, he addressed See the Dark personally:

"My brother, although you are young I know that you are already a proven warrior and so I speak to you as man to man. The Cut Finger people have been kind to me and my woman since we arrived in your camp."

Bright Antelope Woman looked at the Coyotero as he said this; it was the first time that he had described her as 'his woman'. She glowed at her new status and Badlands nodded her assent.

"Kindness must be repaid. My heart is sad that you lost your eye as a boy, though it has not stopped you from killing your natural enemies and this pleases me; a man must kill those who threaten his family or his home. Your mother told me of your prowess in battle."

See the Dark hung his head in modest embarrassment, though he was secretly pleased that his mother had managed to impress the dark warrior. He tried to speak but remembered that the Apache still held the pipe; it would be rude to interrupt. The Traveller continued:

"I notice that you use your right hand to hold a knife or axe. This is your natural killing hand and so your strongest spirit will dwell on that side of your body. Your right eye allows the spirit to look out from inside you and guide your weapon to its mark. There are men whose spirit lives on the left hand side of their bodies but they are rare and do not live long."

See the Dark mused on this. The dark one was right; Shining Horse had always favoured his left hand and now he was dead. The Traveller spoke wisely.

"Your uncle told me that perhaps a gun would be your choice of weapon. He has said that your remaining eye is now suited to aiming a rifle barrel, as the whites do"

See the Dark nodded but looked downcast; a rifle was out of the question until he had captured one in battle or stolen one from the *vehoe*. He watched as the dark one reached back and brought out a long buckskin case from the rear of his lodge. He set this down in front of Dark who looked at it and then at his mother. Viajero spoke again:

"Take it. This is my gift to you. Use it to bring meat to your family and to kill your enemies."

Thinking it was a new bow, See the Dark grasped the skin case and lifted it up. It was heavy; it was not a new bow. A stab of guilty relief washed over him. Untying the sinew cord that bound the flap, he reached inside and pulled out a rifle. It was the Traveller's old gun that he had seen in the saddle bucket when he had first arrived with the People.

At first, See the Dark was not sure that the Traveller had actually given him the gun; he had never heard of such a precious gift being given amongst the *Tsis-tsis-tas*. Perhaps it was just to borrow and use to help fill the camp cookpots. His mother saw his indecision and confirmed that the N'de had indeed given him the rifle as a gift. With a small closing motion of her hand, she prompted him to offer thanks and to give a gift in return.

Viajero sat back against the frame of saplings and smiled benevolently; he passed the pipe to the younger man. Dark carefully drew in a mouthful of smoke and blew it out in a cloud; it sped towards the vent hole in the lodge. His mind raced; this was his first real social occasion where he had been at the centre of things. True, his naming ceremony had involved him but he had not been expected to speak then; now he was. Badlands Walking Woman watched her son anxiously. It would not do to stumble over words like a child. See the Dark had to get this right.

Pointing the pipe stem to the sky to indicate that he spoke truly and honestly, See the Dark made his response:

"My brother, I give thanks to you for the gift of this gun. I accept the gift with pride from such a powerful warrior as the Traveller. I will use this well, both in the hunt and in battle. The gun pleases me greatly and it has been used many times to kill your enemies. You know best how to shoot this – I would be honoured if you would teach me the ways of this rifle. I will try to be a diligent pupil and learn your skills."

Viajero listened with pleasure to Dark's soliloquy as the boy's mother translated it, carefully crafting the words to achieve the best effect with the Traveller. The Apache nodded indulgently and agreed to be Dark's tutor. He watched as the mother again prompted her son into action. Dark spoke once more:

"I too have a gift for you. It is small and does not compare to the rifle but I give you this as a token that we might be brothers from this time on."

Dark fumbled around his waist and untied his rawhide belt with his knife on it. It was the knife that he had been given after the arrow had taken his left eye. The knife was well kept with a steel blade and the sheath was pretty. He handed this to Viajero. The Apache smiled and immediately put the knife on his own belt, next to his large hunting blade. He nodded his approval.

"That knife was payment for my eye from a boy named Little Snake. He was taken by the Pawnee during the big raid, we do not know where he is now."

Viajero nodded grimly at the news and took back the pipe. The pipe had gone out so he blew on the smouldering twig to revive the flame and relit the tobacco.

"Those people also injured my woman. When your skill with the rifle is improved, we will hunt them down together. Your fight is my fight."

Badlands Walking Woman sighed silently with relief; there had been no social catastrophe. Her son had acquitted himself well at the ceremony and there seemed to be a growing bond between him and the N'de. The Apache would be useful on the war trail with the Cheyenne when the Pawnee were called to account. She watched as the two men handled the rifle, the Traveller demonstrating how it should be held and sighted properly and, despite the language difference, See the Dark was nodding enthusiastically and copying the actions. They would be well suited as comrades in arms. She smiled at Bright Antelope Woman; it was the coming together of two families.

After some light talk, Badlands Walking Woman and her son stood up and were about to leave the Apache lodge when Bright Antelope remembered – there was another gift for See the Dark.

See the Dark could not wait to show his father his new rifle. He had been taken by surprise when the N'de woman caught his arm and spoke to the Traveller. She seemed to be reminding him of something. Viajero nodded and took the small deerskin pouch from around his neck and handed this to See the Dark. The young Cheyenne was puzzled and sought out his mother's explanation. She spoke to Viajero and Bright Antelope, quizzing them so she understood completely. Then she faced her son:

"Open the pouch. It is your new eye"

Dark took the smooth black obsidian stone from the pouch and turned it over in his hand, admiring the shiny surface and the small etching of a deer on one side. He grinned and leaning down to the cookpot, skimmed some of the warm grease from the top of the stew. He plastered this over the sphere, lifted the bandage from the top of his head and gently squeezed the globe into his trembling eye socket. It hurt; and a few tears came involuntarily out of the unused duct. Dark turned away to hide them but rapidly whipped his head round to face them again.

The shiny black eyeball, terrible in its contrast to his good eye, stared out of Dark's head. His mother gasped and Viajero nodded his approval. Bright Antelope was pleased to see that her etching had swivelled round to the front of the Cheyenne youth's face and now looked proudly out of this young warrior's head. It had not meant to be such a significant gift when she had given it to Viajero; this was a better use for the stone from the Mescalero country.

All recognised that the One-Above had planned this – just as he had planned the coincidence of horses, grasslands and the People. The Mescalero stone fitted perfectly into this youth's skull. The One-Above had meant this to happen – he had determined that the stone should be picked up in the lands far to the south; he had caused Bright Antelope to give the stone to Viajero and he had used the Coyotero to carry the stone here. It suddenly seemed a powerful talisman, a gift that was much more than a casual present given in friendship. All four recognised the string of events that had resulted in this day; Badlands Walking Woman shuddered with the enormity of it. Their two families were now joined forever by a simple round stone.

No-one said it at the time but the black eyeball had changed Dark's appearance. His boyish, unlined face had altered – gone was the smooth, youthful plumpness around the jawline and the rather apologetic look in his right eye. A harder, more austere aura now emanated from the young man.

Parents recognise the point where their children turn forever into adults – this was Dark's time. His mother was sad; she clung desperately to the images of him as a baby splashing in a sunlit river or playing around the village as a boy. Even when he had first taken a life during the Pawnee raid, Dark's shy smile did not desert him. Now that smile seemed to have been eclipsed by this strange new object in his eye socket. His stare was cold and more confident. He had the face of a killer.

Chapter Twenty Two

---- o o o ----

Yellow Bear sat in the shade of tree by the river and applied paint symbols to a well scraped buffalo hide. The whitened skin was stretched taut over a sapling frame that leant against the tree bole. He sat cross-legged in front and, with a series of willow twigs dipped into different coloured paints, drew in the simple outlines that represented the events of recent Cheyenne history. He had kept such a record ever since the spirits had spoken to him and he had decided to become a medicine man.

Noting a similar robe on a visit to a Lakota camp some years ago, he had decided to copy it. He had given the ancient lodgemaker, Sings Loud, a good trade blanket for her expertise in dressing and curing a suitable skin. He had begun the drawings in the centre and had gradually traced out an expanding spiral of the unfolding events of Twisted Wolf's *Suhtai* Cheyenne band as Yellow Bear saw it.

The first symbol at the centre represented himself - a sticklike warrior dropping his bow and taking up a turtle shell rattle. Next came a series of hoof prints denoting a successful pony raid against the Crow that year. Some way along the spiral story, a symbol showed the loss of See the Dark's eye; a simple, black circle represented the boy's head with a vivid red hole on the left side of his face. The spiral continued its unfolding journey, tracing out the Cheyenne version of recorded history. In happier times, the hide had hung in public view outside Yellow Bear's lodge and fathers and grandfathers brought along the young of their families to tell the stories associated with the stark drawings.

The gaunt Suhtai had yet to recover his reputation fully after the loss of the Cheyenne children in his care. However, easier summer living seemed to make people kinder to him and Bad Elk had encouraged a resurgence of spiritual belief to bring the band closer together. He used Yellow Bear as his spokesman on these matters and ensured that the medicine man had influence at the council fires. The

Pawnee raid, the time of the snows and the hardships undergone then had sapped the will of the People and forced them down a selfish road. They had to be brought back and slowly this was happening. Yellow Bear was gradually sought out again for family ceremonies and celebrations that required a spiritual overtone. He was grateful to Bad Elk for his wise handling of the band during a troubled time.

Bad Elk had not stepped down from his role as the leader of his People. He had wanted to but Smoke on the Moon and Broken Knife had dissuaded him each time. The small band was content with Bad Elk and no-one spoke against him. So, the brother of Smoke on the Moon accepted his new life as leader of his small tribal band but often sought counsel for his plans from Yellow Bear. The medicine man had been grateful and surprised by Bad Elk's patronage – to him, the son of Great Horse had wisdom enough of his own.

Smoke on the Moon had now taken to reporting what he was doing to Bad Elk. Bad Elk had laughed when he pointed out the change of habits they were getting into – the elder brother seeking the counsel of the younger. Smoke was happy to do it and was proud of the role his sibling had taken on.

The soldier societies had been busy during the year with Smoke and Broken Knife directing their efforts. They had ranged far and wide for horses and had taken many from the wild. They had bartered for some as surpluses arose during the life of the village; their chief suppliers were the Comanche far to the south.

Bad Elk, assisted by See the Dark were constantly seeking ways to overcome the losses inflicted on them by the Pawnee. With much experienced manpower away collecting horses for many weeks at a time, the younger Cheyenne males were being brought into the service of their people much earlier. Meat was still needed in the expanding number of lodges and whilst chokecherries, plums, wild onions and turnips grew in abundance near the village, they were not enough to sustain an active life on the Plains. Hunting parties of youths and boys were constantly out, often leaving the village dangerously denuded of fighting strength as they did so. Women and old men now stood guard over the village.

White Rain Woman, whilst growing her affection for See the Dark, was in front of some of the more extreme changes to the tribal band. Her killing of the Pawnee warrior during the raid had sparked something in her. Five of the single women, led by her, decided that they liked this warrior role and had formed their own society despite the derision of the single men. They were careful to avoid a direct comparison with the male soldier societies led by Smoke and Broken Knife but refused to disband even when put under pressure to do so. They all painted themselves the same way – one half of the face was decorated with a jagged streak of white forked lightning, the other half with the same thing in red. The women sang their own songs, held meetings, practised with weapons and had persuaded Yellow Bear to make offerings and chant blessings for them.

A sceptical Smoke on the Moon ceased his objections when he realised that this women's society actually wanted to fight when the Cheyenne took their revenge on the Pawnee. He knew that the warriors killed in the raid would take a generation to replace though some remaining boys would soon be of age to fill the pony saddles of the war parties. No, every bow and lance would be useful, every rider, male or female could take a Pawnee life. These were difficult times and difficult decisions but the women were not slaves and could not be kept at home while only men went on the war trail. And so the Forked Lightning Women soldier band came onto the battle strength of the Suhtai.

Buffalo hunts had gone well though the beginning of the previous winter had been an opportunity missed. In normal times, The Dust in the Face Moon would have been the perfect season to harvest the hides of four-year-old buffalo cows. These skins were agreed to be the best in age and condition for making lodges but the Pawnee raid had denied them that. The Cheyenne would have to make up in spring and summer what they could not get in winter. For this year, numbers of hides would be more important than quality.

Everyone took part in the hunt as the need for many hides overcame old traditions. The soldier societies still maintained order before the chase but with the lack of experienced hunters, all riders were allowed in at the kill. Youths, boys and even the Forked Lightning Women chased the lumbering animals and shot down as many as they could. It was an exhilarating moment for all; the People were back to some semblance of their old life.

Smoke and Broken Knife were embarrassed that the hunt was not as well planned or ordered as usual. The excited whooping and yelling from the over-enthusiastic buffalo killers had driven the herd far from the main camp and it was not until late the next day that the last of the youths and women were accounted for, plodding back into camp leading overloaded horses. They had chased their quarry for many miles, killed several buffalo each then had to skin the huge animals, butcher the meat and drag their trophies back to the village. Much of each carcass had to be left where it lay, ponies could not carry or drag any more weight. All were exhausted with the effort. However, the timber and earth lodges of Crow Star were still a close memory and no-one wanted to repeat the experience of living in them again. So from the growing pile of lodge hides, tipis were gradually stitched together with the busy awls of Sings Loud and her group of helpers. Slowly the People recognised their village again.

Four of the youths that had been left without parents banded together and became Contraries. But it was a hard and isolated existence. After a few weeks, three had returned to what passed for normal village life but the fourth, Thorn, had dedicated himself to that difficult trail. His mother had been snatched by the Pawnee and his father scarcely spoke to him now; he could not forget the hurt of Thorn wanting to keep his child name. He had no adult models but he too, like See the Dark, had seen Contraries at the huge tribal gatherings of his nation.

So, Thorn often rode his horse sitting facing its rump, washed in dust and dried himself off in the river and generally did the opposite of that expected of a Cheyenne. He lived in a spare and austere fashion under a hide canopy stretched from tree branches and anchored with rocks to the ground. He shivered with cold on hot days, ostentatiously wearing his buffalo robe and then stripped off to a mere breechclout if the chill winds blew, wiping imaginary sweat from his brow. He constantly practised with his weapons and, as

Smoke observed, rapidly became one of the best bow shots in the tribe. The few remaining children would often visit Thorn's shelter to chorus 'Hello' just so that they could hear him reply 'Goodbye'. They ran away shrieking as he approached them, as children often recognise when someone is approaching the edge of madness.

Yellow Bear pondered all these things as he awaited inspiration for his next painting. He turned suddenly as he realised that someone was behind him, watching him. It was Bad Elk.

Without waiting to be asked, Bad Elk sat down and watched the medicine man at work. Yellow Bear faced the hide again and dipped a twig into the black paint. With some difficulty he applied paint onto the rough skin, drawing several copies of the same symbol – an oblong with a leg at each corner. Bad Elk watched patiently trying to understand the pictures and then he recognised what they represented. They were burial scaffolds – Yellow Bear had recorded the biggest event of last year, the Pawnee raid. Bad Elk spoke to the medicine man:

"My friend, it is good that you draw those signs; it means that we will never forget our past or forget that we still have to take revenge on our enemies. The soldier societies are preparing themselves for this."

Yellow Bear nodded in agreement though did not speak or turn away from his work. After a moment's pause, he dipped the twig back into the black paint and drew two diagrams that represented the earth lodges. Again a moment's thought and he switched to the red paint, going back to the symbols of the funeral scaffolds. Here he added in the unmistakable outline of a child being abducted by a warrior with a spiked scalplock. The People may have been more forgiving about Yellow Bear's disgrace but it seemed that the medicine man would not let himself forget. Bad Elk saw a tear fall from the eye of the spirit diviner and looked away. He then spoke of the reason for his visit:

"There is another event for you to paint. It may be important…"

Yellow Bear turned round and sat facing his chief and waited for him to explain.

"We have a visitor from our families in the south. He says that the *vehoe* soldiers are planning a road between their forts that will pass directly across the buffalo range of our southern cousins. The road makers are in the Smoky Hill country. The soldiers will not go back and say that they will return in spring to build bridges to make the road permanent. Our southern bands are angry but they do not wish to attack the soldiers – not yet anyway."

Yellow Bear nodded at the information. Everyone knew that a large mobile column of bluecoat soldiers was even now assembling up at the soldier fort known as Kearney. The Lakota were to be punished for killing Grattan, the young soldier chief, the previous summer. The Cheyenne would want to avoid that. The medicine man spoke in his slow deliberate way:

"Your information is important and should be recorded. We are being squeezed like a soft fruit between the palms of two hands..."

He held up his skinny, paint-flecked hands to demonstrate. The palms hovered horizontally, several inches apart.

"Each of my palms is a river: here in the north is the *veho* river – the Platte and to the south the Flint Arrowpoint River – the whites call this the Arkansas. Much of the Cheyenne country is between the two. Both these rivers carry the wagon roads of the *vehoe* as well as the soldier forts. We are surrounded in our own land. Now you tell me that the whites are building roads in between these rivers – this will disrupt our buffalo herds and drive away the game. As night follows day, there will come white towns and farms. Soon there will be nothing left."

Yellow Bear brought his palms sharply together to illustrate the point. His angular face looked grimly at Bad Elk:

"We may not have to fight the *vehoe* this year but eventually we will have to stand and keep them back. Otherwise the People will flicker and die like the flames of a poor campfire. Only our ashes will remain, to be scattered by the boots of the soldiers."

The thin spirit diviner then turned back to his buffalo hide and considered how to record this depressing fact in symbols.

Bad Elk was lost for a reply but knew Yellow Bear was right. The new chief stood up and left Yellow Bear to his work. He walked to the top of a small rise and looked around his village with a growing sense of accomplishment that lightened his mood.
The encampment buzzed with life. To the north, the entire side of a long hill gleamed and danced in the sunlight; it was the pony herd grazing the slopes. Numbers of horses had steadily risen as the stock had been replenished and now over five hundred glossy coated mounts whinnied and snorted as they were prepared for their lives of service to the People. Women broke and tamed the stockier specimens for the travois and picked out the more docile ones for their children and elderly relatives. Here and there, youths rode swiftly on newly acquired pintos or piebalds, revelling in the natural spirit of a painted horse. Soldiers from the two societies worked on their favourites to note the traits of each mount; a good hunting pony was not necessarily a good warhorse. The activity and bustle pleased Bad Elk – it was good to see the old signs of Cheyenne life again, though how much longer it could be sustained was a puzzle.

Off to the western edge of the village, a pile of prepared buffalo hides was now rapidly dwindling as Sings Loud and her band of women neared completion of all the lodges necessary to re-house the People in proper Cheyenne tipis. Making the lodges had now been transformed from a driving imperative into a much more social event as the end of the task came into sight.

The dedicated band of women sang their own lodge-making songs now; they were a close sisterhood of equals who had performed an important role. There was much laughter at jokes, derisive yells at the unskilled and clumsy men who ventured close and a growing awareness of their improved standing in society. These women called themselves The Sore Fingers and invented their own hand sign, keeping it a secret from their male relatives as it was rude and gently impugned a warrior's manhood. Burnt Hair, Bad Elk's wife, often used the sign with her sisters who hooted at any baffled males watching.

Loud and enthusiastic yells on the other side of camp signalled the arrival of a boys' hunting party; all were afoot as their ponies each dragged a frame laden with meat. Bad Elk watched the scene with satisfaction and pride. The boys had been away from camp for four days; some were as young as ten years but each had understood the need to keep his aim true and the camp supplied. Two of the boys had been orphaned during the Pawnee raid but they were welcomed back with much affection by their surviving relatives. The boys piped squeaky songs about their hunting prowess while their sisters, aunts and mothers clapped their hands in delight. Women, washing skins in the river, waved and dashed across to claim their share of the bounty.

From his high point, Bad Elk also scanned the horizon; not because he was expecting enemies, though it always paid to be vigilant, but because Smoke on the Moon and a small delegation from the soldiers were visiting the Arapaho to the south. They had gone to seek alliances for their impending revenge raid on the Pawnee; they would be back in a few days.

A shot rang out from a nearby ravine and Bad Elk walked over to investigate; shooting was not uncommon near the village and the chief was not alarmed. Some warriors, if they had the powder, fired guns off in celebration. Another shot followed as Bad Elk traced the source of the noise. The shooting was deliberate and not wild; both shots had sent the same echo from the bottom of the shallow ravine so the shooter had not moved his position.

Bad Elk crested a rise and looked at the flat floor of the rocky valley. There, some hundred feet below, lay See the Dark and the Traveller aiming and test firing the young Cheyenne's rifle. Bad Elk mused on the strange bond between the two men – different ages, different tribes, different Gods. Life often laid strange trails for men to follow. Those two would probably take to the war trail together to wreak vengeance on the Pawnee. His once-gentle nephew and the dark skinned man killer would make a bloody combination.

Chapter Twenty Three

---- o o o ----

Smoke rode away from the Arapaho village with a heavy heart. The talks with these staunch allies of the Cheyenne had not been a success; they were always eager to take to the war trail with the *Tsis-tsis-tas* but there had been a marked reluctance to try the new, organised way of fighting that Smoke was determined to use.

The arrival of the Cheyenne party amongst the Arapaho had been the occasion for much feasting and celebration. The noisy Arapaho encampment got even noisier. Drums thudded, women sang, warriors yelled, children laughed and dogs barked. Later, an Arapaho buffalo-calling dance was performed for the Cheyenne guests amid much eating.

Smoke had brought carefully selected presents for the Arapaho war chief, Looks at the Sun. Waiting until the time was right and to ensure the best effect, six pinto ponies, well chosen for wind, speed and stamina, were led, at Smoke's command, prancing and snorting into the village. On the back of each horse was a fine buffalo robe, each from an early kill of Two Teeth cows. In addition, painstakingly dressed cougar skins, edged in red trade blanket were wrapped around bunches of arrows; each arrow straightened to perfection, an iron tip nocked and bound solidly into each shaft. Ball and powder, though a serious depletion of Suhtai stocks, were in rawhide parfleches draped from the cantle of each Cheyenne saddle.

Looks at the Sun was pleased with his presents. Smoke knew him of old; the Arapaho was a great warrior but inclined to be boastful and sensitive about his place in tribal society. The gifts played on his sense of self-importance; Smoke had prepared the ground well. Though, as he found during his speech, not well enough.

Looks at the Sun rose in the middle of the feast and, as the general hubbub faded, spoke to his people:

"We welcome the son of Great Horse, war leader of the Medicine Arrow people to our humble lodges and to share our food. It is an honour to have such a warrior with his party of friends among us. He bears gifts from one great warrior to another. He tells me that his people are much troubled after a fight with the despised Pawnee and seeks our help in taking revenge…."

Smoke sighed. Looks at the Sun had made the Pawnee raid sound like any normal fight ; there was even a hint of censure that the Cheyenne had been defeated by their own shortcomings in battle and needed the Arapaho to make things right. The Cheyenne war chief bit his lip and said nothing. Looks at the Sun continued:

"And so, I offer all the help that the Medicine Arrow People will need…"

The Arapaho chief's sense of timing was as good as Smoke's. Out into the firelight leapt a young boy of about ten years old. He was painted for war and carrying a large hatchet and shield. The boy capered around the fire, shaking the large axe and whooping with a high-pitched and squeaky voice.

Looks at the Sun roared with laughter and his people joined in. It was a good joke – an untested Arapaho boy symbolised the contempt that his people felt for the Pawnee. Just one of their youngsters would be a match for any number of those despicable half-men with the spiked scalplocks. The Arapaho gathering hooted and jeered.

Smoke, as usual, took the joke in the wrong spirit. The appearance of the boy slighted the exhausting battle that the Cheyenne had fought against the Pawnee.

In normal times he would have agreed with Looks at the Sun – the Pawnee were contemptible village dwellers and crop raisers, only occasionally sneaking onto the great grasslands to steal a few buffalo from under the noses of their betters. They were no more than thieves and beggars. Yet these very same thieves and beggars had whipped his experienced Cheyenne fighting men to a standstill. The Pawnee had gathered their available manpower, planned their attacks properly and had returned home victorious. It had been a rare moment of success for the Pawnee and it hurt Smoke on the Moon to think that his band had paid the blood price. The Arapaho would need to be told the truth and his plan for defeating their mutual enemies.

Wrapping his robe around him and carrying his eagle feather fan, Smoke got to his feet:

"My brothers of the great Arapaho nation, we of the Medicine Arrow People thank you for your hospitality and for the honour you have shown us by allowing us to witness your Buffalo Calling Dance. With such powerful medicine from that dance, the Arapaho will never go hungry…"

There was hooting and howls of assent from Smoke's audience; the many years of alliances between Cheyenne and Arapaho meant that most understood what Smoke was saying immediately. Others, unused to the harsh Suhtai edge to his accent, struggled a little.

"Thank you for the help you have offered to defeat our enemies…"

He pointed to the boy warrior, now slumbering in the firelight overwhelmed by excitement and tiredness brought on by waving the heavy war implements around. People cackled and Smoke forced a smile.

"Unfortunately, even such a fine specimen as your boy will not defeat the Pawnee this time. The name of the Pawnee war chief that we fought is Stone Turtle. My scouts have only recently found this out from our Lakota cousins. This man, whilst an enemy, deserves respect…."

The Arapaho were in no mood to accord respect to any Pawnee and rudely barracked the Cheyenne leader. Smoke struggled to be heard, Looks at the Sun signalled for silence.

"He deserves respect because he defeated my soldiers…"

The Arapaho people gasped in amazement. This was the first time that any member of the famous Medicine Arrow People had admitted defeat by a Pawnee.

" Stone Turtle had the advantage of numbers it is true but the thing that turned the tide against us that day was that they were organised and fought as one…

.. We Tsis-tsis-tas fought with our usual bravery but we also fought according to our usual customs and rituals – each individual man delivering only a one-handed blow to the enemy. The enemy fought as a group and delivered a killing blow. If we had not managed to get mounted, the numbers of our funeral scaffolds would have been greater."

The Arapaho fell silent, though one or two just urged Smoke to fight harder. Smoke bit back the urge to bury his hatchet in their stupid skulls.

Looks at the Sun had made no firm promises of assistance to Smoke. His traditional warrior's mind could not grasp the enormity of battle without single combat – how could his young men gain honour and glory? What brave deeds could ever come out of all going into battle at the same time? Where would be the opportunity to ride out in front of your friends, to show how you ignored danger and demonstrated your courage? No, without the promise of shedding blood in an honourable way, battle was best to be avoided. Smoke on the Moon's Cheyenne may have become deranged or visited by the spirits of misfortune after their defeat by the Pawnee. Looks at the Sun would ask his tribal spirit diviner about the omens for an alliance with the Medicine Arrow folk, though in his own heart he knew that they would not be propitious.

Smoke's horse crested the rise above his village; the boys out with the pony herd saw the returning party first and raced to the village to tell Bad Elk, shouting the news to all. Smoke took in the progress that had been made since his departure – a full camp of skin lodges, much meat on the drying racks and a large and valuable horse herd. Soon his people would be back to normal but equally soon they would have to find Stone Turtle and kill him. But they would have to do it alone.

Chapter Twenty Four

---- o o o ----

As summer faded, good news had reached Bad Elk's band. Stone Turtle's band had been found. The information had come from a captured Pawnee woman now held by the Oglala band of the Lakota. Relatives of Sioux women married into Cheyenne villages had brought the news. Smoke on the Moon, however, fumed with frustration.

The enemy village had been found up north near the Loup River but allies to assist in wiping out the Pawnee were in short supply. The Arapahos had declined, thinking that bad spirits dogged the Cheyenne. So too had the Lakota, who had troubles enough of their own with the expected march of the bluecoats against them; many Sioux bands had camped to the south of the Platte on the advice of the Indian agent from Fort Laramie to show that they were not hostile. Another refusal had come from the Kiowa; these were uncertain times with the presence on the Plains of so many soldiers. Other Cheyenne bands thought the same – the bluecoat roadmakers in their southern buffalo country had unnerved them.

It was also late in the raiding season. The Pawnee village was a long ride away and it would be impossible to get up there and back before the snows.

Smoke on the Moon had only his own fighting men to count on and said so at the council fire. The Forked Lightning Women soldier society had protested at this and insisted that their numbers be added to the battle strength; Smoke had demurred and accepted, knowing that a war party was out of the question as things now stood. Stone Turtle's village was just too strong to attack and it was too late in the year to go after him.

The warm airs of late summer had given way to northeasterly winds bringing the chill weather. The village had returned to the original Cheyenne pattern of life – summer had been a time of ease after the hard work of recovery from the devastation it had suffered. Winter food stocks were high and lodges were all complete, including one for the Apache couple in thanks for their help during the times of hunger.

Viajero was proud that he had fitted in to this small band of the Medicine Arrow People; Usen had brought him here and his destiny now lay with them. Bright Antelope Woman now carried his child and there was imminent promise of raiding and killing – he was content.

During the early summer, suitors from other bands had met the widows of the original Suhtai warriors killed in the raid and married some of them. One or two of them had sought out White Rain Woman but she refused their advances; See the Dark had seemed pleased when she told him but she had been surprised when he had not suggested that they married. He went off to think.

Following tradition the newly married men had moved into Smoke's village to join the women's' kinfolk and slightly increased the band's fighting capacity. This pleased Smoke and Broken Knife. All would be needed when the time came.

Badlands Walking Woman, who had lost two children since See the Dark had been born, now found herself pregnant again. She asked Yellow Bear to seek spiritual guidance to keep this child alive.

See the Dark now spent most of his time at the lodge of Viajero and Bright Antelope Woman. White Rain Woman often went with him though she would remain outside. Viajero would sometimes ask if the woman was his chosen companion for life's trail; Dark would blush but not commit to any answer. For now he was glad to be in the company of the Traveller; his knowledge of the N'de language increased rapidly, giving greater strength to their friendship.

It was while he sat outside the Apaches' lodge, idly ploughing furrows with his fingers through an army of ants spilling out of their nest, that he came up with the idea of how to beat Stone Turtle.

Chapter Twenty Five

---- o o o ----

See the Dark looked down the barrel of his rifle from high on a rocky outcrop that overlooked the wagon road. In the distance, about a mile beyond the thin blade of the weapon's iron front sight, two wagons creaked and swayed towards his position.

Dark had often wondered why the *vehoe* went west. Did they not have enough land in the east? Perhaps the hunting wasn't good there or some other whites had driven them away. It was difficult to know as Dark had only met one white man, the yellow-haired man with the big rifle, and his grasp of the white man's tongue then had been too poor to ask.

Viajero lay on a rocky flat on the other side of a narrow defile from his young Cheyenne companion. He could see Dark occasionally looking at him from his vantage point; the boy would be checking that he could see Viajero's red bandana. It was a splash of colour against the grey boulders and clumps of green greasewood, though it was not visible to the advancing *indaa* on the trail.

This was the first time that both men had ventured on a joint expedition. There was a chill in the air, both warriors lay under buffalo robes with the tanned hide outermost. The colour of the hide blended with the pale shades up in the rocks and helped their concealment. Soon the whites would stop for the night and then the warriors could launch their plan.

See the Dark was getting used to his new rifle though he was often surprised by the trickiness of the gun. It was odd that he could not always hit a target even when he was firing from the same spot in an unhurried way. Still, Viajero was a patient teacher and constantly made Dark repeat shots at different targets and at different ranges until he was satisfied with the results. Dark's right eye was instantly able to align the front and the rear sights when he looked down the steel barrel, just as his uncle and Viajero had prophesied. Other men with two eyes had to close the left one and adjust their vision when they sought a target for an accurate rifle shot. Dark, however, had been surprised by the violence of the weapon firing. The explosion from the muzzle did not shock him but it was the more immediate danger to his remaining eye as shards of copper percussion caps, powder debris and smoke flew up at him when the hammer fell. The rifle would blind him if he wasn't careful.

Both Viajero and Bad Elk shared in the young warrior's tutelage. Dark's uncle was known as a proficient rifle shot and he and the Apache understood the basics of firing bullets with gunpowder – the more powder that was poured down the barrel, the further the bullet travelled. Both knew that the fire from the spark released the spirit in the powder and made it bark. Dark's teachers were not profligate with powder and ball; and certainly did not squander their own. Viajero never used his Sharps rifle for practice or to illustrate a point and Bad Elk was the same. Powder could only be obtained from the *vehoe* – they made it, traded it and could demand high prices. They knew that some Arapaho women had been traded for barrels of gunpowder by their menfolk. Bad Elk had always joked that the *vehoe* would never take his ugly wife in exchange for powder – he would have to pay *them*. Of course, he never said this in front of See the Dark; Burnt Hair was his aunt and she had spoiled him as a boy.

Frugal as they were, the powder that came with Viajero's gift soon dwindled away, as did the lead ball and copper caps. They would need more, especially as a war party against Stone Turtle was now a possibility.

Three generations of the Pendleton family now lurched along what had become known as the Oregon Trail; the two laden wagons heading towards the narrow defile where the warriors waited. The sun was getting lower and they would need to find a place to camp, ready for an early start next day.

Time was a factor in the travelling season and the Pendletons had just lost five days repairing the lighter of their two wagons. The weather was generally mild but the need to press on and avoid other delays was a strong driving force. And they were not yet at the halfway point of Independence Rock where the hardest part of the journey would begin. Getting the timing wrong would mean wintering in deep snow in the unforgiving stone fastness of the Rockies. Such a situation would be unwelcome to a large wagon train. For the Pendletons' small group it would mean certain death.

For now though, the Pendletons had no choice but to try and make up the time; there was always the chance that bad weather or some other mishap had delayed the main train, now a week ahead, so they could catch up. The wagon train captain had been worried about them but the pressure to get the majority of his charges across the mountains before the snows and into the fertile valleys of the Willamette had precluded the offer of any real help. He would tie red cloth to trees or bushes to ensure that, even in bad weather, the stragglers could still find the way west along the trail.

The repairs had taken too much time. Jacob Pendleton had cursed his younger brother's recklessness when outfitting to cross the Plains. Jacob's own Conestoga wagon was sound and had been well cared for back in Ohio. Indeed, the trip down to Independence before they even crossed the Missouri had been an excellent testing ground for his rig. To be sure, there had been problems but only minor ones; nothing substantial on the wagon broke; only the well-used iron tyres wore out and they were easily replaced by the wheelwright in Independence.

Spencer, the younger brother, had travelled with Jacob down to Missouri on horseback after selling his small house and orchard; he would outfit himself and his family when they got to the jump-off point. And so, three generations of the Pendleton family had initially shared the cramped and lurching wagon bed on that first part of the great adventure.

Spencer Pendleton was of a different breed to Jacob; it was sometimes difficult for strangers to think of them as brothers – Jacob, stolid and resolute whilst Spencer, though married with two small daughters, was slapdash and irresponsible and seemed to tumble at every fence he took in life. He often said that he was an 'artistic free spirit destined to be untrammelled by life's cares and woes'. Jacob took this to mean that he was afraid of hard work.

The wagon that Spencer had bought from a gleeful farmer just outside of Independence displayed the younger Pendleton's remarkable lack of judgement on practical matters. He shrugged off details like soundness of its wooden construction or even if the wheels turned. Spencer bought the wagon because it was pretty – a powder blue frame with bright yellow wheels. The farmer had quickly pocketed the money and ran indoors, thanking God that there were still fools born every day. But despite protestations from Jacob, and downright rude remarks from the wagon train boss, the blue prairie schooner with the yellow wheels took its place in the great cavalcade west. Spencer was blissfully unaware that only the paint held it together.

Jacob walked beside his team of spotted Ohio oxen as the large wagon bed rumbled comfortably over shale flats; he listened carefully for the sound of squeaking or cracking in the axles but there was none, he had greased them well. He carried a stock whip to keep the oxen lively but he tried not to crack it. His two young sons, currently herding a milk cow and riding a spare draught horse behind Spencer's wagon, didn't like the sound and thought it cruel. Jacob humoured them for now; he just hoped that they would never have to eat the oxen.

Waving his long whip in the air to catch his brother's eye, Jacob pointed to the defile and shouted:

"Sun's gittin' low, Spence. We'll camp among them rocks over there."

Spencer raised his hat in acknowledgement and made a mock bow from his driving seat:

"Your servant Sir!" he yelled.

Jacob laughed and shook his head in disbelief; the boy knew shit about wagons and fixing wheels but he was sure as Hell entertaining.

See the Dark watched the wagons trundle past, below the rimrock. On the other side of the canyon mouth, the Traveller now sat on his haunches to get a better view, cradling his rifle across the tops of his thighs. When the wagons had gone round a bend behind an ancient rock fall, Viajero signalled to his companion and both made their way to the canyon floor to where their ponies were tethered. Already mounted on a third pony was Two Talks, See the Dark's boyhood friend; the young Cheyenne had sought him out to speak to the *vehoe* in their own tongue. Dark remembered his language failings on the riverbank with the yellow-haired white man.

The trio waited and watched the sun lose height and power; they would need to judge it right. Too dark would be too late and too threatening, but they would need to let the *vehoe* set up camp first and be settled. Then they would go calling.

The Pendletons had set up camp with the speed and efficiency that many pioneers had acquired on the long journey west. The two wagons were unhitched from their teams and a rough lozenge shaped box had been formed by the simple expedient of resting each long wagon tongue inside the spokes of each wagons' rear wheel. The draught horse was hitched inside the tongues whilst the four mules were hitched on a half rope in a small clearing. The two large oxen and the brown and white Ayrshire milk cow were hobbled but able to get to the sparse grazing just outside of the small encampment.

A campfire blazed and crackled in the middle of the enclosure. The three Pendleton women, one the matriarch of the family, were setting about preparing the meal. Spencer's two little girls played with a doll on the high seat of Jacob's Conestoga. Jacob was scooping water from the cask on the side of his wagon into a cookpot whilst Spencer was untangling the harness from his mule team and laying it out in preparation for their early start at first light. A long barrelled Springfield rifle rested against one of the wagon tongues.

The trio of Indian riders came cautiously round the bend but halted in the deep purple shadows, now cast in dark bands across the grey dust of the trail.

See the Dark carried a heavy responsibility. He had argued at the council fire that Stone Turtle could be defeated. His idea came to him when he had dug out the ants' nest just to watch the scurrying inhabitants do what they did best – bring order out of chaos. He had idly ploughed his fingers through the dry earth and separated the ants up into groups and had smiled as confusion seemed to reign with the insects. Then it struck him. The Cheyenne would need to do the same with the Pawnee – divide them into smaller groups and kill them.

He had broached this idea at the council fire. At first he had been criticised, it would be impossible to split the Pawnee into smaller groups – the Cheyenne were not strong enough. The Pawnee lived, as everyone at the campfire knew, in large villages inside earthen lodges that would be resistant to arrows and even gunfire. Scornfully, Broken Knife reminded the gathering that Pawnees venerated corn and that is why they planted crops and lived in strange houses. Buffalo were a mere second in their life totems – the 'Men of Men', as the Pawnee boastfully called themselves, only ventured out to steal buffalo that rightly belonged to the Cheyenne. The men with the spiked scalplocks were opportunists on the Plains; they did not belong there.

Dark had thought his argument through. With a note of triumph in his voice he had told the excited gathering that the Cheyenne would not need to divide the Pawnee – the Pawnee would do it for them. Seeing puzzled faces, he reminded them that the Pawnee would split into smaller camps for the winter buffalo hunt. Those smaller camps would usually be strung out close to a river, like beads on a necklace. The camps would not be built of earth but of the more vulnerable buffalo skins. The number of Pawnee warriors in each camp would be small. So a Cheyenne war party could hit each village in rapid succession, each time outnumbering the small groups of Pawnee warriors strung out and separated from their kin.

Dark produced a piece of flattened tree bark to illustrate his point. The captured Pawnee woman who had betrayed Stone Turtle to the Lakota had done the drawing. Dark considered whether it might be a trick to lead the Cheyenne to disaster but dismissed it from his mind. If he had voiced his fears then, they would never take revenge on the Pawnee. The drawing showed a river as a black wavy line running north to south. Along the east side of the river were four circles, each one representing one of the probable winter buffalo camps of the Pawnee. A small group of sandy hills was shown to the west of the river. The river was one of the tributaries of the Loup, the Cheyenne could find it. Only Bad Elk, Smoke and Broken Knife had seen the drawing before but had watched closely as Dark set out his plan.

Dark saw that his words had captured attention. He had continued to state his case – they would have to attack the Pawnee now. The villages must be hit after they had split for the winter but before the snows came. All the Pawnee horses had to be run off to avoid pursuit and then the war party would have to ride hard, back down to where Smoke's village would be in a well chosen spot, close to other Cheyenne bands or allies.

Smoke had been impressed with the wisdom and battle sense of his son and immediately supported it. Broken Knife too was enthusiastic though erred on the side of caution – winter war parties were not unknown but if the elements were against them, risks increased. But he waved these aside and came up with practicalities…..

They would need to set out in less than two weeks if they were to arrive at the Pawnee winter camps before the Big Hard Faced Moon brought the snow and deadening cold. They would carry forage for their ponies and cache food stores on the way out to feed them on the return journey.

And…Broken Knife had looked pointedly around him…it would be better if they could strike the blow with guns in addition to their bows and lances. They would need guns as soon as possible with as much powder and ball as could be obtained in the few short days left before they rode out. The Cheyenne should take this from the whites. In the red heat of anticipation of raiding and killing their enemies, no-one argued against it.

The three Indian riders could see the *vehoe* wagons. They were out of rifle shot and downwind of the stock but they were nervous. They took in the scene at the campfire and could see all the whites that they thought were in the wagons. All, that is, except the two boys.

In answer to an unspoken question from the other two, Viajero nodded to them to walk their ponies forward. Bad luck dogged them from the first step.

A sudden shift in the wind carried the scent of the Indian ponies to the Pendleton's domestic stock. The mules brayed, the horse jerked at its head rope, the oxen crow-hopped into the bushes and the milk cow, unused to being hobbled, fell to its knees as if in supplication. The riders had not gone twenty yards when the two small Pendleton boys dashed out from a cleft in the rocks, dropping armfuls of firewood and ran to the wagons yelling in squeaky voices:

"Indians! Indians!"

Two Talk's pony bucked at the intrusion into its leisurely walk, the boys had been like a pair of clattering sandgrouse taking to the air. Two Talks was almost dumped over its neck but regained his saddle and stirrups in time. Viajero snorted in annoyance; he had wanted to surprise the *indaa* before they could get to their weapons. Now he saw, whilst still forcing his pony to walk, that one of the white eyes had grabbed the long rifle and was running to the wagon shaft with it up in the aim. The second *indaa* scooped the two youngsters into the compound and thrust them and all the womenfolk into one wagon bed. He then ran, cocking an old fashioned flintlock pistol, and joined the other man at the wagon tongue. Under his breath, See the Dark sang an old song that his mother had taught him about courage.

Jacob relaxed from the aim and rested the butt of the long rifle on the wagon tongue and watched the Indians approach. He had seen Indians before at the trading posts along the Platte but they had mainly been drunk or panhandling coins so that they could get drunk again. No, these were different… they weren't painted and did not seem of hostile intent but you could never tell with these gut eaters. He looked across at Spencer who had the cocked pistol in both hands and was pointing the muzzle towards the oncoming riders; his hands were shaking with the tension and the weight of the weapon. Jacob leant over and pushed the pistol barrel down until it pointed at the ground. The Goddamn 'free spirit' would get them all killed if that old horse pistol went off without warning.

As the Indians came closer, Jacob could make out more detail. The older one seemed to have darker skin than the other two; he looked as if he would be a handful in a fight. The one who had almost been thrown by his horse wore a white man's linen shirt and looked inoffensive enough but he did have a bowcase slung over his shoulder. There was something strange about the third one who, mouthing the silent words to some strange incantation, rode towards him. It was only when a stray shaft of fading sunlight caught the black shiny stone in his eye that Jacob's blood chilled a little. This wasn't a social call for coffee, sugar or hardtack.

Jacob cradled the long rifle in the crook of his left arm and held up his right hand in what he understood to be the Plains sign for 'peace'. The three halted their ponies at the wagon tongue and looked at the *vehoe's* right hand; Viajero and See the Dark looked up at the sky where Jacob's fingers pointed but could see nothing of significance. They both looked at Two Talks who shrugged:

"I have seen this sign before from the *vehoe*. I think it shows that their hands are empty of weapons and that they mean us no harm."

"His weapon is in his other hand, I'm not fully blind," retorted Dark sarcastically. Two Talks remained silent and looked intently at the elder *veho*.

All three stayed in the saddle and watched the white man for some seconds. An old white woman peered around the wagon canopy and called out to the man. The man smiled slightly and then stepped back towards the firelight.

Jacob seeing no answering sign to his 'peace' hand lowered it and pointed to his mouth and said slowly and distinctly:

"Do you want to eat?"

Two Talks did not need his language skills to interpret this and quickly swung down from his saddle; the others followed his lead. They ducked under the wagon tongue and moved towards the welcome glow of the fire and the smell of hot food.

Jacob Pendleton was always cautious. He would never have invited them to the campfire if his mother hadn't called out:

"Jacob, bring them closer to the campfire. I've got Pa's shotgun here so we got three guns, they've only got two. And I cain't hit them if they're over there. Invite them to dinner and we'll kill all three of the red bastards if we have to."

Not for the first time did Jacob Pendleton blanch at his mother's language; there must be something about her past life that he didn't know. He beckoned the quaking Spencer to join them.

At the campfire, all sat in a circle. The Cheyennes and the Apache sat cross-legged on the ground whilst Granny Pendleton emerged from the back of the wagon dragging her wooden rocker with one hand and carrying the shotgun with the other. Spencer dashed across to help his mother. The two wives took plates of food for the children still peering wide-eyed from the tailboard at the strange dinner guests.

Jacob's wife set out portions of food onto three tin plates, each with its own spoon, and handed them to the Indians. She hoped they wouldn't take the spoons; they were silver and part of her marriage gift from her sisters back in Ohio. She shuddered slightly that the spoons would come into contact with the mouths of savages but hot water and lye soap would cleanse any disease that these wild men might have.

The Indians ate hungrily and conversed in low tones. Jacob, Spencer and Granny sat and watched the scene, occasionally taking a forkful of stew or a bite of biscuit but their hands never strayed far from their weapons.

Two Talks shovelled the food into his mouth and belched loudly; the Pendleton matriarch glared at him. Two Talks smacked his lips and announced to his companions:

"The food is good, they must have salt with them, I can taste it."

"Never mind the food, it is well known that you will eat anything if it is offered with an open heart" retorted Dark.

"Good food" Two Talks said in English to the old woman – it was always best to seek favour with the elders; she would control the others. Two Talks had been brushing up his language skills when he spoke to *vehoe* at the trading posts. Granny beamed and inclined her head at the praise; her daughters-in-law had done all the cooking but that was unimportant for now.

"What do you want?" asked a querulous Spencer, getting right to the point. "Coffee, sugar, salt?"

Two Talks recognised the words but shook his head; it was a little earlier than he had planned but now was the time for his language skills. He carefully spoke out the three rehearsed words so that there would be no confusion:

"Powder, ball, caps"

There was a sharp gasp from Jacob as the halting English words clarified in his brain. A white man could give almost anything else to a redskin, including the worst snake oil whiskey but firearms and anything to shoot from them was taboo. He acted quickly. The three Indians suddenly found themselves looking at the muzzles of three weapons. Tension barged its way to the campfire.

"Shoot the gut eaters Jacob!" yelled Granny and raised her shotgun. Just in time, Spencer, for once thinking in a rational way, grabbed the shotgun from her but resumed the aim on the dark skinned one. No good shooting gut eaters when there might be more of them about to make a bigger fight of it. Getting them out of the camp was the best bet.

"No powder, no ball, no caps" snapped Jacob, shaking his head to emphasise the negative and stood up. Spencer did the same, keeping their weapons trained on the savages. Jacob motioned with the rifle barrel that the Indians should mount and leave. Jacob shouted for his eldest son and the boy, overjoyed to be involved, leapt down from the wagon tailboard and took the flintlock pistol from his uncle; he trained it on one of the Indians, his mouth set in a thin, firm line of determination against his pale skin.

Two Talks stood and looked contrite. He had forgotten a vital element of their negotiations:

"Trade. Yes, trade. Trade for powder, trade for bullets….come" and walked over to the ponies. Jacob motioned to the other two Indians to stand still. Two Talks untied a large bundle from his pony and spread it on the ground. He pulled it across to the campfire so all could see. With a flourish of triumph, the Cheyenne proudly pointed to the valuable goods on display.

The wives of the Pendleton men now walked tentatively forward and looked at the array, laid out on a fine bull buffalo robe. Both knelt down, primly tucking long aprons under their knees to keep the dust off their dresses, and felt the robe. It had been well cured and dressed; soft and supple with dense brown hair – a warm addition for chill nights to come. Other treasures were also offered, two pairs of moccasins, each with fine beadwork of blue, red and white; a smaller buffalo calf robe, almost yellow in colour and three deerskin shirts, well cut and carefully sewn tight with thin sinew. Jacob's wife looked up:

"These are fine things Jake. This buffalo robe could replace that old blanket of ours that keeps getting wet when the rain blows in. These skin shirts would wear better outdoors than the good wool ones. Can't you spare some powder and lead?"

But Jacob was adamant – no trade for materials that could get them or any other white pioneers killed. He put the rifle back up into the aim and pointed at Viajero:

"Git out and don't come back. If I see you again, I'll nail your damned red hide to my wagon to keep the water out. Take your flea-bitten stuff and make tracks."

Viajero moved slowly to his pony followed by See the Dark and Two Talks, who was hurriedly re-tying his trade bundle. All were tense but subdued; they mounted in silence and rode back down the trail accompanied by Granny's jeering and the thin, relieved laughter of Spencer and his nephews.

Out on the dark grasslands, the three men rode abreast; a dark cloud feathered its way across the moon. Two Talks talked the whole time; he was almost jocular, rejoicing in his dual language skills and happy that they had got to eat. Viajero was silent; he had wanted to see what Dark would do and was disappointed that a fight had not ensued. Still, the *indaa* had more guns and the three of them could have been killed on a fruitless task. But it was galling to leave empty handed.

After a long spell, See the Dark suddenly turned his pony. He did not speak to the others as he did this and so was not missed for a few moments. It was only because of the change in his silhouette against the lighter sky above the horizon that the others knew that he was heading back the way they had come. They too reined their horses around and joined Dark. The moon suddenly came out and highlighted the face of the one-eyed youth – his normally copper toned skin was granite grey, his jaw and cheekbones seemingly chiselled and unmoving. The black obsidian globe in his eye socket gleamed as though shot through with white fire. Dark spoke softly but with conviction:

"Those *vehoe* made two mistakes – they didn't disarm us and they didn't kill us. Now they will learn."

In the darkness, Viajero smiled.

Chapter Twenty Six

The men in the Pendleton family were already awake and checking that their animals had not strayed overnight. The oxen bellowed in recognition as Jacob walked out, smiling, to unhobble them and bring them to the harness. The brown and white Ayrshire, thin from lack of good grass, lowed pleadingly so he stopped first to untie her and let her get used to walking around, unencumbered by the rope loops around her ankles.

It was while Jacob was bent over the cow's feet that Viajero's arrow thudded into his rib cage, the iron point slicing easily through flesh and cartiledge before puncturing the stomach wall, its feather flights sticking incongruously out from under his arm. The cow stepped back in alarm as Jacob slumped, wheezing, into the greasewood clumps. Viajero saw him try to stand and call out so sent another arrow into the *indaa's* chest. The white man was flung backwards into the bushes, crashed through the thin twigs and lay still.

Spencer Pendleton, tending minor sores on his mules' backs some yards away, had not seen the flight of either arrow but had heard the crashing of the bushes and went towards the sound. What the Hell was Jake doing? Granny and the two wives were getting out of their wagons, shaking sheets and blankets – they would air them over the bushes when the sun rose properly. They had not seen Jacob fall either.

Viajero and Two Talks quickly changed position in some rocks beyond the greasewood. There was no sign of See the Dark.

Spencer, who had been calling out and joshing his brother for answering a call of nature when there was work to be done, suddenly stopped. Jake would normally have answered, slinging back a sharp wisecrack and reminding Spence of his lowly position in the family.

Suddenly, just as in many blood chilling dime novels he had read, Spencer's hair prickled on the back of his neck and he sensed danger. Pulling out the flintlock pistol from his belt, he cocked the hammer back and checked the few grains of fine powder in the flashpan. A sharp explosion and gout of grey smoke exploded almost in front of him and a heavy lead ball smacked with enormous force into his groin. At first he thought that he had shot himself and yelled in pain as he fell to his knees.

Viajero was angry. See the Dark should not have wasted bullet and lead on the younger *veho;* he could have been killed with a knife. To compound the mistake, the man was not dead. Across from where the *veho* lay screaming, he saw the old woman come charging out of the wagon camp with the shotgun at the ready. Two Talks had leapt out of the rocks to finish off the white man with his hatchet when the white man stopped screaming and raised the pistol.

Spencer had only fired the old pistol once before they had set out on their trek west. The Indian coming towards him seemed familiar and he recognised the grubby linen shirt from the previous night's encounter. These weren't docile gut-eaters after all. He pulled the trigger.

Two Talks only saw the muzzle flash from the pistol at the last moment and leapt off to one side. The pistol ball raked through his hip, chipping the bone before bursting out the other side; a gout of blood, more dramatic than serious, accompanied the bullet out of the exit wound. Two Talks fell heavily and lay winded.

Granny Pendleton loosed off one barrel of the side-by-side shotgun as she saw Spencer go down. Then, with one barrel still to fire, charged down the dusty track to get her sons. She yelled every profanity that she knew and some she had just made up. The shouting gave her courage.

The lead shot rattled off the rocks as See the Dark raised his head to come back into the fight after reloading. Pellets zinged off around him and clattered off dry rock; that old woman was dangerous. Taking more careful aim, he fired again and the woman dropped in her tracks, a bloody portion of her tight grey locks exploding from her head as the ball smashed through her skull.

Viajero had taken the opportunity afforded by the old woman's attack to get to the wagons. The wives of the *indaa* were cowering underneath the larger wagon with the two girls and one of the boys. They had not seen the Apache come but the elder of the Pendleton boys had.

Across the small campsite, through the wisps of smoke of the dying cooking fire, a small, determined figure appeared with the Springfield rifle. Tom Pendleton swung the heavy barrel upwards and, knowing he could never hold the weapon in the aim at the shoulder, held it at his hip and pointed it at the dark skinned Indian that had eaten their food the previous night.

Viajero turned his head; he had been concentrating on the women. He laughed when he saw the boy struggle with the rifle but dived off to one side as the explosion came and the bullet whistled past his legs, clipping the leather of the top fold of his long moccasin. The boy was brave and deserved respect; he would have to be killed like a true adult enemy. Bringing up the Sharps, Tom Pendleton's light frame was smashed back against the wagon boards as his mother screamed.

See the Dark moved in swiftly to finish off the younger *veho* still screaming from the wound in his groin. It needed three blows form his war club, a stone bound in shrunken sinew to a smooth ash handle, to kill the young man. The side of the man's head caved in from the pounding and leaked dark blood and pink brains. Dark picked up the pistol; he was disappointed that it was not a repeating weapon like that of the Traveller. Still, they were here for guns and powder and they would take three weapons home to arm the soldier societies.

The three warriors gathered at the wagons and debated what to do with the surviving women and children. Captives were always trouble when taken from any tribe; they would often act submissively then escape at the first opportunity to lead their relatives back on reprisal raids. White captives would be even worse; the *vehoe* would actively hunt for them; bluecoat soldiers were already crossing the buffalo country of the Lakota and could turn on the Cheyenne at any time. No, it would be best to kill them all after they had looted the wagons. Screeching with joy in anticipation of their rewards from the *vehoe* camp, they set to their task.

The two Pendleton women and their three remaining children stood in a tight cluster, the girls clinging to the skirts of their mothers. Jacob's youngest boy, Michael, placed himself defensively in front of them all. They didn't need to speak damn Indian talk to know their fate was being discussed. The wild and raucous yelling of the Indians unnerved them further. All were ashen-faced and trembling in shock from the sudden and violent loss of their family but they had spoken about such dangers before they had ever set out on the wagon road. The time to cope with these dire emergencies, though all had earnestly prayed that they would never have to, was at hand. They had little time to act.

Viajero and See the Dark searched the wagons, triumphantly holding up the two small casks of gunpowder that they found in the wagon beds. Three satchels of lead bullets of varying sizes and percussion caps completed the haul.

They yelled their delight at Two Talks who, clutching his bleeding hip, was nonchalantly guarding the captives. Some iron tools were thrown into the camp clearing from the larger wagon – an axe, claw hammer and saw clanging down beside the now dead fire. Food was ransacked and wrapped in blankets to load onto their ponies. Clothing was torn from leather bound trunks and scattered, Sunday best dresses of the Pendleton women were thrown onto the ground and left. Two Talks tried on a top hat but threw it into the bushes when it fell off. He picked up a heavy woollen work shirt and threw it over his shoulder; it would be useful in the winter. Neither Viajero nor Dark wanted any of the *vehoe* clothes to touch their skin; they could be contaminated and weakened.

During the orgy of looting, Two Talk's attention wandered. He failed to see the two women slowly turn around, pulling the young ones round in front of them, using the billowing folds of their long skirts to hide what they would do. By the time Two Talks noticed what was happening, Mamie and Libby Pendleton had killed their children.

Chapter Twenty Seven

---- o o o ----

Yellow Bear's spiritual powers returned when *Maheo*, the Sacred One, hit him with lightning.

It was not forked lightning of course, the sort that can split a tree or kill a buffalo but a ball of exploding white fire that rolled down a hillside during a storm and knocked him off his feet. He later described it as 'colliding with the sun'. He was burnt down his right side where the ball lightning caught him and the red weal, from shoulder to ankle, would remain with him until his death. The medicine man had no idea his powers had returned until he staggered back to his tipi to sleep.

That night he should have been at the council fire to listen to See the Dark's plan to defeat the Pawnee but the lightning strike had made his vision poor and his ears rang with the sound of a constantly rushing wind. He preferred to lie down and recover.

With his ears still full of howling wind, the thin framed Suhtai dropped into a sleep full of strange dreams. He often dreamt; in fact, as the band's spirit diviner it was expected. But since the Pawnee raid, his powers to see and interpret his dreams had vanished; it was his punishment from Maheo for losing the children and women entrusted to his care. On this night however, he seemed able to stand back and watch his dreams as a detached observer. Even while asleep, Yellow Bear knew that this was an exciting development; this is how it was before the raid.

He stood and watched as red and black smoke roiled around inside his head; the coloured clouds, however, kept obscuring something that took shape behind them. Yellow Bear's spiritual eye concentrated hard and then saw what it was. Gradually, the smoke cleared and a crooked branch of a tree, standing vertical, emerged. The branch was barren except for five circular leaves that stood out on their separate stalks to the left side of the branch. Then, the smoke curled in again and the branch was gone.

Yellow Bear slept deeply but awoke with a start at daybreak. He remembered the image from his dream and hauled his buffalo robe pictograph from the rear of his tipi. Without eating and ignoring his custom of speaking to Maheo each morning, he took up his paints. Spitting into the caked paste in the hollowed out part of a small log, he stirred the mixture and dipped his hazel twig into it. He drew a representation of the branch and its five leaves on the rough white surface of the hide and blew on it to hasten the drying process.

Now he needed to find Bad Elk. The medicine man had no idea what the drawing represented but the vividness of the dream and his ability to remember and record it, at least, showed that some of his powers were returning. Bad Elk may know something.

Bad Elk emerged from his tipi yawning and walked off to urinate. He came back to his lodge to find Yellow Bear at his tipi flap, the buffalo hide calendar over his arm.
The band chief welcomed Yellow Bear, asking about the pain from his burn marks, and went inside his lodge, beckoning the medicine man to follow him. In the darkness of the lodge, Burnt Hair was folding back the sleeping robes but wisely left to tend to the cooking fire outside when the men came in. Bad Elk had seemed to treat her better now that she had shown her mettle with the Sore Finger sisterhood, helping to restore the village lodges. It had been no mean feat and Bad Elk had been among the first to admit it. He just wished that she was a little prettier.

Yellow Bear spread out the buffalo hide and pointed to the symbolic branch and leaves that he had drawn:

"My friend, you often praise me for being wise though I do not always deserve it. My powers to listen to the spirits and to take guidance from them have been much diminished since I lost the children...."

Bad Elk was about to speak against that idea but, holding up his hand, Yellow Bear continued:

"As you know I was lucky enough to be struck by lightning; Maheo controls all things and I am sure he sent this to me…."

Bad Elk pondered whether this had been a lucky occurrence. He had once seen the blackened remains of one of his ponies, crackling with blue sparks, after being hit by a bolt of lightning. The luck that Yellow Bear had was that he was still breathing.

"I believe He sent it to help restore my powers. Maheo made me dream this."

Yellow Bear dragged the hide around so that Bad Elk could see the symbol in the light coming from the open flap.

"All my powers are not yet returned as I cannot interpret what this means. But the vision was strong and I stood inside my own head, as in the old days. I think I may be of use to our people again."

For the first time in many months, Yellow Bear smiled.

Bad Elk's pulse had quickened as soon as he saw the symbol but he forced himself down the path of deliberation. He made Yellow Bear explain that the symbol represented a tree branch and its strange, circular leaves. He added that it had been partially obscured by black and red smoke, a sign from previous dreams in happier times, of battles to come. Scarcely daring to breathe, Bad Elk crawled to the far edge of the lodge and retrieved the tree bark drawing done by the captured Pawnee woman with the Oglala Lakota.

With a flourish, he placed it next to Yellow Bear's symbol – the drawings were almost identical. Yellow Bear had never seen the woman's drawing before, it was for a war plan and the soldier society leaders had kept sight of it to a minimum, entrusting Bad Elk with its safe keeping. The faces of both men drained of blood when they saw the significance of the coincidence.

Yellow Bear had dreamt of the Pawnee villages and confirmed their location. The only difference was that the Pawnee woman's diagram put four winter villages on the east bank whilst Yellow Bear's symbol and dream put five villages on the west bank. Time would tell who was right.

Chapter Twenty Eight
---- o o o ----

The Cheyenne war party arrived at the edge of Pawnee country as the ground turned to iron. Their scouts had eventually found the villages on the Middle Fork of the Loup River. From the sandy hills shown on the Pawnee woman's drawing, they had watched their hated enemies go into temporary winter camp before they ranged out after the buffalo. The skin lodges that the Pawnee had now set up would offer no protection against the arrows and bullets of the Cheyenne. Soon the 'Men of Men' would wish that they had stayed at home in their houses fit only for prairie dogs.

Smoke and Broken Knife smiled as they heard the report of the 'wolves'. Yellow Bear would be pleased – the camps, five of them, were all on the west bank as his dream had predicted. Yellow Bear was serving his people again.

The two war leaders now took their column of warriors and withdrew to the sand hills off to the west of the camps. They would rest the ponies after their hard ride, feed themselves then collect their blood price from the Pawnee.

Fires were not permitted in case of giving away their position, Smoke and Broken Knife huddled in their buffalo robes in a cold camp and discussed their plans.

They had managed to assemble almost fifty warriors to fill the saddles of the war ponies. Each warrior had brought along a second mount that was now under guard in timber a day's ride away. Four very disgruntled ten-year old boys had been instructed to look after the horses. Like everyone else, they wished to be in the fighting but the horses would be important for the hard ride home. The boys had accepted their task knowing that their turn would come one day. At least they were out on the war trail with their relatives and heroes. They smiled bravely as their comrades set out on the final leg to the camps.

White Rain's Forked Lightning Women made a strange but confident little group in the war party. Fully armed and well mounted this would be their first battle. Some of the Thunder Bears still muttered about the worth of their women in men's work. Smoke had made each of the women promise that if the bleeding time for any one of them came before the fight, that person would mount up and ride home without touching any of the others. The women, knowing what had happened to Raven Heart during the Pawnee raid, agreed. They were put in charge of running off the enemy pony herd. Three youths would help them. This small group would form the first strike at the enemy.

Eleven other youths, ranging from thirteen to sixteen years and also untested on the war trail were to be the next part of the attack. They had no guns but each had a bow and a case full of arrows. Each carried a hatchet and shield. Two carried their fathers' lances and were determined to put blood on the blades. Four soldiers from the war societies would accompany them to add weight and steadiness to the assault.

There were four independent warriors. Viajero, See the Dark and Two Talks were all armed with guns now. Two Talks had taken possession of the Springfield rifle from the fight with the *vehoe* wagons and had spent several days sawing off a length of barrel to make it more manageable from the saddle. The fourth warrior was Thorn, the Contrary. He would probably fight alone according to his beliefs.

Finally, there were the military societies. Bolstered by recent marriages within the band both the Striking Snakes and the Thunder Bears could now boast over a dozen warriors each. Thanks to Broken Knife's plan to take weapons from the vehoe on the wagon roads, over half of them now carried firearms of some sort. These two groups would do most of the killing.

The war party would rest for some hours then attack as the morning star appeared.

Smoke and Broken Knife ended their discussions; they would soon remind the others as to their roles in the coming fight. Both were worried that a relaxation back into the old, individual ways of fighting by any of their small party would leave them exposed to another defeat. The Pawnee would not just sit still whilst their village was attacked. If Stone Turtle was in any of those five village circles, he could re-organise his warriors if he saw a weakness. Neither could relax enough to sleep on the hard ground but stayed awake and ate jerked buffalo meat, talking in low tones.

Smoke voiced his concern :

"That Pawnee woman captured by the Lakota could have been lying. Those villages on the river may not be Stone Turtle's people."

Broken Knife considered his reply and spoke only after he had given due regard to Smoke's worries.

"You may be right; those villages may not belong to the one who should pay the blood price. But we have had a long ride to get here and below us lie the homes of our enemies. Those lodges may hold some of our captured women and children. If we are right, we get to kill our enemies and recover some of our own. If we are wrong, then at least we get to kill the Pawnee."

Slightly mollified, Smoke nodded in the gloom.

Lying by their picketed horses, See the Dark and Viajero couldn't sleep either; only Two Talks snored lightly under his thick buffalo robe, white wisps of his breath curling out from the hair.

Viajero, silent as befitted an Apache on the war trail, rubbed away the crystals of ice forming on the cold barrel of the Sharps. He thought of other nights in warmer places, though his desert home was often freezing when darkness fell. He cast his mind back to the wickiups on the Gila River but was dismayed to find that he could not now remember what his White Mountain Apache wife looked like. He would, however, always remember his son's face, though not as a happy laughing child – only as a dismembered head, cold to the touch with terror still in its eyes.

Still, he would soon be a father again. Bright Antelope Woman had been sent by Usen to guide him on his life's path; she and the baby were a gift from God. Before setting out, he had pulled Bright Antelope's dress down over her shoulders and traced the scars on her back from the Pawnee weapons. He would take that image into battle with him; those 'Men of Men' would pay dearly. He felt the thrill of the coming battle sweep over him like a wave of fire; Viajero was now back to his old self. He smiled in satisfaction.

See the Dark shivered slightly and hoped that his confident plea for battle would not turn against him. Bad Elk's band could not sustain any more losses. At least many now had guns and that would make up for lack of numbers.

They had not killed the white women at the wagon fight. Even Viajero had been shocked when the three children slumped beside their mothers, blood spouting from the deep slashes across their throats onto the brown linen of the trail dresses. Up to that point Viajero had wanted to violate the women and then kill them. Neither See the Dark nor Two Talks were interested in rapes; the women looked like worn out ponies, haggard and grey with fatigue. There could be no pleasure there.

The two Cheyennes had stood aghast at the killings and merely looked with horrified curiosity as the Pendleton wives crouched low and snarling over the bodies of their offspring, pointing their kitchen knives in the direction of the warriors. The women were obviously possessed. Viajero brought the Cheyennes out of their frozen state by roughly pushing them to pack their spoils from the wagons.

The mules were unhitched from the half lariat where they had been overnight and loaded with sacks of food and the casks of powder. Blankets were tied at each end with cord and served as packs for the iron tools and the weapons. Other small items were pushed into leather satchels and canvas bags found in the wagon beds. The draught horse, tied inside the wagon camp, was led out on a halter. It would be a fine beast for pulling a travois.

As a last act, Viajero took his hunting knife and stabbed the oxen and Ayrshire milk cow in their necks. All bawled and wheezed in pain but gradually sank onto their sides and rattled their last breaths. If they were not going to kill the women (and even he shied away from butchering the insane) then the women must have nothing to ride on to get help. And anyway, oxen and cows moved too slowly for a fast escape back to the Cut Finger camp.

True to their Cheyenne upbringing, See the Dark and Two Talks had scalped the men. The old woman had lost part of her scalp with the rifle wound so they left her. Viajero, never much interested in scalps, had offered the opinion that if their camp was ever raided by the white soldiers, then the evidence of Cheyenne involvement in killing these settlers would be hanging from their lodge poles or their lances. See the Dark and Two Talks had considered this for a moment; it seemed a shame to return without real trophies of the fight. But good sense prevailed – they threw the bloody hanks of hair into the bushes and rode off.

See the Dark knew that the fight at the wagon camp had been small scale compared to what he now faced. Now he would fight strong enemies on their home soil. Throughout the small camp that night, Maheo was invoked many times as the Cheyenne prepared for battle.

Chapter Twenty Nine

---- o o o ----

Bad Elk's village erupted with delight. Their first indication that all had gone well with the war party was the drumming of hooves as over a hundred and fifty Pawnee mounts were driven into the small valley adjoining the camp. The four boys who had guarded the spare Cheyenne horses in the timber had the honour of running the stolen stock in. They rode madly through the tipis, calling on all to come and behold their spoils from the Pawnee battle. Though snow had fallen, the boys rode without robes, hot and flushed with victory.

Bad Elk rushed from his lodge when the boys rode in and scanned the surrounding hills for sign of the main party. Smoke on the Moon would want to pass on any word of casualties before the war party returned in full triumph. Relatives would need to be told and mourning commenced.

Unpicketing his pony from outside his tipi, he sprang onto its back, pulling himself on by grabbing the animal's twisted mane hair. Shouting for Yellow Bear, he rode up to the lodge of the medicine man and instructed him to gather the people. Then, pulling the head of his horse round, he rode off into the foothills back down the trail used by the stolen horses. Bad Elk had a light heart; Smoke would not have allowed the reckless entry of the boys with the Pawnee horses if the war party had suffered many dead or had been defeated.

Trotting slowly, Bad Elk kept looking along the skyline of the low hills. Then he saw what he was looking for; a solitary rider crested a rise and reined in his pony. Bad Elk stopped and watched carefully.

The rider on the ridge was carrying a buffalo robe tied into a ball. How many times this ball was thrown into the air would signify the number of dead. Bad Elk watched impassively as the rider threw the ball once. Unbelievably, though Bad Elk had been expecting more, only one death was signalled. Nonetheless, though it was an incredible piece of good fortune for the war party, the dead warrior belonged to someone in the village and they would have to be told. He spurred his horse forward to join the rider on the ridge and learn the name of the one that had been summoned by Maheo.

The small, mixed band of Suhtai was flushed with the success of their encounter at the Pawnee winter camps. Much feasting and dancing was organised and it would last for several days – only when the last of the stories of the brave war deeds had been told would the fires allowed to fade and the camp prepare for the reality of another winter. But the People were content. The spirit of the Tsis-tsis-tas was strong again; they had heroes and they felt invincible.

Smoke's war party had held off from its triumphant return until the dead warrior had been announced and the five wounded, being bounced around on makeshift travois, were safely back in the village.

The loss of Thorn, the Contrary, had been almost expected. He alone had decided to ignore the battle plan of Smoke and Broken Knife and had paid the price. On that freezing day, he had stripped down to his breechclout and moccasins, complained loudly about the heat and charged into the first Pawnee camp whilst the Forked Lightning Women were running off the pony herd.

Thorn had certainly caught the Pawnee off guard and fought fiercely, rapidly dismounting and closing with the bewildered 'Men of Men' on foot. Soon though he was overwhelmed and cut down; the second wave attack by the Cheyenne youths confirmed that Thorn had fallen. His body could not be recovered.

Smoke and Broken Knife had planned their return home in some detail. It was designed to lift the spirits of the People and demonstrate the potent fighting force of the Cheyenne was back amongst them. And it had worked well. Clad in the same battle accoutrements that they had worn against the Pawnee, the whole party rode wildly into the village. Shouting and yelling their war deeds and songs, the battle-tested Cheyenne warriors thundered into the camp circle with guns firing, lances raised, plumes fluttering in pony manes and savage joy on every painted face. Their relatives stood and watched, yelling and yipping like coyotes. Drums thudded, shots were fired, dogs ran round barking and howling, horses whinnied and snorted and pandemonium reigned.

An air of celebration took hold of the camp. It had been a long time since their happiness could flow because of a common event and they made the most of it. Snow was cleared from a flat area of ground across the river and cooking fires lit. Laughing women carried piles of fresh meat and bundles of seasonal roots and vegetables across the stream as small children dashed between them, shrieking with pleasure at getting in their mothers' way. Other girls trimmed and tied up bundles of firewood and carried them to the clearing. Wooden uprights were set, with some difficulty, into the hard ground and lodge poles cut and tied as cross pieces. Brushwood was woven into a windbreak around the fires and buffalo robes were laid out to sit on. Criers rode through the lodges to announce what was happening; the entire village would gather to eat and hear the stories of the great battle fought in the Pawnee country.

Darkness fell quickly and a light, dry snow was in the air, illuminated like a million small stars as it caught the firelight. Whilst this was a formal feast of thanksgiving and celebration, there was a hubbub of noisy chatter as the People gathered to eat and listen. Friends and families sat together, shuffling across the buffalo robes until all those who could be present were fitted in.

Those who had taken part in the battle sat apart from their families in a semi-circle facing the crowd, they would recount their brave deeds for the pleasure of the village. From left to right, they sat in the groups that had conducted the attack and they would speak in that order. Viajero, See the Dark and Two Talks made a strange little band of independent warriors between the youths and the soldier societies. The White Mountain Apache, now dressed in Cheyenne fashioned skin shirt, leggings and robe, did not seem so much of an outsider now. See the Dark and Two Talks had spent all day getting ready and their war shirts and beaded leggings were almost white in the firelight.

Close to the front of the crowd, Badlands Walking Woman, her belly now heavy with Smoke's next child, sat like a contented buffalo cow. Beside her, Bright Antelope, not as far into her pregnancy, lolled back on the robes and wondered when they would eat.

Yellow Bear stood and opened the proceedings with prayer and offerings to Maheo. Small bits of food from each cooking kettle were placed around the fire as he intoned the sacred chants and held each one aloft to the four cardinal points. The prayer reflected what all felt – thankfulness that the war party had returned almost intact with a great victory to its name.

Bad Elk, as ever seeking greater cohesion of his band, had made it widely known that Yellow Bear's prophecy about the location and number of Pawnee villages had been accurate. The medicine man's dreams were now as potent as ever, the spirits spoke to him again. Yellow Bear was whole. The camp was pleased and content. Now they wanted to hear all about the Pawnee fight….

Battles, as the elders had often said, are fragments of confused action seen by the participants, no one man can see the whole battle. The stories of the fighting groups reflected this. The Forked Lightning Women knew they had been successful in running off the series of pony herds from the string of Pawnee villages along the Loup. But they had no idea if the rest of the plan had worked until the remainder of the war party caught up with them for the long, hard ride back to the spare horses corralled in the timber.

White Rain Woman had been the driving force in forming this unique female soldier society. She was determined and spirited; some men previously avoided marrying her because of these traits. But now she had sat astride her pony, leading her small band of sister warriors and youths, ready to play her part. As the morning star rose on the Middle Fork of the Loup, she led the first wave of the Cheyenne attacks. Smoke's instructions were still ringing in her ears – 'Ride hard, stampede all the horses from the villages and don't stop'.

White Rain had done just that. The guards on the pony herd were startled by the sudden outbreak of shrieking and yelling as a bunch of women and boys thundered towards them on ponies snorting clouds of breath smoke in the crisp, freezing air. The Pawnee guards couldn't understand why their women would be doing this and laughed. Only when two of them were toppled by arrows did they realise that these riders were not of their own kind. The scattered ponies of the Pawnee herd jerked up their heads in alarm and galloped off south, driven by the yipping voices of their new Cheyenne owners. The Pawnee guards soon recovered and tried to ride down the horse thieves.

One caught up with White Rain Woman and snatched at her flapping sleeves, gaining a purchase on the deerskin material. White Rain though had been ready and was anxious to test her newly made hatchet. Though the weapon was made from flint, the blade was finely knapped to a knife-like sharpness and deeply embedded in a good ash handle. She had made it herself and it was well-balanced in her hand.

Turning in her saddle, she chopped wildly at the face of the Pawnee clutching her. A satisfying stream of blood issued from the wound though he did not let go. Indeed, he was almost at the point where he could get a better grip and drag White Rain from her pony. With one desperate swing, her whole body behind the blow, she buried the hatchet in the Pawnee's open mouth, cleaving through teeth and soft tissue until grating to a stop on his spinal column. He was dead in the saddle and fell heavily into the flying dirt. White Rain was pleased at her handiwork and screeched her victory song. She could see why the men loved war so much – it made them feel so alive amongst so much death. She rode onwards seeking more victims.

For the first four villages along the river, this tactic worked well. Guards were surprised and overcome as a growing wave of stolen ponies crashed into their own stock. The seed of panic in the horses spread rapidly and the ever swelling wave of horseflesh thundered on according to plan. Nearing the fifth village, there was more light in the sky and the drumming of so many hooves brought alerted Pawnee families tumbling from their sleep.

From the back of her plunging pony White Rain, now with three kills to her credit, controlled her group, occasionally stopping to make sure they were all accounted for. Then, kicking her mount back into motion, she rode beside the herd of stolen stock. As the first light of dawn caught the backs of the milling, snorting avalanche of ponies, she was surprised to see that they were of poor quality. Better ones would be picketed outside the tipis of their Pawnee owners. They would be better prizes. It was then that White Rain made her fateful decision. Calling to her companions to ride on, she charged alone into the small cluster of skin lodges.

A tall Pawnee warrior was already on the back of a sleek, black hunting pony outside the nearest lodge, nocking an arrow onto his bow. White Rain hit him with the full force of her stocky sorrel. The black horse screamed and reared in alarm then fell sideways, on top of its owner against the taut skins and lodgepoles. The black horse quickly regained its feet, trained to do so by its master. Unfortunately, its master was now under its rear hooves and yelled in pain and indignity. White Rain, excited by her success, grabbed the reins of the black horse and rode off screeching in triumph. The black horse would be a great trophy.

This was short lived. After a short distance her sorrel suddenly stopped, badly winded by its recent collision. Unprepared for the perverse nature of horses, White Rain Woman was dragged from the saddle by the charging black pony and crashed to the ground. The rein slipped from her hand and she found herself alone and on foot in a hostile Pawnee village.

The people listened intently to White Rain's account. Most were torn in their feelings – they admired her and her sister warriors for being on the war trail at all; it was a fine achievement and they had brought back many horses. But amongst the elderly there was some sucking of teeth and knowing nods as they realised that she had put herself in peril by disobeying the pipeholder.

Badlands Walking Woman had no such doubts. She was afire with the story; she envied the bravery of the slim young woman and guiltily wished that she hadn't been pregnant at the time. Bright Antelope Woman was less impressed. She snored lightly, her head leaning on Badland's shoulder.

As the next group in the battle, the youths took up the story. Their version was an excited, funny and often confused account of their deeds. Though attempts were made to restrain them by Smoke and Bad Elk, they got to their feet as a group and acted out the many incidents that had characterised their personal war with the Pawnee. This undisciplined and unconventional way of storytelling was taken with good humour by all. The boys mimicked charging the villages, the faces of the shocked Pawnee, the charging horses and the killing of their enemies. The villagers hooted their approval.

When it came to relating a killing or counting coup, the boys quietened down and stood aside to let their companions tell their own tales. Smoke motioned to each one that they should hoist the ceremonial pipe to the four cardinal points to denote that their words were true. It was not a time for bravado or lies. The small group had probably killed three of the enemy, wounded four more and could number ten coup counts between them. This account was done shyly and honestly by those concerned. None had stopped to take scalps, they could only judge by what they had seen happen or what was corroborated by others – flashes of action from the back of a running pony. A glow of pride settled on the audience, their young had not let them down.

Two Talks was his usual loquacious self. He made much of his part with the rifle stolen from the *vehoe* wagons. Two Pawnee had fallen to his bullets; he had mastered the art of reloading in the saddle and gave a comic version of this to the enthralled onlookers, making a wry face at the taste of the spare lead bullets in his mouth as he spat them down the hot barrel of his gun. His bow and arrows had ended two more Pawnee lives and he had delayed long enough to count coup on three others. He threw a captured shield into the circle and dramatically ground it under his heel. Always a crowd pleaser, Two Talks sat down grinning.

Surprisingly, Viajero stood up. He had not engaged many of the camp inhabitants previously in conversation and it was widely assumed that his Cheyenne language skills were poor. This was largely true but a special occasion demanded a special effort. An expectant silence fell. On the first row of the seated crowd, Badlands Walking Woman nudged Bright Antelope until she was fully awake.

In his own version of the ancient Cheyenne tongue, Viajero, the White Mountain Apache, spoke to his new family:

"My friends, the mighty words of the *Tsis-tsis-tas* stumble from my mouth like an infant learning to walk but I would speak…"

Young girls, summoned to carry the feast pots amongst the people, paused as the staccato whisper of the dark skinned one from the south reached their ears. Many had not heard him speak before; his voice was almost like a sighing wind with small, explosive grunts for emphasis. It was very alien to them.

"…It was an honour to ride with your warriors to the land of the *Chahiksichahik..*"

Viajero used the Pawnees' own word for themselves – Men of Men. It was a small conceit that was well received by those who understood it. Elders translated the word for the young ones.

"…and to fight alongside them. My own part in the battle was of little account; I killed some of the enemy but I cannot say how many for, as the son of Smoke on the Moon will tell you, I cannot count in Cheyenne..."

Viajero paused, he had practised this part of his speech. See the Dark smiled – the Traveller had made a joke! People murmured their appreciation. More wood was placed on the fire and the scene was illuminated as it blazed. A spiral of sparks twisted heavenwards.

"…As you know I come from the hot country to the south; from the land of the *N'de*. My first family is dead and my home burnt. My home is now here and I was happy to take the war trail with your warriors. My new child will be raised in the Cheyenne way. I salute the *Tsis-tsis-tas*!"

The audience hooted its approval. Bright Antelope Woman glowed with pride; it had taken some very swift lessons with Badlands Walking Woman to get Viajero's speech right. She gnawed happily at a cooked rabbit leg and burped.

Next came See the Dark. His parents watched intently as their son, once dismissed as having no future, rose to tell his own tale. His mother held back a tear as a shadow of the young warrior's shy, boyhood smile crept across his lean and angular face. Badlands looked closely at her son's sunken cheeks – he needed feeding up.

See the Dark, already tall, stood at the fire; his father's air of authority replicated in his offspring. Now almost eighteen, he carried himself with the bearing of an older and more experienced man. This was no surprise to his devoted mother but Smoke only saw this for the first time in the light of that victory fire.

Dark spoke sparingly and modestly. He thought that he had only killed four or five Pawnee in the entire sweep of the villages. But had counted coup on six others and had captured a lance from an impressive Pawnee warrior who had almost killed him with it. Unusually, he referred to Viajero as his war companion and narrated a brief account of how the Traveller had helped capture the Pawnee lance. Viajero sat impassively, staring into the firelight and did not add to the story. There was much nodding of appreciative heads in the crowd as Viajero became ever more accepted into the small *Suhtai* band.

See the Dark stopped in his story telling; his part in the battle had seemed to him to be short and simple. His account reflected his feelings. For a moment, he stood and took in the scene – the smiling, bronzed faces of his family and friends aglow in the firelight, the wisps of steam coming from the replenished cooking vessels and the scattering of gnawed bones from the food. Camp dogs, given as recent presents to replace the ones eaten during the hard and hungry time, circled and pounced on their share of the bounty.

Dark stole a shy glance to his right. It did not go unnoticed by his ever-vigilant mother who focused on the object of her son's gaze. He was looking at White Rain Woman. The young widow smiled back and showed strong, white teeth. Using her hand in a scooping motion, she urged Dark to continue his story. The young Cheyenne warrior then told the piece of the story that he had omitted.

Dark had ridden furiously through the string of villages, anxious to do his share of the killing. Viajero rode at his side, keeping up a high rate of fire from his Sharps rifle as he quickly chambered cartridge after cartridge into the breech.

Dark had exhausted his supply of arrows and now rode with his bow and rifle slung across his back. In his right hand he wielded his war hatchet; not a simple axe but the iron head of a discarded shovel that his father had found years ago. Burnished to glittering brightness and bound tight with sinew to a new wooden shaft, it had been ground down with stone into three cruel blades at right angles to the handle. As the killing mist came down on him, he slashed out at anyone on foot who came near, burying the blades into flesh and bone and then jerking it free with the rawhide loop tied to his wrist.

It was while he was lashing out on either side of his wheeling pony, as Pawnee warriors came to tear him from the saddle, that he heard someone call his name. It was not the Traveller; Dark could hear the crashing of his friend's heavy rifle to his rear. His name was called again, from slightly ahead of his horse. It was a woman's voice.

He swung his pony towards the sound, across the milling swirl of children and women running for cover, their ragged breath and sweating exertions causing clouds of steam and breath to rise. There, difficult to spot in the fleeing throng, stood White Rain who had run to the side of the encampment in the hope of seeing comrades pass by. She was completely ignored by the Pawnee villagers who did not have time to register that an enemy stood amongst them.

Dark spurred his pony towards her and, as his training rides with Bear Runs came back to him, he formed his left arm and elbow into a triangular loop and hooked his thumb onto his rawhide belt. He leaned out from his saddle to the left. Yelling above the tumult, he drove his horse hard towards the young widow. He hoped she would know what to do.

It had been a perfect rescue of an unhorsed warrior. White Rain saw him coming and slashed the front of her deerskin skirt with her hunting knife – she would need every inch of freedom of movement to spring onto the back of Dark's pony. Dark had braced himself for the collision of flesh and bone as the woman's arm had locked into his. The speed of the pony whipped White Rain off her feet and sent her flying onto the rump of the horse where she scrabbled and clawed at Dark's shoulder and braided hair until she was seated firmly astride the pad saddle behind him. She shrieked in her joy and excitement; Dark winced at the unexpected sound in his ear.

Dark sat down but continued to look steadily at White Rain on the other side of the shallow semi-circle; she smiled and cast down her eyes. She looked coquettish and beguiling. Badlands Walking Woman noticed the intensity of the exchanged looks and now knew that there was more between her son and the widow than just a shared saddle on a war pony.

The celebration fires remained lit for four days and gradually the whole village came to know the overwhelming nature of their warriors' victory over the hated Pawnee.

After the military societies had spoken of their part in the fight, it became apparent that this section of the attack had caused the most Pawnee casualties. The experienced warriors had ridden amongst the disoriented and panicking Pawnee families and had killed at every opportunity. Their bullets, arrows and lances had not spared women or children. The Cheyenne soldiers were not here for captives; they came for revenge and found it aplenty on the hard soil of the Loup riverbanks.

During this killing time, a few had forgotten their pipeholders' instructions - that they were to use surprise and numbers to rip through the other villages. They had to be beaten away from getting involved in localised fighting by Smoke and Broken Knife in order to overwhelm the next small settlement. Organised fighting came hard to the Cheyenne.

The soldiers though stressed the difficulty of the fight – the Pawnee did not run away like startled prairie chickens. They ran to get their weapons to cover the retreat of their families and then ran to find their ponies to come back into the fight. Both the Thunder Bears and the Striking Snakes admitted that Maheo had been merciful to them. Those who had prayed that the One-Above and his spirit helpers should protect them, now went off and conducted private ceremonies of thanksgiving, cutting off small slivers of flesh from biceps and forearms as promised blood tokens.

The public hearing of the war deeds was over but there were so many battle honours to be remembered that Bad Elk, Yellow Bear, Smoke and Broken Knife asked each participant with a claim to a coup or killing to re-tell their tales. This was done a few days after the main feast so the surviving wounded could take part. And so, every youth, woman and warrior that had taken part in the battle was accorded the right to wear the markings of their war honours that they claimed. An overriding honesty pervaded, no-one made any false claims but all could paint or fashion some form of symbol that allowed honourable remembrance of their part in the great battle against the Pawnee on the Loup River.

All five of the wounded came from the military societies as they had attacked after the element of surprise had been lost and the Pawnee had started to re-organise and retaliate. Two of those warriors had since died from wounds so the wailing of the relatives of the dead struck a sombre note into the happy temperament of the village.

None of the missing Cheyenne women and children had been recovered. Both Smoke and Broken Knife felt uneasy at this, as if something had been taken away from their complete victory. Whilst Smoke's plan had worked well, he had not considered anything beyond fighting. The Cheyenne prisoners would have had months of Pawnee dominance by the time the attack was launched – their appearance and dress would have changed beyond mere physical identification. Some would have accepted their new life, others would still resent it but would have been unable to escape and meet up with the charging Cheyenne. Yet others may have been back in the main earth lodges, well away from the hunting villages. All this was unknowable to Smoke but it soured the sweetness of victory in his mouth.

Bad Elk's band now faced the coming winter with restored confidence and pride. Though the Cheyenne could not be sure that Stone Turtle had been amongst the dead, the Pawnee would take years to recover from the blow. They would not tempt fate a second time against the might of the People. Even better, Bad Elk had decided that his *Suhtai* band would join the rest of the Cheyenne nation in their annual gathering next summer. He had already sent riders out to proclaim victory to the other bands. Now they could meet and celebrate as one family.

Book Three

Chapter Thirty

---- o o o ----

Henry Armstrong had been found out. He fumed inwardly as he rode across the northern Sioux country towards Fort Pierre, a week's ride away on the Missouri River. The young Englishman still rode with the 2nd US Dragoons' column as they followed Brigadier General Harney to their winter quarters but he had been removed from command of his troop.

Henry had not disgraced himself. Far from it; during the recent fight with Little Thunder's band of Brule Lakota down on Blue Water Creek, he had acquitted himself well. He had led his troop with 'dash and verve' as his commanding officer, Lieutenant Colonel Cooke, had been moved to write in his report to General Harney after the action.

It had been a glorious chase after panic-stricken Indians and Armstrong's pistol and sabre had been busy during the rout, helping to raise the tally of Sioux corpses to eighty-five. The Sioux had known the soldiers were coming but left their escape too late. They had been caught in heavy fire from the infantry in the hills and had fled directly into the jaws of the closing trap provided by Cooke's Dragoons. The fight had been the perfect recompense for the massacre of Lieutenant Grattan and his twenty-nine men the previous year.

But Cooke's praises had sunk Armstrong. Harney, the expedition commander had demanded to know why an English officer had been commanding American troops; national pride had been imperilled. He had ordered Armstrong's removal to logistical duties, out of harm's way. Harney, like many senior officers, was also a politician; if Armstrong had been killed on active service with his Dragoons, there could be much more severe diplomatic repercussions with the government of Great Britain. So Henry had been reduced to what the British Army called a 'supernumerary'. Henry's own description of the status was more prosaic as he had complained to his fellow officers – 'It's like being a spare prick on a honeymoon – nothing to do and bugger-all use'.

So now, huddled against the early chills of winter and riding slowly along the line of the White River, Henry Armstrong – English cavalryman, erstwhile US Dragoon and killer of America's enemies – found himself without a job. But three hundred years of breeding from his ferocious and cunning forebears never left Henry downhearted for long. He was already plotting to use his newly found independence. He would seek a place in some other mounted unit on another Plains campaign. The Sioux had been humbled and it didn't take a mathematician to figure out that the Cheyenne would be next.

On a spring day in 1857, Henry Armstrong admired himself in the mirror. At long last the US Army seemed to be taking campaigning on the Great Plains far more seriously; equipment seemed to be getting better. Gone was the squashed, rather shapeless cap of the Dragoons in his past life – a useless piece of clothing in Henry's view – replaced by the Hardee hat; a brimmed, black felt campaign hat designed specifically for the newly formed US Cavalry. It not only looked better but it was practical. It would keep the sun out of his eyes and the rain off his head. The right side was hooked up to the crown by a brass eagle and contained a small, black plume. Henry smiled at himself; yes, it would suit him very well as a temporary member of the United States First Regiment of Cavalry.

His transfer from the 2nd US Dragoons to the 1st Cavalry had been achieved with relative ease. The Dragoons had been glad to offload him, not because he was bad at his job but because Henry was a political embarrassment. Brigadier General Harney did not want to offend the Department of the Army but neither did he want a young English Cavalry officer coming to grief on one of his expeditions. No, better to palm him off onto those that were less politically aware

– the new First Cavalry would be ideal, they were already short-handed; they could have him. The Colonel commanding the 1st Cavalry, Edwin Vose Sumner, would respond favourably to Harney's suggestion to take along a battle-tested officer, even if he was English. The internal machinations of the US high command did not interest Henry; he was just delighted to be back on active service.

Henry looked out of his window onto the blue grass pasture to the south of Fort Leavenworth. New horses for the cavalry were constantly arriving, being saddle broken by experienced troopers then turned out to graze on the luxuriant stems.
Recruits to the regiment, some of whom had only just arrived from Jefferson Barracks a few days ago, spent all the daylight hours training for war. Equipment was renewed, clothing issued, weapons cleaned and supply wagons fitted up for service on the Plains. There was much to be done and not a little nervousness about how well they would perform in any coming battles.

Henry had no such worries; he already knew what fighting Indians was like. He had accepted with good grace his attachment to the commissary and quartermaster's section. The young man temporarily in charge, Lieutenant Stuart, seemed to know his business and was an excellent horseman.

Later that day, Henry joined the assembly of regimental officers as Colonel Sumner outlined the plan. Henry liked the plan for its boldness and simplicity – the combined force would sweep and destroy the Cheyenne between two rivers - the Platte and the Arkansas.

Sumner's booming voice resonated confidence and aggression; the expedition would ride out in two columns – his own to the north and west along the Platte towards Fort Laramie and Major Sedgewick's to the south, roughly following the Arkansas River before heading northwest to rendezvous with Sumner on the South Platte.

They would sweep borders of the Cheyenne country and bring them to battle. If that failed they would join forces and thrust deep into the heart of the Smoky Hill country and destroy the Indians wherever they could be found. The Cheyenne were to be severely punished for their depredations of the previous year along the Platte River Road.

As Lieutenant Stuart was assigned to Sumner's column, Henry found himself attached to the northern force. His heart sank slightly as he realised the implications. Happily, there would be two companies of cavalry but Sumner would also be travelling with a ponderous line of fifty wagons, spare horses and mules as well as the commissary beef herd. It wasn't a column designed for fast pursuit of mounted and belligerent Cheyennes. However, Henry wisely bit his lip and said nothing. Perhaps if it came to a battle he could be spared from the commissary lines to use his sabre and pistol.

In the early twilight, Henry wandered out of the post. He often joined in the carousing that the younger officers used to vent to their energies but not tonight. He was in a more contemplative mood. He saw the glow of a cheroot near one of the wagons that was silhouetted against the sunset sky and strolled over. It was the wagon master for the expedition, Mr Lowe. Lowe's opinion was worth listening to. He offered Armstrong a cheroot.

Lowe found Henry's blunt English accent a curiosity and questioned him about his family and military background; Henry, normally affronted by such personal probing, was relaxed and patient. Service to the United States government had mellowed him considerably; the more informal ways of the Americans, especially the Westerners was almost engaging, even relaxing. Though, of course, it would never do to have them to dinner at home.

To his surprise, Lowe spoke of the Cheyennes as human beings and he knew something about them - their way of life, religious beliefs and even their superiority as horsed warriors. It was the first time the Henry had learnt that the Cheyenne names for rivers were different to the English versions.

The translations of the Cheyenne words brought home to the young Englishman just who the real inhabitants of this vast country were.

Henry's sympathies were not, and could not be, fully with the Indians; after all the United States was merely colonising a land they had acquired, just as his own nation continued to do worldwide. But it just seemed unrealistic to expect the Cheyenne and all the other tribes to sit back and meekly accept this domination by foreigners. No, they would fight - and Henry was glad. Henry Armstrong would still kill as many Indians as he could find but he would not bear a grudge if one of their arrows or bullets ended his life. As a professional soldier, it seemed to be a fair trade. The excitement of living life to the full as a young man in return for an early but glorious death – Henry was sure the Cheyenne would understand that.

That night, Henry did an unusual thing - he prayed. His prayer was a simple invocation – if there was to be any action, he wanted to be in it. Ungratefully, he added that he hoped Sedgewick's more mobile column to the south would not find any hostiles. God must have been in a good mood; Henry Armstrong's prayers were answered to the letter.

Chapter Thirty One

---- o o o ----

"Fat dog weather," said Henry, trying to prompt a conversation. Lomax struggled back from the brink of snoozing:

"What?"

"This heat, it's like a fat dog lying across your face. Actually happened to me once; damn thing nearly suffocated me."

In truth, Henry could never remember exactly what had happened as he'd only been old enough to crawl around the floor at the time. But the cook had told him later – he'd fallen asleep, nose down in a litter of puppies, and the old Labrador bitch had wandered back into the kitchen and sprawled across her brood, her belly covering Henry's face. He had felt the body heat first and then the numbing weight that stopped him opening his mouth to breathe. Cook had hauled him out as he was turning purple.

"Well, there's no fat dog here. Just horses, steers and stinking mules," observed Lomax testily, sitting half up and resting himself on one elbow. Parched dust covered the back of his blue campaign shirt as though he'd been dragged through a flour mill. Not that Henry looked any better; a sunburned triangle of skin showed through his pants leg, his boots were scuffed and caked with dried mud and the brim of his Hardee hat clung on to the brass eagle that fixed it in place against the crown. Lomax took a pull from his canteen and offered it. The water was warm and tasted of lye, Henry swished it around his mouth then spat into the dust, the dark splash drying quickly under the white hot sky.

"Hard to believe we had rain, hail and a tornado only three days ago," said Henry conversationally. "I thought you and Sedgwick's boys would never find a place to cross the damn river."

"We weren't supposed to join you, your column was meant to join *us,"* answered Lomax and rubbed the hair beneath his hat brim energetically, dust particles cascading out and revealing that he wasn't actually grey before his time. "Not our fault that the Old Man didn't want to get his feet wet."

Henry lay back, contented as a man with holes in his pants and dust inside his shirt could be. Lomax's grumbling was almost soothing. Soldiers always grumbled, it was as natural as breathing. The two columns of the expedition had, at least, arrived on the South Platte at the appointed date. Henry had heard Sedgwick's column before it came into sight – a thirty one gun salute from their mountain howitzers had boomed downriver to celebrate the Fourth of July. But it had taken another three days before a safe ford across the river could be found and the columns re-united.

It had been good to see everyone again; handshakes and backslapping and telling of tales. Neither of the columns had had much excitement, though a buffalo stampede against Sedgwick's four cavalry companies had 'almost required a change of underwear' according to Lomax. Only the coolness of Captain Sturgis in organising a wedge of troopers firing continuously into the approaching animals prevented them from being trampled into a bloody slick on the floor of the Arkansas Valley.

"Did you see any Cheyenne?" asked Henry, noting the lye taste was still there in his mouth and spitting again.

"Not a Goddamn one," replied Lomax. "None that were alive anyway, just a few burial lodges. Even those could have belonged to some other tribe of gut eaters." Lomax held all Indians as savages and he wasn't alone in that view. "We saw plenty of Arapaho though. They were pretty peaceable but wouldn't tell us much about where the Cheyenne were."

"Just to be expected I suppose, "said Henry "I hear that they've been allies with the Cheyenne for a long while now." But he was speaking to empty air, Lomax had turned on his side and was snoring gently.

Henry lay back too and watched a red kite wheel in the sky. His own march with Sumner's column had also lacked action. To Henry, it was pointless being a soldier if pistols remained in holsters and sabres unsheathed. Of course, it was exciting to ride out on the Plains with a full-blown punitive expedition but seven hundred uneventful and weary miles in the saddle had taken the edge off his enthusiasm. He looked down to the riverbank as the notes of the bugle reached him.

He nudged Lomax in the small of the back with his boot tip. "Officers' Call, Lunsford. Shift yourself."

Lomax yawned, scratched and rammed his campaign hat on his head. The dust flew and trickled down onto his moustache.

"We'd better get down there," said Henry. "I'd hate to be late for one of the Old Man's speeches."

The two men made their way down to the river, blowing down their nostrils as the dust rose, for even careful steps caused swirls.

Henry took his half-hunter from his pocket and flipped the protective cover from the glass. It was almost noon and the light was twisted out of true. The ground was simmering as though on top of an underground stove. If he listened carefully, he was sure he could *hear* the heat, like a single bass string being strummed some way off. Shapes flickered and shimmered; he had to concentrate for a few seconds on everyday objects just so he could identify them properly.

Cavalry horses stood on rope lines in company order, tails swishing against biting flies; troopers groomed their mounts or walked them down to water as their turn came. Further off the white tents of the infantry looked as if they were floating in the air, their ropes pinned only to a miasma. Beyond them the mules, the *remuda* of spare horses and beef herd spread across the bare hills, though none strayed too far from the river.

Henry sat down and then shifted uncomfortably as sharp grass stubble poked through the thinning fabric of his cavalry pants. He pulled a leather bound journal out of his campaign shirt and sat on it. He'd done this so many times that the imprint of his backside was starting to show as two polished crescents on the dull hide; the damn thing was as getting as curved as a saddle seat.

Lomax collapsed beside him and tried to snooze again, stretched out on the unyielding tussocks. He had wrapped a dirty muslin square around his face to keep the flies off. The cover rose and fell over his mouth as his breathing evened out. Henry let him be. Yesterday, to celebrate the meeting on the river, Lomax and George Bayard had swum to the north bank, to symbolically join the command together again. Though the South Platte was only around four feet deep at that point, it was fast flowing and about a half-mile wide. Troopers had cheered them on, clapping as they emerged exhausted from the river, clothes bundles held in their teeth. He deserved a sleep.

Fellow officers arrived and sat down, cursing and slapping as mosquitoes rose from the river and homed in on fresh blood. Soon pipe smoke billowed out to ward off the whining assault.

A stocky, barrel-chested man strode over, accompanied by a nervous looking note taker. Henry nudged Lomax awake. The Colonel stopped in front of the sprawl of dusty blue uniforms and stood with his hands on his hips. One or two made a half-hearted attempt to rise as he arrived but he impatiently waved them back to the ground.

"This is no way to conduct a war, gentlemen - two months in the saddle, seven hundred miles and fifty broken down men. Even worse - not one Goddamn Cheyenne has been brought to book."

Edwin Vose Sumner always spoke in a booming voice, as though he was in a theatre and had to project to the distant cheap seats. It was a commendable tone for battle but close up, it shook back teeth and rattled nerves.

Henry rolled his eyes in exasperation, though he was careful not to let his Colonel see it. Sumner was a good Commanding Officer but tetchy about small things like unexplained grimaces or doubtful looks. He thought that they betrayed a lack of confidence in his leadership and was always on the lookout for such slights. Still, Sumner made sure that he shared the hardships of such marches with his men and that stacked up well with the rank and file. They would follow him anywhere.

The Colonel strode back and forth in the dry grass tussocks, the dust rising and settling on his boots:

"Boys, our scouts tell us that the Cheyenne are gathering south of the Republican. We've seen neither hide nor hair of 'em so far but now they're gaining comfort in numbers – just like these damn skeeters."

He swatted the insects away from his face. "We're here to punish and, by God, punish we will. The Cheyenne have stopped avoiding us and now they're just waiting for us to come calling – so let's not disappoint 'em."

Of course the Cheyenne would be waiting for them. They had known that the Army was coming since before the expedition set out. What did the Old Man expect? Futile scouring along the Platte and Arkansas was one thing. Now it was going to get serious, the untested 1st US Cavalry was about to invade sacred Cheyenne homelands. You could lay good money that they'd be waiting.

Wiping his brow, Henry ran greasy fingers through his long hair and stroked his emerging beard, though it was barely more than long stubble. He wished his moustache could have been more evident; it was the curse of the fair skinned. The expedition had left Leavenworth over eight weeks ago and his whiskers evoked no manly pride at all. It looked like he just needed a damn good wash.

The gold signet ring from his mother was grimed with sweat and dust. Its rich shine had given way to a dull yellow glow that barely reflected light; the oval face, with his intials 'HLA', was scratched and pitted from constant work with saddlery and harness. His mother, a great believer in the social graces, would throw a conniption fit if she could see him now in his dusty blues, sitting on the very journal that she had instructed him to keep. His meat-bound intestines blasted belly gas onto the tome as an additional insult.

Henry's mind wandered then snapped back. Damn! Someone was asking a question about rations and the estimated time of finding the Cheyenne. Daydreaming had meant that he had missed the answer but he stole a glance across at the culprit. He should have guessed that it would be Frank Wheaton; a dull man, at least in Henry's view, obsessed by columns of figures. Henry mentally shot him with an extended finger.

Henry lit a cheroot and looked round at his companions – good sorts most of 'em, if you kept them away from the drink. Several notorious topers in the Regiment now looked almost healthy as hard living drove the sutler's whiskey out of their guts. Even the Frock Coat Militia, the contemptible shiny britches with a love of desk work and hearts set on influential staff postings in Washington, only complained in private.

Sumner had paused and was sitting on the ground, deep in conversation with Wheaton and Lieutenant Stuart, the acting quartermaster. The sprawlers remained lounging in the sun, some with hats over their eyes; Henry lay on his back, the journal now a pillow. It was too hot to look eager and attentive for long.

"Well, bean wrangler, whaddya think?"

Henry peered from under his hat brim at Lunsford Lomax.

"I think you should have done us all a great service and shot Frank Wheaton when you were both with Sedgewick's column. And don't call me a bean wrangler; I'm the Assistant Commissary officer."

Lomax grinned: "I meant, what do you think about going after the Cheyenne? You've fought Indians before – how's it all going to come out?"

Henry sat up and eyed Lomax suspiciously, as if he hadn't asked a serious question. Still, the chance to deliver advice to those too slow witted to move away wasn't to be missed:

"How will it come out? Well, let me see – the Cheyenne can ride better than most of these mounted ploughboys. Their horses can eat this scrub grass and thrive, while ours need to be stuffed with oats just to get them moving. The Indians know the country inside out and what else…? Oh yes, they'll be fighting to protect their families on home soil. There, I think that does it."

"We're screwed then?" said Lomax.

"You're damn right."

"But the 2nd Dragoons defeated the Sioux up on Blue Water Creek two years ago. Indians aren't invincible," persisted Lomax.

"No," admitted Henry, "there we managed to get close enough to trap them and panic 'em into running. The infantry flushed them out and straight into the path of the Dragoons."

Henry remembered the thrill of the running fight with the Brulé Lakota of Little Thunder. It had been his first time in action. The Dragoons had wreaked havoc amongst fleeing families with pistol and sabre and the new rifles of the infantry picked off those that tried to hide in the limestone cliff caves. Later, when the details of Grattan's arrogant dealings with the Sioux emerged, Henry thought that the Indians had got a rough deal.

A cloud of small black specks sped towards him and he blew a stream of blue smoke as discouragement. The insects ploughed through it and bit him anyway. He fanned them away with his hat, adjusting the brass eagle on the pinned up brim. The black plume had long ago been battered into submission and whisked away by the constant wind on the Great Plains.

Lomax was about to speak again when there was ripple of movement from the Colonel and his staff. Sumner got up and strode onto a small hummock. The waiting officers looked up:

"Our combined columns will form one, fast-moving field force and push south east to find these heathens. The wagons, sick men and the broken down horses will be sent back to Fort Laramie. We'll take six companies of cavalry, three of infantry, a pack mule train with the beef herd and the howitzers. I'll re-organise the command accordingly and I want us to be heading for the Republican in less than a week. We'll rendezvous with a supply train in twenty days. My written orders will follow; you are dismissed to your duties, Gentlemen."

A short, sweet soldier's speech and, at least, Sumner would get rid of the damn encumbrances in order to increase their speed of march. Henry rose stiffly and brushed the fine dust from his shirt. Cheroot dangling from his lip, he saluted as Lieutenant Stuart walked up to join him. Stuart was about to speak when Henry remembered the cheroot; he ripped the stub from his mouth and saluted again.

"Why Henry, you are the very model of military correctness in the field and a fine example to us uncultured Americans." Stuart smiled through his Virginia lilt.

Henry replied in kind. "Well, Mister Stuart, you will know that my attachment to this expedition was not only for my Indian fighting skills but to raise the social tone of this Regiment. Old Bull-of-the-Woods," - Henry gestured towards Sumner - "particularly said that I should concentrate on the sorrier specimens, such as your good self."

James E.B. Stuart laughed. Henry Armstrong had a way with insults that made men welcome them.

"Well Henry, none of us look too fashionable right now. Why, my poor Momma would die of embarrassment if she saw how many patches I had on my shirt. She has a great interest in nature but I doubt that it extends to seeing her son's buttocks hanging out of his britches."

It was to be only a short moment of camaraderie. Stuart led Henry off to one side and put a hand on his shoulder.

"But there is a cloud in the sky, old friend. When we march out again, I'll be getting my company back. Heading up the Commissary and being the acting Quartermaster is not really my style so it will be a parting of the ways. Frank Wheaton will be your new boss. And Henry, do try to treat him delicately – he is sadly lacking in the humour department."

Henry gaped in disappointment. Plodding along with the commissary wagons for seven hundred miles along the Platte had been made bearable by Jeb Stuart's good humour. Sparkling repartee was not Wheaton's strong suit. Finding the Cheyenne couldn't come soon enough.

"But what about me?" Henry asked, his voice verging on a whine. "I'm one of the few here who've actually fought Indians. With fifty men going back to Laramie we'll need every man in the saddle that can handle a pistol and sabre."

"Now Henry," said Stuart, shaking his head "We all know that you defeated the Sioux almost single handed but glory must be shared. The Glorious First must cut its own crop of the red devils." He adopted a mock theatrical pose, the back of his palm across his forehead and stared at the sky.

"I inherited the gift of prescience from my Great Aunt Maude back in Patrick County, before she took up with the snake-oil salesman and fell into bad ways. I can foresee the future – for me there will be glory but for you there will only be dust and mule shit. Enjoy yourself!" Stuart clapped him on the shoulder and walked off laughing.

"Bollocks," said Henry Leviticus Armstrong to no-one in particular.

Chapter Thirty Two

---- o o o ----

A visitor had ridden into bad Elk's camp. The man was a Pledger from the *Omissis* band of the Cheyenne and he brought great news; a Medicine Lodge and Sun Dance was to be pledged deep in the heart of the Cheyenne country. All bands were to attend and join their kinfolk for the great celebration; all were to move together towards the Red Shield River where the ceremonies would last eight days.

It was just the news that Bad Elk had been waiting for. His band had camped safely south of the Tallow River for the winter after the war party had returned from the attack on the Pawnee villages. Outside his lodge he sat and smoked with the Pledger and proudly told him of their recent victory against the Honehetaneo. This feat should be recognised by the wider Cheyenne family, Bad Elk's soldier societies had much wisdom to impart on warfare. The Pledger had agreed and nodded thoughtfully:

"It's good to hear that you have done well against our enemies, though the Dog Soldiers may not like it. They are usually at the forefront of any Cheyenne fighting."

"Well, we did ask for help but they decided to stay away. Anyway, we Suhtai can fight our own battles" said Bad Elk, nettled that the Pledger had mentioned the Dog Soldiers as though they were the only ones capable of battle. He decided on a mischievous approach:

"We didn't need the Dog Soldiers as our women and children also fought in the Loup battle; it was more than enough for the Pawnee."

Bad Elk, his face impassive, watched the shock register on the Pledger's face and smiled inwardly. Tell *that* to those overpainted southerners, he thought.

Spring had been late this year and Bad Elk's village had moved from the muddy bottomlands to higher ground to avoid the run-off from the recent rain. Only now was grass growing to revive the horses and put them back in condition for the summer hunting season. Cottonwoods, hackberry and ash were also greening along the tributaries of the river where they camped. The move to the Red Shield River would bring them within easy reach of the southern buffalo herd and fine summer feasting with their families.

The Pledger, however, had brought Bad Elk other news that surprised him – many other bands of their northern families had also camped south of the Platte that winter. Some of the younger hotheads from other Cheyenne bands had been active and aggressive along the *vehoe* wagon routes in the late summer and early autumn of the previous year. There had already been one small battle with bluecoat soldiers last year and other confrontations would surely follow. The whites would want revenge.

Even whilst collecting their winter annuities from Bent's Fort, the southern bands of the Cheyenne had heard that soldiers would be coming after them. As a result, nervous and angry bands of the People had grouped together for security over the long winter months. According to the Pledger, all but one of the Cheyenne bands were now camped between the Tallow and the Flint Arrowpoint Rivers.

Bad Elk was astounded; his own band had not been blameless in the attacks on the whites, of course, but the few minor attacks on white wagons had merely been to arm his people for the battle with the Pawnee. The killings at the Pendleton wagons had been a necessary part of taking the supplies they needed. He had not heard of the widespread actions of his kinfolk. His band had no quarrel with the whites and he certainly did not want to stand against well-armed bluecoat soldiers unless he had to. He was pleased that the People would gather soon and decide what to do.

Chapter Thirty Three

---- o o o ----

"How many pack saddles?" asked Henry incredulously.

"A hundred, I believe" said the new Commissary Officer. "We have some but we'll have to make the rest."

"Make them? Jesus Christ, we needn't chase the Cheyenne now; they'll have died of old age by the time we get to the Republican."

"Now, now, Lieutenant Armstrong." Frank Wheaton never called him Henry. "We'll just have to get on with it."

Henry simmered as an uncomfortable silence fell. He already missed the cheery exchange of insults with Jeb Stuart.

Wheaton examined the crosstrees of a packsaddle, holding them up in the bright sunlight to see how they worked. He and Armstrong would have to try and get along; God knows how many miles they would have to ride together before the expedition finished. He tried a different conversational tack:

"Your middle name – I saw it on the muster roll. Leviticus is very Biblical – are your folks prominent in your church back home?"

"Well, they attend church of course. The parish church is on our land and my folks - er, my family has its own pews there. Have done for centuries. We sit at the front and all our workers sit behind us. It's just the natural order of things, old man. The Great and the Good and all that."

Henry smirked as he watched the morally upright Wheaton struggle to ignore the bait of the unacceptable social divide in a place of worship. Wheaton would not be drawn.

"Indeed, Lieutenant Armstrong, but your name? Leviticus?"

"Oh, that. Well, Leviticus is indeed from the Old Testament – the Revengers' Chronicle as my father calls it – it has that bit in it, you know: 'An eye for an eye and tooth for a tooth'. Revenge, you see."

"But why would a respectable and prominent Englishman like your father want to give you such a bloodthirsty name?"

This was the first time that Henry had ever heard his father referred to as respectable. In fact the old devil was a severe landlord to his tenants, a grinding skinflint and a lecherous scourge amongst the entire female community, the vicar's wife included.

"Well sir, my family were mounted raiders in the sixteenth Century in the English Borders. We were Border Reivers. And my father has a sense of family history that he likes to reflect in my names – so even Henry can be shortened to 'Harry', which can mean to pursue the enemy or to ravage land. So, Henry Leviticus covers all the options."

Wheaton looked uncomprehending and shocked. John Bulls were supposed to drink tea from fine china cups, hold civilised discourse on Shakespeare and Milton and generally set the social tone – not to blather on about bloodletting and revenge. Thank God for '76.

Henry though was now in his stride. He pulled up his right shirtsleeve to reveal a thin strip of red linen knotted around his pallid upper arm.

"See here – when I was baptised, my right arm was covered in this cloth. When they dipped me in the font, the linen was to make sure that none of the holy water touched my right arm. This is the bit they used when I was a baby; I wear it day and night. My father made me promise."

Wheaton was puzzled: "And that means..?"

"It means that my right arm was never included in any pact of Christian behaviour. I am free to strike my enemies with a clear conscience."

Henry rolled down his sleeve and laughed. It was the only thing that he had in common with his father, this love of their slightly disreputable family history. As a boy at home, he would sometimes be called to his father's study and together they would open the heavy, brass-bound family bible and trace the spidery ink lines of their violent ancestry.

With an illicit sip of whisky from his father's tumbler, centuries old stories linked to each name would be repeated – of murky nights in the saddle with a burning peat divot at the lancehead, of the killings and the plunder, the Hot Trod and the Debatable Lands. Henry's father would grow wistful and his eyes would fill – now all he had were his ledgers, troublesome tenants with their constant disputes and the rolling mossy acres of the Borderlands. It was no substitute for saddle and sword.

Frank Wheaton shuddered. These English ruffians were more like the damn Cheyenne than honest Americans.

Chapter Thirty Four

---- o o o ----

Scouts continued to report the movement of the soldiers on an almost daily basis. Two large columns of pony soldiers, wagons, large guns and walking soldiers had come together on the Fat River and were pushing through Cheyenne country to find the main village of the Tsis-tsis-tas. The scouts had seen their Army counterparts probing forward carefully, the column rolling slowly but inexorably behind them. Confrontation was only days away.

The place to fight the soldiers had now been decided – it would be on Turkeys Creek, not more than half a day's ride north of the village. Bad Elk had stood up in the council when this had been mentioned. It was impolite but he made an important point - the location of the impending battle was too close to the village. Even if all went well in the battle there was still the chance of the large soldier column splitting into smaller groups and finding the Cheyenne homes vulnerable and close.

All the council chiefs seemed taken with the persuasive talk of two young medicine men; they reassured Bad Elk that the young men's magic lake medicine would defeat the whites far away from the village. Unconvinced, Bad Elk rose again and demanded that the village be moved further away from the soldiers' line of march. He was pulled back down by Smoke and Broken Knife, embarrassed that their camp chief did not agree with the rest.

A Dog Soldier chief called out:

"The Suhtai chief, needn't be afraid – after all he will have his women and children here to fight for him."

The sarcasm was unmistakeable; the Pledger must have passed on his derogatory comments to the Dog Soldiers. Several in the great council gathering gasped at the rudeness but did not castigate the Dog Soldier who looked smugly triumphant. Bad Elk glared at him but said nothing more.

He was unsure too about the magic proposed by the two young medicine men as neither was known to him. The names of the two men were Ice, sometimes referred to as Hail, and Grey Beard, sometimes called Dark. Ice was of the Omissis band and Grey Beard was a Dog Soldier. Both were from apparently honourable families and enjoyed a high reputation for their spiritual powers. He didn't deny the fact that they had magic powers; they just had not been proven to him.

Whilst Bad Elk had doubts, Yellow Bear had none. He seemed to be the only one of the People who had flatly refused to believe their magical claims. He didn't trust the two upstarts and said so; he had dreamt about them and his dreams had confirmed his gut instinct – the two young Cheyennes who claimed to have magic powers were lying.

Bad Elk, Smoke on the Moon and Broken Knife returned from the latest gathering full of restive thoughts. The meeting had been conducted in an almost dreamlike way; Ice and Grey Beard were often the main speakers, vocally supported by the majority who longed for war. Only the old men were anxious but their weak voices were drowned out in the clamour for a clash of arms. Smoke and Broken Knife could speak up for themselves when they needed to but they too seemed overwhelmed by the aura of confidence in the magic powers of the two young men. Confidence bred lethargy, it was as though they were crawling down a narrow tunnel and could only head one way.

Bad Elk's head hurt with the complex decisions he had to make and wished that he had never been selected as chief. But he believed that he was right – he would find a way to maintain common cause with the Cheyenne decision to go to war whilst protecting his own small group. They had already suffered much during the recent past; he would not let them do so again.

The war leaders and chiefs now met every day to discuss what they would do. Confidence abounded in the great medicine of Ice and Grey Beard though, in private and only in the company of his own band, Yellow Bear continually reported his dreams about the young men; their powers were suspect and disaster would befall the Cheyenne.

Bad Elk, Smoke on the Moon and Broken Knife took Yellow Bear seriously. The medicine man's powers had indeed returned last year and had pointed them to the Pawnee lodges to help in their victory. Their spirit diviner could now find buffalo again and this had helped bring in communal fresh meat over the winter. It would be a foolish man that now spoke against Yellow Bear.

And yet, the two young Cheyennes that he took against were charismatic and seemed to speak with honesty. They claimed to have magic that would make the bullets of the *vehoe* have no power against the People. The lead balls would roll harmlessly out of the gun muzzles and fall to earth.

All the Cheyenne had to do, when the bluecoats came, was to wash in a special lake that the two young men could lead them to. The two aspirant medicine men also claimed to have a white powder that guaranteed the effectiveness of any shot fired from a Cheyenne gun. The young men had allied themselves with those wanting to fight the *vehoe* and their guarantee of safety for all those who fought was a powerful influence over the Cheyenne. Many wagons and columns of soldiers were riding across their sacred earth; only spilt *vehoe* blood would stop the relentless march. Ice and Grey Beard were right. So the Cheyenne turned to them and sought their magic.

All Bad Elk's subtle skills, of remaining at one with the majority of the Tsis-tsis-tas whilst heeding the pragmatic advice of his own band's spirit diviner, would be needed over the next few days. The Sun Dance and Medicine Lodge ceremonies were over but as they now were still grouped within the larger circle of Cheyenne lodges for communal hunting, outside opinion mattered. Yellow Bear's dreams would divide loyalties if they were made public. Bad Elk just hoped that the white soldiers would leave them alone so that the powers of Ice and Grey Beard would not need to be tested.

Chapter Thirty Five

---- o o o ----

"So what's in the journal, mule boy?" asked Jeb Stuart, leaning over and trying to grab the leather covered book. Henry grunted, said nothing and kept the journal out of his friend's reach.

"C'mon Henry. Let's see what you have to say about life on the trail with the US Cavalry."

Unsettled, Henry did as he always did with the book; he sat on it. But Stuart was in a playful mood. Others gathered round.

"We ride out tomorrow and I want to know if you have given us all a fair shake. I want to see poetic paragraphs of beautifully crafted prose about the nobility of comradeship in the cavalry, the dangers of the Great Plains and the sacrifices we may have to make when whipping the redskins. At the very least, I want to see that you've spelled my damn name right."

George Bayard dived at Henry and held him to the ground while Stuart slid the supple leather out from under Henry's rump. He ran to the light of a lantern hanging on a wooden pole at a corner of the officers' mess tent to get a better look. He flicked through several pages before he made the contents public:

"Gentlemen, I will now give you a full reading of the journal of Henry Leviticus Armstrong, late of Her Majesty's Light Dragoons – Entry One – '20 May 1857 – set off from Fort Leavenworth'. Entry Two – '6 July 1857 - arrived on the South Platte'. Hell, Henry, I've had laundry lists longer than this." Stuart and the others exploded with laughter.

George Bayard chipped in: "Two months in the saddle and only two sentences. Jesus, boy – at that rate the story of your entire life would fit on a whore's dance card."

Henry snatched the journal back, reddening slightly but recognising the atmosphere of camaraderie that always preceded a dangerous march. The mood of the assembled officers was light; the hard work preparing the expedition for a swift move to the Republican was done, they could relax a little. So he would indulge them:

"Gentlemen," Henry paused, "and in this company, I use the term loosely..."

There was a chorus of good-natured boos and catcalls; Stuart clapped appreciatively, others joined them from the mess tent to hear Henry expound his dubious theories. It was often good entertainment. English sarcasm had a cutting edge to it they liked.

"It is a well-known scientific fact that the brain of the average Englishman can hold up to ten times the amount of information than the head of the average colonial peasant, sorry – I mean, American officer."

Louder catcalls, groans; tufts of grass were thrown. Henry grinned, it was a good start.

"Thus, all the boring details that made up our trip along the Platte are firmly retained in here." He tapped the side of his head.

"I'll just fill them in later and the journal will read like a Penny Dreadful of a young hero's adventures in the wilderness. All I need do is to add a few more Indian attacks, some rescuing of damsels in distress and perhaps mention a few elephants – it'll sell like hot cakes."

Hooting and applause. Cigars, cheroots and pipe bowls glowed in the dusk. Sumner strolled from his ambulance to see what the commotion was about. Unrecognised, he sat at the back and watched the young Englishman go through his routine; the boy had done well with Brigadier Harney against the Sioux back in '55.

It was a pity that Harney had been such a politician instead of a soldier - he had removed Armstrong from combat duty after the Blue

Water fight and had him assigned him to less dangerous logistical work. Sumner had no intention of repeating that mistake – Armstrong, Englishman or not, had seen active service against hostile Plains tribes and would be useful when they found the Cheyenne.

Of course, he wouldn't tell him yet - it would do the boy no harm to sweat it out with the commissary for a few more days – dealing with mules built character.

Chapter Thirty Six

---- o o o ----

The three sat in silence in the sunshine a short distance from Smoke on the Moon's lodge; they had asked others to join them before Bad Elk's thoughts were to be aired. Bad Elk could not compel anyone to do his bidding, he would have to persuade and cajole to win support. He sighed; life was much easier when he had just been a hunter.

Badlands Walking Woman sat outside her lodge. Her new son lay next to her as she expertly fleshed an elk skin pegged out on the ground. The chubby brown limbs of the boy thrashed around in the summer warmth; an arc of urine rose skywards from the small form. Smoke looked across with pride. See the Dark came out of the lodge just in time to be splashed and grinned at his brother. White Rain Woman also emerged but she had not been pursuing any female duties. Instead she carried a bundle of newly straightened arrows and walked off to her own tipi.

Bright Antelope Woman, who carried her new daughter on a cradleboard, soon joined Smoke's wife. She sat down beside her and looked over to where the men were gathering:

"They look worried, is everything all right?"

"They're men, they like a simple life – they are happy to go to war but worry about their families" replied Badlands. "The battle with the soldiers must come soon but they are afraid that we are too close to the bluecoats if anything goes wrong."

Bright Antelope unswaddled her child from the cradleboard and lay her next to the boy; the babies mewled and grunted at each other. She mused a little:

"I thought that the magic of the Tsis-tsis-tas was strong and we would have no reason to fear…"

A tremor ran through her body as she remembered her treatment at the hands of the Pawnee. If the grassland people could be so cruel, what would the *indaa* be like?

Badlands put a comforting hand on her friend's shoulder:

"My husband says nothing about the battle except that all will be well. But he has had many long talks with his brother and Yellow Bear and always returns looking worried. I have never seen this in him before, even before they went off to attack the Pawnee."

She stopped talking and watched as others approached the willow tree where Smoke, Bad Elk and Broken Knife were waiting. Yellow Bear walked past her to the meeting place, his long strides on skinny legs were recognisable even in a busy camp. Viajero trotted in from the other side of a cutbank, as always, his Sharps rifle was in his right hand. See the Dark and White Rain strolled back to the group and sat down slightly apart from the others. Around them was a forest of multi-coloured lodges; tipi poles reaching up into the blue vastness of a perfect summer sky.

The large encampment teemed with life; riders trotted back and forth, hunting parties returned with meat and game whilst groups of relatives stood and gossiped. Yelling children and brindled dogs, both roaming in packs, raced around the lodges. In the background were the constant noises of the pony herd as horses whinnied, snorted and occasionally barged into neighbours that took their grass. Drying racks sagged under the weight of the summer abundance.

Bad Elk's meeting was not a gathering of elders or a formal council, he just wanted to express his thoughts and gather the opinions of others before speaking directly to the rest of the band. First, he asked all present to speak in turn and tell him their thoughts on the coming battle.

Both Smoke on the Moon and Broken Knife said that they would lead their military societies into battle against the pony soldiers.

They did not know whether the magic powers of Grey Beard and Ice would work but they were committed to defending the Cheyenne way of life and would ride out regardless. Bad Elk nodded but kept silent. The soldiers were responsible for war against the enemies of the Cheyenne – there could be no other response.

Bad Elk gestured to his nephew with his chin; the young man was starting to gain recognition and influence in the tribe and often had useful thoughts about weighty matters. His opinion would be of value. For his part, See the Dark was sure that the magic spell used when they washed in the lake would protect them against the bullets of the vehoe. He too would ride against the bluecoats.

Viajero, sitting on the outside of the circle, was surprised to be asked his opinion and carefully framed his response. He was unsure of the magic claimed by the young men but he now felt himself to be a part of the Cheyenne family – he would ride out with his friend, See the Dark.

Without waiting to be asked, White Rain Woman declared that she and her small band of female warriors, now grown to eight women, would also ride out against their enemies.

Bad Elk sucked his teeth in annoyance; this was new ground. Women were considered to be almost sacred within the tribe – they brought forth life and nurtured all those around them. He had had little objection when the Forked Lightning Women had gone off with the war party against the Pawnee to revenge the wrong visited upon their kinfolk – that had only seemed fair. But now it seemed that they wanted more – more fighting, more intrusion into a man's world, more opportunity to give their opinion when it had not been sought; where would it all end? Bad Elk bit his tongue and kept quiet.

See the Dark was less constrained and hissed:

"The women should not go against the bluecoats; there are many white soldiers, all with guns. The strong medicine of Ice and Grey Beard does not cover women."

White Rain knew that See the Dark was only worried about her safety but immediately hit back, saying that she was not aware that Cheyenne medicine power protected only the men. To her knowledge, neither Ice nor Grey Beard had ever said this and anyway…

Bad Elk held up his hand to stop the bickering. He had already foreseen difficulties leaving the female soldier society behind, so he had a task for them and a compromise for the others. But first he asked Yellow Bear to speak.

The skinny Suhtai looked careworn but defiant. A small group of ponies cantered past their meeting place driven by young boys; the dust kicked up by their hooves settled on Yellow Bear and gave him the appearance of a much older man as the greyish white particles settled on his hair and skin.

"You all know that my dreams have troubled me for these many nights. I have invoked Maheo and Maheyuno, the One Above's spiritual helpers to guide me. I am sure that the signs in my dreams all point to the same thing. Ice and Grey Beard have no powers..."

See the Dark had assumed a much more benevolent version of Yellow Bear's dreams; Smoke had only told him that Yellow Bear had some doubts about the coming fighting. This was the first time that he had heard the severe criticisms of the young men and was a very different story. Dark, in turn, had not mentioned the medicine man's doubts to White Rain. Yellow Bear's pronouncement made her gasp. He continued:

"My dreams are the same. I see two man shapes at the council fires of the Forty-Four Chiefs of our People. The man shapes are made of water – I can see right through them. These shapes are Ice and Grey Beard. They have no substance. Their magic will only bring us disaster."

Yellow Bear did not intend to discuss how he knew these shapes were the two young Cheyenne magic bringers; he just knew and had no more to say. Let Bad Elk's band heed his advice or ignore it, he had done his duty and told them. He drew his palm flat through the air to conclude his speech. His eyes glittered with defiant resolve.

Bad Elk noted the surprise on the faces of those around him; he also saw that Yellow Bear's words had carried to Badlands Walking Woman and Bright Antelope. Both continued with their chores but kept silent so they could pick up other snippets.

Bad Elk chose his words carefully:

"Our small village now rests amongst the others of our People. It is right that we are here. Not long ago we thought that we would never survive to attend another great gathering. Our burial scaffolds still stand in our old country to remind us how close we came to being rubbed out forever"

Heads nodded slowly in assent as they remembered the time of killing and hunger.

"We need to keep the faith with our People and so it is right that our warriors join their brothers in the coming fight with the bluecoats..."

Smoke and Broken Knife looked relieved. See the Dark and Viajero grunted in satisfaction to each other. White Rain Woman smiled broadly and nodded to See the Dark as if vindicated in her stance to take the Forked Lightning Women into battle. She was, however, premature. Bad Elk continued :

"My opinion is that whether our two young medicine men are right or wrong, our great village is too near to the battlefield and too slow to split up quickly if things go wrong. The bluecoat soldiers are many; even if all their bullets fail they may still come on us and try to attack our weak point – our families. Their scouts will know where we are by now, we are easy to find..."

Smoke and Broken Knife looked uneasily at one another. It was their job to fight the battles of the People but they recognised that leaving the families in easy striking distance of the white soldiers was a risk that they would not normally take.

Smoke remembered that in the planning for the raid against the Pawnee villages, he had ensured that Bad Elk moved the small encampment to a safe area. There had been only a slight risk that the Pawnee would follow them. He recalled See the Dark grinning and saying that the Pawnee would have to chase them on foot as the Cheyenne had stolen all their horses. Slight risk or not, all had felt easier in their minds that their vulnerable village had moved closer to allies and further away from Pawnee reprisals.

See the Dark was about to speak up for the magic of Ice and Grey Beard but had seen the thoughtful look of his father. Smoke's silence seemed to give weight to Bad Elk's judgement. His uncle continued:

"I will ask the people to leave the Great Circle of lodges at dawn tomorrow. The grass is getting thin and the main village may move anyway – I want us to head south, closer to the Flint Arrowpoint river and cross the trail behind the soldiers where they have already passed. I want us to be close to the mountains in case we need to hide. We cannot leave our people exposed – we will not survive a second time. "

There were murmurs of agreement from all under the willow tree. No-one voiced the opinion that they might be thought cowards or unbelievers by the rest of the gathered bands; the opinion of others mattered little when it came to survival.

Bad Elk now turned to White Rain Woman:

"I have a special and dangerous task for the Forked Lightning Women and I would ask that they take it. Most of our fighting strength will be set against the whites. I ask that your female soldiers protect the move of the village when we move to our new place."

White Rain Woman was about to protest when she realised the sacred duty that her military society had been given. After recent grievous losses of women and children, it would be a great honour to protect and preserve what they now had. She kept silent and nodded her agreement. See the Dark smiled in relief but was careful not to let the young widow see.

Chapter Thirty Seven

---- o o o ----

The soldiers had already crossed the north fork of the Solomon; steadily probing east-southeast as their Delaware and Pawnee scouts picked up stronger and stronger signs of Cheyenne presence and proximity. Tension and excitement were high in the slow moving, blue-coated columns as they rode relentlessly onwards in the bright sunshine and warm air.

Henry Armstrong, covered in dust and caked with white mud around his boots and stirrups, sat easily in the saddle as he rode alongside the pack mules in his nominal role as assistant commissary officer.

Far ahead, Colonel Sumner's fighting columns had halted to let their slower brethren catch up. It was tedious work but Henry did not complain even when the infantry companies, now marching at a steady, rhythmic pace, sometimes overtook the mules, catcalling as they went past. He was just glad that the wagons weren't with them now or they would be going even slower. Sumner's decision to restrict the spearhead columns to those capable of combat had been a good one. The wagons were returning to Fort Laramie and with them had gone many broken down horses and men. With those losses and the attachments of cavalry troopers to the mountain howitzer batteries, Sumner's fighting force of available sabres and carbines had been depleted.
Still, at the rear of the column with the complaining mules, the remainder of the beef herd and the Regiment's *remuda* of spare horses, the column looked large and invincible to Henry.

A rider trotted slowly back down the column towards the young Englishman; it was Jeb Stuart. Henry gave him a relaxed salute and Stuart grinned. Armstrong smiled back; he liked Stuart both as a soldier and a companion. Their friendship was about to pay off.

Stuart leaned forward in his saddle: "Old Bull-of-the-Woods will go into camp once we've reached the middle fork of the Solomon. He reckons the Cheyenne are real close and he wants to rest the horses in case we find them tomorrow. Keep your eyes on the skyline, Henry my boy; I'd hate those Indians to run off what's left of our rations."

Stuart turned his horse around and rode off, back towards the front of the column to retake command of G Company. After a few paces, Stuart reined his mount around and called out:

"Oh, by the way, the Colonel has given you permission to ride up with me and G Company tomorrow – I've fixed it with Frank Wheaton. We'll be setting out early, don't be late mule boy!"

Henry was delighted and yelled his thanks to Stuart. At last! This was his chance to be free of the tedium of paperwork and these damn mules. His morale now soaring, Armstrong kept his mount moving forward over the hilly ground. Reaching the tops of the many rises gave him something to look at – he could take in the beautiful, rough country, the glistening of creeks and rivers ahead and the almost complete lack of any timber. Grazing had also been poor and both mules and cavalry mounts were starting to feel the effects. Henry was mounted on a horse that he had bought himself and had seen to it that he kept it in the very best condition as far as campaigning on the Plains allowed. All the other officers in the First Cavalry had done the same. It was a sound insurance policy.

Armstrong knew that though the workaday horses that the troopers rode were generally serviceable – 'A working class ride is better than an aristocratic walk' as his father used to say – but they could be tricky in the charge or the chase, often giving out at critical times in battle. He had seen the results at the Blue Water fight, the sleek officers' mounts out in front with the troopers' broken down specimens blowing hard in the rear. He would make sure that he didn't lag behind at the kill.

Henry was also sure that the Cheyenne were close. Only a few miles back he had seen the signs of a very large Cheyenne village – blackened and charred fire sites, circles where many lodges had been erected then taken down and the trails of horse dung, only a few days old. There had been several hundred tipi rings. That meant a lot of Cheyenne out there, just waiting.

The halt came earlier than Henry had been expecting, on high ground overlooking Bow Creek, the middle fork of the Solomon. Again there was no grazing – the livestock would have water but little to eat. The men were tired too. Leaving the mules in the care of the chief packer and his assistant, Henry rode off to find Lieutenant Wheaton to formally relieve himself of his commissary duties.

After taking his leave from a disgruntled Frank Wheaton, Henry rode through the Company lines. The First Cavalry encampment now looked as if it was on a war footing and was a fine and uplifting sight. Henry felt genuinely sorry for those who never went to war.

Dismounted troopers took advantage of the early camp to tend to their horses - grooming, checking shoes were well seated, giving feeds of grain and taking them to water as a rota was called. There were no bugle calls and cooking fires could only be lit in daylight; all fires had to be out before darkness fell. NCOs moved amongst their men issuing extra ammunition, checking carbine mechanisms for dirt and sabres for rust. The scrape of whetstones against steel was a constant camp sound. Men took the opportunity to write last letters to relatives, as soldiers have always done on the eve of fighting.

As night fell, sentries were posted and alert, horses were tethered close to their sleeping owners on a half lariat and noise kept to a minimum. Everyone slept in his own equipment, booted and spurred. Henry lay awake, wrapped in his cape and blanket, staring at the stars. He fingered his pocket watch, given to him by his father; the ticking soothed his nerves.

There was a yapping and snarling down by the river. He later asked a passing sentry what the noise was. The guard, a nervous youth of around nineteen with a scarring of acne that made his face look like a stretch of bad road, told him that two Indian dogs had come into camp for food.

In the darkness, Henry checked his revolver and carbine again. The Cheyenne were close.

Chapter Thirty Eight

---- o o o ----

As the first fingers of a red dawn pushed into the sky above the middle fork of Turkeys Creek, See the Dark watched the *vehoe* soldiers stir into activity. He had been called into service as a scout and took his duties seriously. With a wolf fur pelt over his body, the jaw and top of the animal's head over his own, the young Cheyenne crept to the side of a sloping ridgeline and peered carefully over the top. Keeping low behind a greasewood clump, he looked across into the white soldiers' camp. His heart thudded and he fought down a desire to sneeze or yawn. On either side of him, his companion 'wolves' took careful note of what they saw; they would meet the main war party on the banks of the south fork later.

The soldiers were stirring but there was no music today from their copper trumpets; each man was brought alert by word of mouth. See the Dark had never seen so many whites. It was an impressive sight – so many horses, so many guns, so much power. He thumped himself silently on the chest to still his quailing heart. He should ride off soon and report – he hoped that he would have time to bathe in the magic lake.

Back in the great village, cooking fires were already lit as the women prepared an early meal for their menfolk. Smoke, Broken Knife and Bad Elk talked for the last time before the war party moved out. Yellow Bear joined them, shaking the stiffness out of his joints as he crawled out of his lodge. The tall medicine man put his hands on the shoulder of each war leader and said that he had prayed for their safe return.

Smoke looked at his erstwhile warrior companion – Yellow Bear was younger than he - but he seemed run down like a tired pony. His eyes looked watery; it could have been with age or tears, Smoke could not tell.

At a tap on his shoulder from Broken Knife, Smoke and the leader of the Thunder Bears then went off to gather their soldiers, paint their bodies and make their final prayers to Maheo.

Viajero had not slept. He was unafraid as always but now had his woman and child to consider. He had consulted Usen, the One-Above, keeping to his own beliefs even though he had been with the Cheyenne for so long. He sought an answer on the question of magic powers claimed by the young men of the Tsis-tsis-tas. But Usen, as he often did at critical times, remained silent.

Though he would not admit it, the absence of See the Dark on the scouting mission seemed to be a bad omen. The boy should be here so they could ride out together. He checked the Sharps and his bag of linen cartridges, strung his bow and tested the sinew string – dampness sometimes made it lose its power. It was taut and deadly.

Bright Antelope Woman brought out his new batch of specially made arrows, their sharpened iron points tightly bound to straight wooden shafts. He slung the arrow case across his shoulder. Ducking outside the lodge, he took out his paint and applied the same vermilion and yellow stripes to his face that had so scared the young *vaquero,* a lifetime away in Mexico. Bright Antelope Woman brought the baby to its father. Viajero touched the baby's face and stroked the cheek of Bright Antelope then untied his war pony from the picket pin, mounted and rode off to join the others. He had no words of farewell or comfort; Viajero was little changed.

Across on the far side of the *Suhtai* lodges, White Rain readied herself and her Forked Lightning Women. Sorrow had already visited the lodges as Sings Loud, the ancient crone who had overseen the rebuilding of the *tipis* after the Pawnee raid, had died the previous night. On her deathbed she had cried out that the days of the People were over. She wanted no part of it. Burnt Hair and others from the Sore Fingers sisterhood, who were in attendance at Sings Loud's last moments, were unnerved by the old woman's cries. The village had wanted to mark her passing so they agreed to take her body with them and erect a funeral scaffold later.

White Rain's women painted themselves, then sat in a circle and sang a song of death. Rain sat for a while after they had left the circle and pondered what the next few days would bring; she offered a prayer to Maheo for See the Dark's safety. They had become close since his rescue of her in the Pawnee country and she was glad to be the woman of a warrior again, even though he was so much younger than she. Her soldier women had often commented on it in the early days but now accepted the pairing as fate. Whilst they shared a lodge, neither Dark nor herself had spoken in detail about whether they would eventually marry. It had seemed unimportant before but now, as battle loomed, she was worried.

But there was work to do. She fetched her pony from the picket and minutes later they were all mounted, urging the *tipi* owners of Bad Elk's band to dismantle their lodges as soon as possible and move out to the Flint Arrowpoint River.

Smoke took his leave of Badlands Walking Woman and his new son, keeping up a cheerful chatter as he cradled the boy and let him grasp the decorated feathers of his warbonnet. He handed the child back to his mother who buried her face in the boy's chubby belly to hide her tears. Smoke brushed the hair out of his wife's eyes and held her face between his palms. He spoke softly to her, reminding her that she was his chosen companion on the trail of life and that she had always brought him great joy. As a man and a Cheyenne warrior he considered himself to be truly blessed. He kissed her on the forehead and promised to meet her beyond the banks of the Flint Arrowpoint. Untethering his war pony and his spare mount, he swung into the saddle with his weapons and rode off without a backwards glance.

Smoke and Broken Knife's soldiers fell in behind the main war party. Over three hundred Cheyenne warriors now followed Ice and Grey Beard to the site of the magic lake. As they reached it after a short ride, the sun came out and made the waters sparkle and glistening points of light dance across the surface. The water looked as though it was alive; magic could surely live here?

Ice and Grey Beard dismounted to sing and pray, the sun rose higher bringing warmth to the hollow where the lake gleamed. A breeze rippled the surface, goosebumps rose on the exposed flesh of the Cheyenne warriors as they dismounted to follow the instructions of their new medicine men. All knelt and washed in the lake, wrists and forearms. Ponies tried to push forward to drink but they were held back by their owners – a magic lake was not for quenching the thirst.

The two young shamans called out, reminding all that the day had come to throw the *vehoe* out of Cheyenne land and make them pay the blood price for their arrogance. The magic, they said, would take away the power of the white soldiers' bullets; the battlefield would be full of useless lead balls that had rolled out of the barrels of the *vehoe* guns and into the grass. Their only problem that day would be to have enough arrows, and their horses enough wind, to follow the fleeing enemy and strike them down.

In the centre of the warrior column, Viajero snorted at the boasting of the two young spirit diviners and took no part in the washing. He knew that See the Dark would never make it back in time to make his preparations at the lake; Viajero wanted no power that would give him an advantage over his young war companion. They were friends and would ride into battle together on equal terms. He ignored the hostile stares from those around him.

Waiting for the ceremony to finish, he idly picked up a small, misshapen piece of wood lying by the lake; the wind must have blown it here. Its shape was familiar somehow and he examined it closely. He smiled as he realised what it looked like. The curled piece of dried wood was the shape of a horned lizard. To the astonishment of those at the sacred ceremony, Viajero laughed out loud. Usen certainly chose the strangest of times to talk to him. He tucked the wood in the waist of his breechclout.

The Cheyenne war party remounted and, following their war leaders now, rode to the south fork of Turkeys Creek. See the Dark was waiting there to give his report. The whites were moving out but their big horses moved slowly; he estimated that they would be at the river by midday. He then sought out Viajero to rest up and wait for the whites to come to them.

Chapter Thirty Nine

---- o o o ----

Sumner's troopers picked their way slowly through the narrowing valley of the Solomon's southern fork. He had ordered that the artillery should wait for the infantry to catch up so the cavalry column, now unencumbered by its slower moving element, quickly outdistanced them.

The three trotting columns of tired horses had to merge into a single line as they rounded the bend in the valley where the river now continued its eastward course.

Henry Armstrong rode happily at the rear of G Company; eating dust was a minor inconvenience if it meant being in at the kill. The Pawnee scouts had already indicated that the Cheyenne were near.

Henry himself had caught a glimpse of a small band of mounted Indians steadily withdrawing along the high ground of the bluffs, following the easterly flow of the river. He grinned in his excitement, those must be Cheyenne scouts. They certainly didn't seem to be panicked by the sight of the large column, they rode upright and alert; watching and riding off then stopping to repeat the process.

The long column now rounded the base of a rocky hill that sliced across the valley. Ahead, as the companies cleared the hill and shook out into their original columns, the valley broadened out to threequarters of a mile across, from the north bank of the Solomon up to the bluffs. Henry could see that the Colonel had halted with some of his staff around him; they were using telescopes to look ahead into the valley.

Standing in his stirrups, Henry tried to see what they were looking at but he could only see a mile or so ahead. There seemed to be a stand of sparse timber at the end of the valley with moving animals in front of it. They could be buffalo, it was hard to tell at this distance. His observations were brought to a sudden halt as the booming voice of Edwin Vose Sumner now reached out to control his destiny.

Chapter Forty

---- o o o ----

The warriors unsaddled their ponies and let them graze on the poor grass between a stand of cottonwoods. The men ate jerked buffalo meat and prepared their minds for battle. Some joked and played the bones game, others talked amongst themselves, tense and nervous with the waiting. A small group of youths had followed from the village, including some from visiting Oglala Lakota bands, eager to see the great battle and witness the last days of the *vehoe* in Cheyenne country. They rode to the top of the bluffs to the north of the river to get the best view. From their vantage point, they could see the river below and, off to the west, the dust from the advancing column of the pony soldiers.

With a high pitched yipping to attract attention, Cheyenne scouts now rode into the valley to the west of the timber. They rode their ponies in circles to indicate that many enemies were in sight. A high fever of excitement gripped the assembled warriors – horses were re-saddled, bridles and girths checked, weapons brought out of carrying cases, guns primed, arrows nocked on bows and lances held at the ready. Everyone remounted and, at a signal from the war chief, all the soldiers of the military societies walked their ponies into a long battle line -stretching from the bluffs north of the river down to the river bank itself.

Smoke was amazed and delighted at the formation; he had never seen the Cheyenne do this before. It brought to mind the disciplined way that they had fought at the Pawnee villages. He looked around him for See the Dark but could not make him out in the jostling press of riders. He sent a silent blessing to his son and thanked Maheo for bringing them both to this place to be united in battle.

See the Dark looked for his father and saw that both the Striking Snakes and the Thunder Bears were at the front of the line close to the river. He wanted to go down and join them but Viajero kept him close to the bluffs. There was much excited yelling and chatter, even though the soldiers were not yet in sight. Viajero was saying something but Dark could not hear what it was.

Viajero rode over on his pony, roughly pushing others aside. When he reached Dark's pony, he grabbed the bridle and held out his hand. It was the piece of wood shaped like a lizard; it had broken in two. See the Dark had no idea what it meant but could see that its significance troubled his friend. Viajero spoke urgently:

"Come. Yellow Bear was right. The magic is broken."

See the Dark hesitated for a moment before pushing the other man away. Viajero did not have to fight. He had already proven his worth to the Tsis-tsis-tas in many ways. But Dark's place was with his people; he would stay.

Viajero shrugged and called out something in his own tongue then, as if resigned to fate, walked his pony alongside that of Dark's and sat silently facing the oncoming enemy.

Chapter Forty One

---- o o o ----

The young Englishman was not unintelligent but he loved the stark simplicity of a soldier's lot in battle – to 'close with and destroy the enemy; seize and hold ground'.
It was a simple mantra for the uncluttered mind. Those who could retain this bright focus and control soldiers in battle, however complex the plan, would win. Those who could not, failed. Henry hoped that Sumner was one of the successful ones.

"Front into line!"

The booming voice was heard by all. It drove them to obey and, strangely, it calmed fears. It carried the authority and confidence that men need at such times.

Henry reined his horse to comply with the order. The untested First Cavalry swung into extended line, guidons fluttering on the right of each company. Six companies, now reduced to around fifty troopers in each unit through sickness and detachment to man the howitzers far to the rear, trotted abreast into the valley. Leather slapped against leather, sabres rattled in scabbards, harness jingled musically and metal accoutrements shone in the bright sunshine. Each man instinctively passed an experienced hand over his saddle tack and weaponry; a final comforting check on carbine, pistol, ammunition pouches and sabre. Those who knew how, prayed.

Henry, as an extra officer rider in G Company, had no real place in the line but thought that a place behind the guidon bearer would be acceptable. That way he would not be seen as too pushy by G's troopers but would be well placed to forge ahead if the order to charge came. He caught himself thinking about these points of protocol and laughed; only the bloody English would give a damn about these things in the approach to a battle.

Whilst the protocol might have been correct, the guidon bearer's back blocked Henry's view so he angled his horse out to the right hand side of him and looked into the valley.

"Jesus Christ!"

The exclamation rose from Henry's lips and it was in good company. It was as though the entire line had just comprehended what was in front of them. Less than a mile to their front were the Cheyenne.

Troopers looked uneasily at each other. The Cheyenne were doing exactly what the First Cavalry was doing – advancing in extended line across the valley. Nothing had prepared them for this.

The Cheyenne made a magnificent warlike spectacle. The soldiers heard the nerve-jangling songs and war cries wash over them time and again. Coloured warbonnets swirled behind the leaders, feathers fluttered on lances and bow staves of the main throng. Painted faces and bodies, alive with savage excitement, added to the splendour. Each man yelled his own song and hurled imprecations against the white invaders. Tough, fresh ponies, sleek with recent grazing but hardened into muscle by long training, pawed the ground; excited and anxious to be given a loose rein.

Henry smiled to himself - two lines of America's inhabitants closing on each other – one only a spit away from the Stone Age, the other at the cutting edge of modern Nineteenth Century military technology.

From the Cheyenne lines, two parties of warriors broke away from the main body to ride around the flanks of the soldiers. The soldiers still rode as if at garrison drill, carbines untouched. Henry saw Sumner order Companies A and B to counter the threat.

Company A galloped towards the group riding to turn the left flank along the northern bluffs. The small group of Cheyenne hesitated then reined their ponies about and went back to join the main body. B Company splashed across the river to close with the second group.

Only a few hundred yards now separated the opposing lines. Henry wondered when Sumner would wake up and let the cavalry do its business. The Indians were close now, shrieking war cries with venom and hate tore at the air. Their chiefs, on prancing excited ponies each painted as colourfully as its rider, rode ahead urging their warriors on. The Cheyenne line surged.

Suddenly there was a shot. Henry saw that it was one of the First Cavalry scouts, a Delaware called Fall Leaf, who had ridden out from the line and fired at the Cheyenne. He quickly rode back into the trotting blue ranks followed by a hail of shots and arrows. This action seemed to be a catalyst. Henry was mildly amused that the war would start by one Indian firing on another.

The bugle, its shrill notes cutting across the almost dreamlike advance, now sounded 'Gallop-March.' Troopers rose in their saddles and let their horses run. The heads of the animals came up and each mount felt the excited quivering of the horse next to it. With a tremor and much snorting the cavalry horses forgot their tiredness and stretched their legs. The ground pounded under the sudden mass movement.

Four deep in company lines, the second rank and beyond spat out the dust of their comrades in front. Troopers put their fears to one side and touched the steel butt plates of their carbines; soon they would unleash a comforting hail of lead into the yelling, painted savages ahead of them.

Sumner's bellowing voice came as a surprise but it was welcome nonetheless.

"Draw sabres!"

"Charge!"

There was a mighty metallic hiss, ending in a singing note of scraped steel as three hundred sabres were drawn from scabbards. The sun flashed on three hundred blades as they were brought up and into the tierce point. Three hundred wrists were locked forward behind hilts as the arms of the troopers prepared for the shock of steel on flesh and bone. Now it was their turn; a loud yell went up from the blue ranks. It was not a word or a formal battle cry – just an expulsion of air to intimidate the foe, expel fear and prepare them for the bloodletting.

Chapter Forty Two

---- o o o ----

See the Dark let his pony surge forward with the rest. His rifle was in his right hand and he waved and pointed this to the sky in his excitement. Viajero rode alongside, singing songs in his own tongue and occasionally standing in his stirrups and snarling threats at the advancing blue ranks; a little foam had appeared at the side of the Apache's mouth but it was whipped away by the slipstream of forward movement. Whatever doubts the Traveller had, he seemed to have lost them now.

The Cheyennes trotted and surged, each anxious to get at the enemy but held back by the war leaders out in front. The warriors were all mixed up now – the Kit Foxes rode amongst the Dog Soldiers, Crooked Lance with Striking Snakes, Thunder Bears with Red Shields. It didn't matter, Maheo was with them. They were fighting alongside their family.

The charge of the *vehoe* brought another bout of wild yelling from the warriors around See the Dark. He recognised one of the uplifted voices off to his left, it was Two Talks, his body slashed with red and yellow paint, his face filled with hate. The young man was now ferociously threatening the bluecoats as they thundered towards the Tsis-tsis-tas. Dark was between two friends; he could ask for no more. It was a good day to die.

Suddenly, the hiss of drawing sabres pieced the din. The sun flashed on the deadly blades and unsettled the warriors. The yelling of the soldiers now drowned out that of the Cheyenne; the ground trembled as the gap between the ranks of horses closed. Large clods of earth thrown up by the heavy cavalry horses flew into the air. The ground shuddered at the oncoming weight of the *vehoe* charge.

The war chiefs stopped, reining in their mounts. The remainder barged into them and stopped also. Ice and Grey Beard were nowhere to be seen; there was no encouragement that the magic, apparently so potent against hot lead, would have any power against cold steel.

There was a milling of Cheyenne ponies as the indecisive obstructed those hot for battle. But the loss of Cheyenne confidence was rapid and all-enveloping.

Bravely they sat on their ponies until the tips of the sabres were only a rifle shot away. A shower of arrows towards the soldiers eased some of the hurt but the whites kept charging. All the warriors now knew the truth – the magic of Ice and Grey Beard had been wrong for that day. Smoke and Broken Knife, trying to rally their military men from the morass of horsed warriors, reined their ponies around and broke away to cross the river.

See the Dark and Viajero did the same, spurring north towards the bluffs. They had lost sight of Two Talks. Below them in the valley, the break-up of the Cheyenne war party turned into a rout as groups of warriors splashed across Turkeys Creek to get back to their village.

The Cheyenne knew the riverbanks well and avoided the patches of quicksand that lurked under the surface. However, the bluecoats had not ridden here before and many became mired down in the sucking ooze. The fresher Indian ponies soon outdistanced the tired cavalry horses but, here and there, small personal skirmishes between one or two individual warriors and bluecoats took place.

Dark and Viajero though had no time to stop and stare. In company with some other badly shocked warriors from the *Omissis* band, they rode hard along the bluffs for a while then, using the cover of the scattered cottonwoods between themselves and the pony soldiers dropped back down into the valley and crossed the river.

Keeping to the bottom of a dried stream bed, the small party headed south. At one point a lone bluecoat caught up with them on the ridge to their right. He was too far away for any decisive shot but fired his carbine at them anyway. The shot missed, Dark couldn't see where it went.

The soldier then yelled something at them in his own tongue that they did not understand and took out his pistol. Viajero turned in his saddle and fired the Sharps, the first time he had done that all day. His shot missed the trooper though it was close as he saw him duck in his saddle. In reply, the pony soldier fired three quick shots from his pistol, the low, flat cracks of the explosions echoing down the slope. The bullets merely kicked up dust, many paces short of the Cheyenne. After the third shot, a bugle sounded far in the distance and the bluecoat pulled the head of his horse around to the north and trotted off.

The *Omissis* warriors soon outdistanced Dark and Viajero; they needed to get back to their families and move quickly. The pony soldiers would come again in the morning to find and destroy the village.

The Apache and the young Cheyenne now rode alone and in silence. They were glad of the respite from the *Omissis*' constant chatter about the poor magic of the medicine men that they had chosen to believe in. Dark was struggling with his own feelings – he felt betrayed and defeated. He was also disgusted with himself for not pushing forward to be killed honourably by the enemy. At least that way his spirit could enter the next world with head held high. But it was too late – he, like the rest of the Cheyenne, had run. It had not been a good day to die.

Viajero was untroubled by the retreat; he had been expecting it. . The broken piece of wood had foretold disaster. Usen had told him in advance. The Apache was happy that Bad Elk's band had left the village early; such a small group might escape the intentions of the *indaa* soldiers when they punished the rest of the People. Now all he and his young companion had to do was to find their families.

Chapter Forty Three
---- o o o ----

Henry Armstrong was exhausted. Glory had not come to him in that wild chase after the fleeing Cheyennes. His well-bred horse had mired down in the quicksands of the Solomon and he had only got it out with much difficulty. Henry hadn't fired a shot or bloodied the edge of his sabre – it had been a disappointing day.

They hadn't killed many Indians and had lost two of their own. His friend, Jeb Stuart had been wounded by a shot from an old pistol carried by one of the Cheyenne and now lay resting under a makeshift shelter; but he was strong and would recover. The rest of the wounded would need to recuperate before they could travel. Reports coming in from those who'd ranged out to find Indian bodies had only found seven so far. It seemed an unsatisfactory end to spending two months in the saddle; more of a skirmish than a decisive battle and, in the end, most of the enemy escaping.

Still, Henry comforted himself that he had at least taken part in the exhilarating charge and had seen the much-vaunted Cheyenne run.

He lay back on his blanket but sleep would not come. Idly, he looked at the canopy of stars above his head and focused on one of them; it seemed to have a red cast to it and, occasionally, it winked. His thoughts wandered back to England and the green North Country of his boyhood. He wondered if his father was still alive and if he would be proud of his son's battles.

Tomorrow his orders were to begin building a sod fort to protect the wounded from any returning warriors. Then the 1st US Cavalry would bury its dead and plunge deeper into Cheyenne country to avenge them. But for now, Lieutenant Henry Armstrong was in enemy country and far from home.

Chapter Forty Four

---- o o o ----

Bad Elk's small and tired band halted for the night on their journey to the Flint Arrowpoint. The Forked Lightning Women had screened and protected the moving village, chivvying along stragglers at the rear and encouraging the others. They took their martial duties seriously and constantly checked the back trail from high points along the way, looking for riders from their own people or, worse, advancing bluecoats.

Cooking fires were not allowed; it would be a cold camp with only dried meat and pemmican to nourish and restore spirits. Lodges were not erected, Bad Elk wanted the village to move far and fast before he allowed them to relax.

Not all of the *Suhtai* had wanted to move. Buffalo Lodge Woman, the mother of White Rain, had firmly believed in the magic of Ice and Grey Beard. There was no need to move, she insisted; she would await the triumphant return of the Cheyenne menfolk from the battlefield. Her husband had been crippled many years before and moving was especially trying for him; a withered leg made mounting a horse difficult.

She knew her daughter, as the leader of the women's military society, had her responsibilities to the majority of the band and reassured her that all would be well. White Rain Woman was not convinced. Her mother's stubbornness had weighed heavily on her mind as she organised her comrades to protect the move.

A wind got up and blew steadily all night. Babies cried but were quickly hushed. Before the morning star appeared, a heavy rain fell and mothers sheltered their children under buffalo robes from the cold, lashing sheets of water. Muddy rivulets ran through the small dispirited gathering of families as they waited impatiently for dawn. Perhaps the morning would bring better news – a rider sent out to bring them back to celebrate a great victory perhaps or, at least, some word of their loved ones.

At first light, Yellow Bear, Bad Elk and the wives of Smoke on the Moon and Viajero climbed to the top of a rocky promontory as, below, the Forked Lightning Women urged tired families to pack up and prepare to head south again. The small, bedraggled band stood and waited for good news.

The rain cleared and shafts of sunlight spread across the valleys and hills over which they had travelled. Yellow Bear walked off alone to a stunted tree, growing out of a rock cleft. He invoked *Maheo* and asked him to bring them a sign that all was well then walked back to join the others.

Badlands Walking Woman had the best eyesight and now stood motionless on a flat rock overlooking the sun dappled valleys. Surely, on such a beautiful morning she would see her husband coming, or her beloved son or just *anyone* with news. But the only movement was a small group of elk, idly grazing in brushwood near a shining stream.

Bright Antelope Woman also scanned the horizon eagerly. Viajero would soon return to take care of his family. She would recognise his distinctive riding style at a great distance. During the cold, comfortless night she had prayed to Usen that Viajero would be spared in any battle. Like Yellow Bear she invoked her God for a sign that all was well. But there was none.

Chapter Forty Five

---- o o o ----

Viajero snored lightly next to See the Dark. The young Cheyenne was awake and his mind churned with the events of the day. He was alive and unhurt but did not know the fate of his father and friends who had been in the charge with him. The mix of bodies and pushing horses during the surge meant he had lost sight of Smoke on the Moon, Two Talks and the rest of the soldier societies. Riders tried to move in every direction once the fear had gripped them and Dark just had the impression of the People scattering as he rode with the Traveller out of the melee. It was a disgrace that would be hard to bear.

The *vehoe* now occupied sacred Cheyenne land and Dark did not know if they would ever get it back. The magic of the two flawed Cheyenne men had failed and See the Dark would never question Yellow Bear's predictions again. Defeat coated his tongue with a bitter sap.

He was glad the village had moved early; it had been a good decision by Bad Elk and White Rain would be safe. He and the Traveller would find them in a day or two if they had been able to cross the Flint Arrowpoint into the southern country.

He stared hard into the sky to try and empty his mind and let sleep overtake him. There was a red star that winked occasionally, he would concentrate on that.

Tomorrow, he and the Traveller would pick up the trail of their families and be re-united. For now, they were in enemy country and far from home.

---- o 0 o ----

Printed in Great Britain
by Amazon